M000023744

THE
NEW MEXICO
GUIDE

THE
NEW MEXICO
GUIDE

Charles L. Cadieux

Fulcrum Publishing
Golden, Colorado

Copyright © 1992 Charles L. Cadieux

All rights reserved

Book design by Richard Firmage

Cover photo, *Taos Pueblo Church*, copyright © 1992 by Linde Waidhofer,
Western Eye Photography.
Back cover photos: *Olla Maidens, Gallup Ceremonial* and *Electric Farolitos–Inn of Loretto,
Santa Fe*, © 1992 by Mark Nohl, New Mexico Economic and Tourism Department.

All interior photos by Charles L. Cadieux unless otherwise noted.

Library of Congress Cataloging-in-Publication Data
    Cadieux, Charles L.
      The New Mexico guide / Charles L. Cadieux.
         p.   cm.
      Includes bibliographical references and index.
      ISBN 1-55591-095-5
      1. New Mexico—Description and travel—1981- —Guide books.
    I. Title.
    F794.3.C33 1991   91–58487
    917.8904'53—dc20   CIP

Printed in the United States of America
0 9 8 7 6 5 4 3 2

Fulcrum Publishing
350 Indiana Street, Suite 350
Golden, Colorado 80401

Contents

═How to Use This Guide═

This book is organized into six geographic regions: the Hispanic Highlands, the Northeast Region, the Northwest Region, the Lower Rio Grande, the Southeast Region and the Southwest Region. Each region has a corresponding map pinpointing its location in the state.

The area code 505 covers all of New Mexico. Remember that when calling another city within the state, you must dial a 1 before the number.

New Mexico is on Mountain Standard Time. This is two hours earlier than Eastern Standard Time (New York) and one hour later than Pacific Standard Time (California).

All hotels, motels and restaurants include price ranges. These are given as follows:

$: less than $25
$$: $25 to $50
$$$: $50 to $100
$$$$: $100 and above

Introduction

MEET NEW MEXICO

New Mexico is called the Land of Enchantment, and it rates the name. I came to New Mexico in 1962 and became enchanted by it over the next 10 years. Then a transfer took me away for 6 years, and I could hardly wait to get back. I returned in 1977, and I'm back to stay. Enchanting New Mexico is my home.

People have always found this area enchanting. As witness, Acoma—the Sky City—is one of the longest continuously inhabited places in North America. Many peoples found it enchanting, starting with the Anasazi—the Ancient Ones—who lived here 2,000 years ago and whose ruined towns still fascinate the explorer. The ancient city at Chaco Canyon was once the biggest city in North America.

The Apache and the Navajo crossed the Bering strait from Asia, and with the entire continent to choose from, they moved to what is now New Mexico. The Indian presence is still important.

My home state was first explored by Europeans more than 400 years ago. The Spanish worked northward from old Mexico, along the Jornada del Muerto ("Day's March of the Dead Man"), to establish the oldest capital in what is now the United States. Santa Fe, the City of the Holy Faith of St. Francis of Assisi, is so interesting that all newcomers want to close the door behind them and enjoy it all by themselves.

The Spanish brought the Catholic faith with them, and New Mexico is still the most Catholic state west of the Mississippi. The padres built with adobe, erecting churches that seemed to belong on the earth—the earth that formed their walls. Many small villages in the mostly Hispanic Rio Arriba—"Upper River"—part of this state appear as they did 300 years ago. In towns such as Chimayo, Tierra Amarilla and Truchas, life is slow-paced and peaceful.

When the Anglos came belatedly on the scene, the Johnny-come-latelies, they completed the tricultural tapestry that is today's New Mexico. It's still very much a land of three cultures—Indian, Hispanic and Anglo.

But lest you get the idea that this is a state living in the past, you should know that America's atomic bomb was developed here, in Los Alamos;

our nation's greatest radio telescope, the Very Large Array, still eaves-drops on radio waves from the outer reaches of the galaxy; all of the nation's astronauts come to the Lovelace Clinic in Albuquerque before they travel into space; and Sandia Laboratories plays an important part in advanced research in today's world.

There's a lot of New Mexico: It ranks fifth in the nation in area, behind Alaska, Texas, California and Montana, with 121,666 square miles of the most varied geography in America. Elevations range from Wheeler Peak's 13,161 feet to the lowest spot in the southeast corner of the state, which is still 2,800 feet above sea level. Big New Mexico has only a million and a half inhabitants, which means that it sure isn't crowded. There's only one large city, Albuquerque. It concentrates more than half a million people in its metropolitan area, leaving the rest of the state even more roomy.

Everyone who comes to New Mexico comments on the light, a light that is crystal clear. This quality of light, coupled with the quality of life, is what attracted so many artists into the artist colonies of Taos and Santa Fe. Enchanted light illuminates the red-sandstone cliffs, the green pine-clad mountains and the sere brown deserts, attracting artists like Georgia O'Keeffe and Peter Hurd.

Painters are not the only artists in this big state. The Santa Fe Opera, one of the oldest and best known, produces both avant-garde and traditional opera in the pines just outside of our capital city during the summer.

Forty percent of New Mexico is in forests, offering cool trout streams and gemlike lakes set among the pines and forming the slopes of ski basins—Taos, Santa Fe, Angel Fire, Red River, Ruidoso and others.

Volcanic calderas and lava flows point to a violent geologic past and offer clues to the modern-day development of geothermal energy. One of the largest known geothermal resources in the world is currently being investigated near Los Alamos, where the atom bomb was developed.

Geothermal energy comes from hot water deep within the earth. But hot air provides one of the biggest events on the calendar—the world's largest hot air balloon festival, which takes place each October. It brings together as many as 600 hot air balloons, and their mass ascensions provide a colorful sight seen nowhere else.

New Mexico is home to the outdoorsman, the hunter, the angler, the skier, the hiker, the birder and, above all, the photographer. The Bosque del Apache National Wildlife Refuge offers a tour to see as many as 60,000 snow geese in one flock, along with a dozen other species of waterfowl. The refuge is home to a population of whooping cranes, one of the world's rarest species.

Healthy herds of elk and mule deer are found in New Mexico, along with one of the nation's greatest populations of wild turkeys. Three species of trout swim in the streams of the high mountains, and access to most fishing is free because it is in the national forest.

That's a short look at how New Mexicans play. But they work also. Research is important, and Los Alamos boasts more Ph.D.s per capita than any other city in the United States. New Mexico ranks high in oil and gas production, has a thriving lumbering industry and exports many million tons of coal to markets farther east. Its cattle-ranching operation employs real cowboys who ride the wide range, tending the dogies.

Molybdenum, potash and uranium mines take riches from the earth—but I have to be honest and admit that the largest single employer is the government. I also want to point out that tourism is near the top as a money-producer in the Land of Enchantment.

I admit to being in love with New Mexico. I'm proud of it, and I want to show you the way to become enchanted with a land of lost gold treasures and natural treasures, such as Carlsbad Caverns. I'll tell you where to stay and where to eat, what to see and what to look for, whether you're flying in and touring with a rented car or driving your own recreational vehicle and living in campgrounds, whether your interest is in meeting the ski bunnies on our deep-powder slopes, researching our prehistory, fishing for trout on the San Juan,—where you can realistically expect to catch trout of more than 20 inches—attending the Indian ceremonials at Gallup or just lazing through ageless adobe villages while the pace of life slows perceptibly.

Come see New Mexico. Here's how!

TEN TOP ATTRACTIONS IN NEW MEXICO

Now that I've introduced you to the Land of Enchantment, you would think I'd leave well enough alone, but I hereby go out on a limb and name the top 10 attractions in my beloved New Mexico. Naturally, many people will disagree with me, but here is one man's slate of the top 10 attractions, ranked in order.

1. **Carlsbad Caverns** (The Southeast Region).
2. **Chaco Culture National Historical Park** (The Northwest Region).
3. **The Very Large Array** radio telescope (The Southwest Region).
4. **Acoma**, the Sky City (The Northwest Region).
5. **Albuquerque's Aerial Tram**, the world's longest (The Lower Rio Grande).
6. **Gila Cliff Dwellings** (The Southwest Region).
7. **White Sands National Monument** (The Southeast Region).
8. **Santa Fe** (The Hispanic Highlands).
9. **Taos**, the city, the pueblo and the Ranchos de Taos (The Hispanic Highlands).
10. **Old Town in Albuquerque** (The Lower Rio Grande).

TEN MOST HISTORICAL SITES
IN NEW MEXICO

1. **Fort Union**, in Mora County, just 8 miles off Interstate 25 on N.M. 161, was set up to protect the Santa Fe Trail, to control the Indians and to serve as a depot for U.S. Army installations. It stands today pretty much as the army left it more than 100 years ago. Interesting and easy to visit, it offers taped narratives and other interpretive features. Stand in the quadrangle and hear the sounds of the cavalry trooping out to battle the Indians. (The Northeast Region.)

2. **Fort Selden State Monument** preserves the fort where Douglas MacArthur played as a boy and where U.S. Army units were stationed to protect the frontier. Its remarkably well-preserved ruins of a typical frontier fort are located halfway between Las Cruces and Rincon, just off Interstate 25, in Dona Ana County. (The Lower Rio Grande.)

3. **Santa Fe's Plaza**, the center of the historic city, is a place where you can sit and imagine the Indians, led by Pope, as they came to slaughter the Spaniards in the Pueblo Revolt of 1680. Hear the creaking of the wagons, finally arriving from the long, dangerous trip across the Santa Fe Trail. Remember that this was the northern terminus of the Chihuahua Trail, which led south from this same plaza, across the Jornada del Muerto ("Day's March of the Dead Man") all the way to Mexico City. General Stephen W. Kearney rode into the plaza with his U.S. soldiers to claim this country from Spanish control. (The Hispanic Highlands.)

4. **Taos Pueblo,** one of the oldest continuously occupied population centers in North America, is a five-story structure in a land filled with memories of Kit Carson, Bent (remember Bent's Fort?) of early-day Mountain Man Rendezvous, beaver trappers and Indian fighters. The lovely church that Georgia O'Keeffe painted is here in this historic center, which is now a skier's paradise. Located in Taos County. Take U.S. 64 southeast from Tres Piedras or N.M. 68 north from Española. (The Hispanic Highlands.)

5. **Coronado State Monument** is on the northwest outskirts of the town of Bernalillo, just off Interstate 25 and N.M. 44, 15 miles north of Albuquerque. Here the earliest Spaniards spent a miserable winter and avoided starvation by stealing the corn of the Indians who built a pueblo there. The ruins of the ancient pueblo are interesting and easy to visit. (The Lower Rio Grande.)

6. **The Trinity Site**, where the first atomic bomb was exploded on July 16, 1945, is NOT open to the public, except on rare occasions.

Check with the Chamber of Commerce in Alamogordo about tours, offered once or twice a year. The atomic bomb shortened the war and saved many American lives. The Trinity Site is on the edge of the Jornada del Muerto, the "Day's March of the Dead Man." (The Southeast Region.)

7. **Lincoln State Monument**, in Lincoln County, best reached via U.S. 380, halfway between Carrizozo and Roswell, is the setting for much of the story of Billy the Kid. Excellent living history presentation, along with the chance to tour the setting of the Lincoln County Wars. (The Southeast Region.)

8. **Pancho Villa State Park**, where the famed Mexican revolutionary raided U.S. territory, is located on the Mexican border at Columbus, on N.M. 11, south of Deming. We may think of Pancho as a *bandido*, but to most of the Spanish-speaking peoples on both sides of the border, he is a hero, the man who twisted Uncle Sam's tail and lived to tell about it. (The Southwest Region.)

9. **Three Rivers Petroglyphs**, 8 miles of good road off U.S. 54, 17 miles north of Tularosa in Otero County. One of the best collections of ancient Indian writings chipped onto black rocks, the petroglyphs pose more questions than provide answers. Who were the people who drew these thousand-year-old pictures? Why did they choose this rocky ridge? Were they boasting of kills, or are the drawings religiously significant? Good picnic and camping area run by the Bureau of Land Management. (The Southeast Region.)

10. **El Morro National Monument**. The first Spanish explorers carved into the soft red-sandstone walls, *"Pasamos por aqui . . ."* ("There passed this way," in English). The Inscription Rock chronicles the passing by of mountain people, Spanish padres, U.S. Army detachments and the earliest of the Spanish *gobernadores* in graffiti of 400 years ago. There's a nice campground and an excellent visitors center nearby. The monument is just off U.S. 53 in Cibola County, southwest of Grants, on the way to the famed Zuni Pueblo. (The Northwest Region.)

THE REGIONS
OF NEW MEXICO

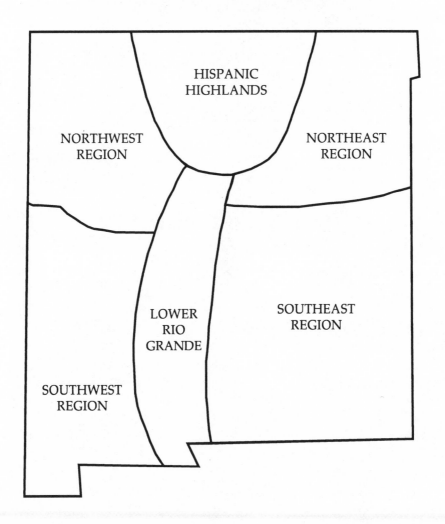

HISPANIC
HIGHLANDS

NORTHWEST
REGION

NORTHEAST
REGION

LOWER
RIO
GRANDE

SOUTHEAST
REGION

SOUTHWEST
REGION

THE
HISPANIC HIGHLANDS

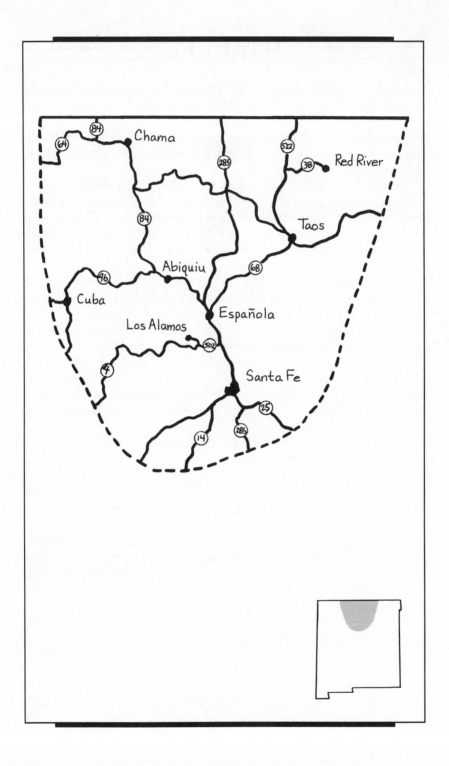

Santa Fe

Located 7,000 feet above sea level against the slopes of the Sangre de Cristo Mountains, Santa Fe is the highest state capital in America. It's the oldest capital in the United States and has been called one of the three most interesting cities in America, along with Charleston, South Carolina, and New Orleans, Louisiana. I'm not sure that Charleston and New Orleans really measure up.

New Mexico's tricultural history is nowhere more evident than in Santa Fe, which was the seat of government in this portion of New Spain long before the United States of America existed. Santa Fe is situated among a grouping of eight Indian pueblos and shares their past. It is the destination of the Sante Fe Trail and part of the title of the 1940s' hit song "On the Atchison, Topeka, and the Santa Fe."

Although Santa Fe's citizens number only 58,000, the town is the state capital. It boasts a thriving art colony and carefully nurtures its eighteenth-century look—preferring its historic Spanish colonial architecture to the look of modern-day development. Even newcomers want to forestall growth and preserve Santa Fe's unique identity.

Santa Fe is a city of narrow winding streets, of hundred-year-old shade trees, tan adobe walls, red chile *ristras* and a quiet serenity all too rare in our modern world. It had a symphony orchestra before the first log cabin was built in Chicago. Some folks admit that to be true but claim that the city has done nothing since those days.

More than any other city in New Mexico, Santa Fe has an individuality of character—it is the *only* Santa Fe.

HISTORY

Santa Fe was founded in 1610 by Spanish explorers pushing up from Mexico into the Indian country. The name of its streets (such as Paseo de Peralta, Guadalupe, Otero, De Vargas) attest to the Spanish influence. The Spaniards named it *La Ciudad del Santa Fe de San Francisco de Assis*, or "The City of the Holy Faith of Saint Francis of Assisi."

The Pueblo Indians rebelled and drove the Spanish out in 1680 but were reconquered. There has been a good bit of bloodshed in the scenic plaza that is the heart of the city. Too few people for such a big territory, *los españoles* never really consolidated their occupation, but they left a lasting signature on the entire state.

The Santa Fe Trail was started by merchants and fur traders who became the suppliers for Santa Fe. Despite bloody attacks by hostile

Indians, American merchants forced open this lifeline to the city—after all, Santa Fe is much closer to Kansas City than it is to Mexico City. Economic reasons were probably more important than political reasons, but Americans became the guiding forces in Santa Fe in the first half of the 1800s, completing the tricultural nature of Santa Fe's heritage— Indian, Hispanic and Anglo.

———— GETTING THERE ————

Santa Fe is located on Interstate 25 and U.S. highways 84 and 285. Commuter buses and airlines carry passengers from Albuquerque's busy Sunport to Santa Fe, making the old city close to the population center of the state. **Mesa Airlines, 842-4414**, has about three flights per day between Albuquerque and Santa Fe. Rental cars are available at the airports.

Amtrak serves Lamy, 17 miles from Santa Fe, with shuttle service between the cities. The Lamy ticket office telephone is **988-4511**; Santa Fe telephone for the shuttle is **982-8829**.

Greyhound, Trailways and **TNM&O buses** serve Santa Fe, **858 St. Michael's Dr.** Santa Fe telephone for schedule information is **471-0008**.

There's a good municipal airport in Santa Fe situated at the end of Airport Rd. off Cerrillos Rd., providing a 6,344-foot runway and lighting for private planes. Call **473-7243** for information.

———— FESTIVALS AND EVENTS ————

Fiesta

The biggest celebration in Santa Fe is the Fiesta, which takes place during the weekend following Labor Day every year. The event is 300 years old and celebrates the reconquest of the city by Don Diego de Vargas in 1682. Fiesta features the queen and her court, the current Don Diego de Vargas and his retinue of 17, two parades, bands, mariachi music, singing and dancing. The fun begins Fri. morning, with the Pregón de Fiesta and mass at Rosario Chapel, celebrated by Archbishop Robert Sanchez of Santa Fe. The Fiesta ends with the burning in effigy of Zozobra, "Old Man Gloom," to dispel the sadness of the year and to make way for joy in the coming year. Santa Feans have been practicing this Fiesta for 279 years, and they've got it down right. For more information, call the **Santa Fe Convention and Visitors Bureau, 984-6760** or **1-800-777-CITY, 201 W. Marcy St.**

Indian Market

The Indian Market takes place during the third weekend in Aug. Now in its sixty-ninth year, the Indian Market is the largest juried Indian arts and crafts show in the world and draws about 75,000 people. For more information, call the **Southwestern Association of Indian Affairs, 983-5220.**

Spanish Market

The Spanish Market, held during the last full weekend in July, is a juried exhibit of Hispanic arts and crafts and attracts larger crowds every year. Call the **Spanish Colonial Arts Society, 983-4038.**

Music Festival

All through July and Aug., the old city puts its musical face forward. The world-famous Santa Fe Opera presents five operas, and the Desert Chorale also performs. For a listing of this year's dates and performances, call the **Santa Fe Convention and Visitors Bureau, 1-800-777-CITY**, the **Santa Fe Opera, 982-3851,** or the **Desert Chorale, 988-7505.**

Rodeo de Santa Fe

Ever since the mid-1940s, the rodeo has been held on Rodeo Rd. near Richards Ave. in southwest Santa Fe. With purses totalling $35,000, the rodeo attracts top riders, ropers, steer wrestlers and bull riders from the U.S. and Canada. It lasts four nights, with one Sat. matinee, and pleases some 20,000 spectators annually. All the usual rodeo competitions are included, plus a good parade. Call **982-4659** for more information.

—— OUTDOOR ACTIVITIES ——

The **Santa Fe ski basin** is just minutes from downtown Santa Fe and offers slopes for beginners to advanced skiers. See the Ski Areas of New Mexico section.

Trout streams and lakes are numerous in the immediate area, and access to these waters is provided free by the U.S. forest service. **Hiking trails** lead into both the Carson and the Santa Fe national forests, with trailheads easily accessible by car. If you are willing to walk 3 miles, you'll get away from the ribbon clerks and have privacy while you fish or hunt. Well stocked with rainbow trout, the small lakes and streams of the national forests are good fishing from early May through Oct. These same national forests offer good **hunting,** in season, for mule deer, elk, blue grouse and doves. For information about hunting and fishing, contact the state game and fish department, Villagra Building, or call **827-7911.**

Golf in Santa Fe is somewhat limited. The Santa Fe Country Club, located in south Santa Fe on Airport Rd., opens its course to the public but not its clubhouse. Call the pro shop at **471-2626** for information. Green fees are about $11 on weekdays, $16 on weekends.

Horse racing is one of Santa Fe's top attractions. Just west of Interstate 25, a few miles south of town, the Santa Fe Downs offers horse racing four days a week from May 26 through Labor Day. Call **471-3311** for more information and post times.

Whitewater Rafting

The Rio Grande changes its nature; north of Santa Fe it is a fast-flowing narrow river that dashes itself against the rocky sides of the Rio Grande Gorge. Below La Bajada (the downslope), south of Santa Fe, it spreads out and covers a lot of ground, becomes shallower and flows more peacefully.

Where it is a fast-flowing river, the Rio Grande offers some excellent **whitewater rafting.** Degree of danger and degree of expertise required varies with the season. When the spring runoff is at its highest, the Grande is a brawling, boisterous stream that challenges the nerves and ability of experienced river rafters. As the snow melt decreases, the flow slows down and the river becomes an interesting trip, but lacks the excitement of the higher water. Many firms in and around Santa Fe offer excellent whitewater rafting trips. You can get information from the **New Mexico Department of Tourism** at **1-800-545-2040** if you're calling from out of state. In state, call **827-0291.** Or if you want to save a call, contact the following outfitters directly. They can arrange everything for you to sample the whitewater of the Rio Grande:

Rojo Tours, at **983-8333,** Mon.–Fri., 9 A.M.– 5 P.M., or 986-0000 **ext. 445,** Sat. and Sun. **228 Old Santa Fe Trail, Santa Fe, NM 87501.**

New Wave Rafting Company, Route 5, Box 302A, Santa Fe, NM 87501. Call **455-2633** in winter, or **984-1444** in summer.

Rio Bravo River Tours, PO Box 524, Santa Fe, NM 87501, 988-1153.

Los Rios River Runners, PO Box 2734, Taos, NM 87571, 758-1550 or **776-8854.**

A word of advice on scheduling a whitewater rafting trip: Shop around for price breaks, but don't make your decision on price alone. If possible, see the equipment and talk to the person who will be leading you across the white water, then make your decision. Whitewater rafting is safe and exciting. Give it a try!

—————— **SEEING AND DOING** ——————

Before you start out to see Santa Fe, let's get one thing straight. You're going to walk, not ride in your car. Parking spaces are priceless in this city, which was laid out to accommodate the needs of the seventeenth century—those certainly didn't include automobile traffic. Park in one of the paid parking areas, as close to the central plaza as possible, and start out. Most of the many attractions are within half a mile of the St. Francis Cathedral.

Visit the **oldest church**, even with its unsubstantiated claim of being the oldest church in America. San Miguel Chapel at **401 Old Santa Fe Trail** and De Vargas St. was built in the 1600s by Tlaxcala Indians, who came from Mexico as servants of the Spanish conquistadores. The church was damaged severely in the Pueblo revolt in 1680 and rebuilt in 1710. It displays the San Jose Bell, thought to have been cast in Spain in 1356 and brought to Santa Fe through Mexico City. Archaeologists found that the site had been inhabited by Pueblo Indians as early as A.D. 1100. Right next door is a gift shop, occupying what is thought to be the oldest house in America. The church is just a short walk off the central plaza, and it's well worth a visit. For more information, call **983-3974**.

Escalera Famos, "famous staircase," is in the Loretto Chapel, built in 1873 to house the Sisters of Our Lady of Light, who came to establish a school for young ladies in Santa Fe. The staircase contains two 360-degree turns, a double helix with no visible central support. Legend has it that a master carpenter appeared out of nowhere, built the staircase and disappeared without even asking for his pay. The chapel is located at **211 Old Santa Fe Trail**. Call **984-7971** for information and admission fee.

St. Francis Cathedral, right off the central plaza at San Francisco St. and Cathedral Place, seems slightly out of place in this very Hispanic town, because its styling reflects the fact that it was built by French archbishop Jean-Baptiste Lamy in 1869. The archbishop and the church itself feature predominantly in Willa Cather's classic *Death Comes for the Archbishop*. Ask to see the wooden statue of St. Francis of Assisi and the famed *La Conquistadora* statue. On the Sun. after the feast of Corpus Christi, *La Conquistadora* is carried through the city to Our Lady of the Rosary Chapel. When visiting St. Francis Cathedral, please remember it is a church and treat it with respect. For further information, call **982-5619**.

Cristo Rey Church, on Upper Canyon Rd., is the largest modern adobe structure standing today. It was built by its parishioners, using dirt from the site to form the adobe bricks. It commemorates the four hundredth anniversary of Coronado's exploration of the Southwest (and you thought Plymouth Rock was old!). It was built to house the great *reredos*, "stone altar screens," which are probably the greatest artworks of the Spanish colonial period in New Mexico.

Santa Fe Outdoor Opera, located in a beautiful "outdoor" setting just 7 miles north of the city on U.S. Highway 84/285 near Tesuque, presents grand opera—the classical, the forgotten and the avant-garde. Internationally acclaimed, the company usually presents six different productions during the summer. The first performance is special, featuring a gala reception for the audience before the opera and waltzing under the stars after. For schedule and other information, call **982-3855**, or write **Santa Fe Opera, PO Box 2408, Santa Fe, NM 87504**.

Santuario de Nuestra Senora de Guadalupe was built around 1796 close to the same time America declared its independence and started building the United States. Its 3-foot-thick adobe walls house the largest and finest oil paintings of the Southwest. The most famous rendering of Our Lady of Guadalupe was painted in Mexico City by Jose de Alzibar, who signed and dated it in 1783. The big work of art was brought a thousand miles up the Camino Real on muleback! For more information, call **988-2027**. Admission is free.

Palace of the Governors, which makes up the north side of the central plaza, is the oldest seat of government in the United States. It housed the Spanish governor when it was first built in 1609–1610, 160-odd years before the Declaration of Independence was signed in the English part of North America. Since 1913 it has been the museum of history for New Mexico. It features historical exhibits of New Mexico's colorful past— Spanish, Mexican, Indian and pioneer American—and a good collection of old firearms and historical costumes. After seeing the exhibits, you'll want to shop the Indian market under the wide front portico, where turquoise and silver jewelry and other Indian artwork is sold. Admission is $3. For more information, call **827-6483**.

Museum of Fine Arts, west across the plaza from the Palace of the Governors at **107 W. Palace Ave.**, offers a collection of more than 8,000 pieces, most of them classified as New Mexican art. Georgia O'Keeffe and other well-known New Mexican painters are featured, and exhibits change regularly. For more information, call **827-4455**.

Museum of International Folk Art, located about 2 miles southeast of the plaza, is the largest folk-art museum in the world. Specializing in Hispanic arts, the museum houses a collection of 125,000 pieces, including the world-famous Alexander Girard collection. The newly added Hispanic heritage wing offers a wonderful display of Mexican art. Folk-art demonstrations and workshops are presented through the summer. You can spend an hour or a month—enjoyably. For further information, call **827-8350**.

Museum of Indian Arts and Culture, next door to the folk-art museum, features an exhibition of masterworks of Southwestern Indian culture. This museum does a fine job of interpreting the culture of Pueblo, Apache and Navajo Indians, emphasizing the important part played by Indian cultures in forming modern-day New Mexico. For information, call **827-8941**. Admission is $3.

Indian Arts Museum, at **1369 Cerrillos Rd.**, displays the works of the students and faculty of the Institute of American Indian Arts in Santa Fe. On the first Sun. in Dec., the museum holds a sale of the students' work. Displays open the first Sun. of June and continue through the last weekend of Aug. Open Mon.–Fri., 8 A.M.–5 P.M.; free admission. Call **988-6281** for more information.

Randall Davey Audubon Center, at **1800 Upper Canyon Rd.**, is the regional headquarters for the National Audubon Society but once was home to renowned artist Randall Davey. You can drive to the end of the Upper Canyon Rd., but if you do, you'll miss the pleasant walk through the length of it. Starting at El Zaguan, one of the oldest apartment buildings in America, you'll browse, shop and stroll the 2 miles of this historic roadway, past art galleries, shops and restaurants. It's one of the oldest barrios in the city. Call **983-4609** for tour specifics.

Barrio de Analco is one of the oldest continuously occupied streets in North America. Settled by Mexican Indians in the early 1600s, it is now called East De Vargas St. Interpertative plaques tell the story as you walk along this historic avenue.

Sena Plaza, across Palace Ave. from St. Francis Cathedral, is a quiet little enclosed area, circled by shops that face exquisite gardens. Also housed here is the well-known restaurant La Casa Sena. This historic spot was given to Alferes Diego Arias de Quiros in 1692 as a reward for helping with the reconquest of Santa Fe after the Pueblo Revolt. Major Sena, a friend of Kit Carson, bought it in 1867. The Sena family lived here until 1927, then deeded the historic spot to a group of Sante Fe people. It is still private property but always open to the public.

Cross of the Martyrs is reached by a long brick walkway, starting at the corner of Paseo de Peralta and Otero streets. Informational plaques guide the visitor up to the great white cross commemorating the Franciscan monks killed in the 1680 Pueblo Revolt. Not just a piece of history, the cross offers a wonderful view of the city below.

NEARBY ATTRACTIONS

Visit San Ildefonso, Pojoaque, Tesuque, Nambe and Santa Clara, all small and interesting Indian pueblos. None is more than a 40-minute drive from Santa Fe.

NIGHTLIFE

Not famed for its nightlife, Santa Fe nevertheless offers some excellent entertainment in downtown lounges. Local favorites Rueben and Antonio play excellent classical guitar at several spots in the downtown area— ask at any lounge for current information. The La Fonda Hotel at **100 E. San Francisco St.** has entertainers Al and Norma Tell on a regular basis and books outside acts from time to time. Call **982-5511** for information.

SCENIC DRIVES

The **Turquoise Trail** starts in Santa Fe and travels through historic towns of Golden (the site of the first gold rush west of the Mississippi), Cerillos (which once boasted 21 saloons) and Madrid (a coal-mining ghost town that now is home to artsy-craftsy folks and several types of nonconformists). An extension of the Turquoise Trail takes you to the top of the Sandia Mountains. From that 10,000-foot-high perch you have a fantastic view of Albuquerque, and your horizon will stretch all the way to Mount Taylor, 75 miles to the west. The trail then skirts through Albuquerque and heads back to Santa Fe on Interstate 25, with a fascinating stop at Santo Domingo Pueblo, which is still home to more than 3,500 Indians.

National forest drives start in Santa Fe and wind through the high mountains of the Santa Fe and Carson national forests. Order national forest maps of the Santa Fe and Carson forests for $2 each from **USFS Regional Office, 517 Gold, Albuquerque, NM 87102.**

Cochiti dam, reservoir, pueblo and golf course are just an hour's drive away. Whether you are interested in trying one of the nation's most challenging golf courses, fishing for bass, crappies, northern pike and catfish, or just enjoying a quiet picnic, Cochiti can satisfy your needs.

El Rancho de las Golondrinas, the most historic of southwestern ranches, is 15 minutes south of Santa Fe on Interstate 25 at exit 271. Buildings were repaired and restored to offer a glimpse into the Hispanic past of New Mexico. Visit a complete working rancho of 1780. In Spanish colonial times, this was the last overnight stop on the thousand-mile Royal Road from Mexico City to Santa Fe.

Actually, this is more a complete village than a museum. The annual **Spring Festival** is the first weekend in June, and the first weekend in Oct. finds the **Harvest Festival**. Featured during those festivals are Spanish folk dancing and music and authentic Mexican foods. Costumed interpreters demonstrate pioneer methods of spinning, weaving, soap making and other domestic chores of 1790. This highly recommended place is open Wed. and Sat., June–Aug., at 10 A.M. Cost: $3 for adults, $2 for those 12 to 18 years of age and $1 for those under 12. For more information, call **471-2261**.

WILDLIFE

Mule deer, elk, bighorn sheep, blue grouse, trout streams, fishing lakes, fish hatcheries, bandtail pigeons and doves all are within half a day's drive of Santa Fe. See Outdoor Activities section.

———————— WHERE TO STAY ————————

ACCOMMODATIONS

La Fonda—$$$-$$$$
Right on the historic plaza, La Fonda bills itself as the Inn at the End of the Santa Fe Trail. La Fonda was already there when Santa Fe was founded in 1610. This hotel offers much more than history: It is the meeting place of the city. If you don't choose to stay at the La Fonda, at least walk through its historic lobby and shops for the flavor of Santa Fe. **100 E. San Francisco St., 982-5511** or **1-800-523-5002**.

The rooms at La Fonda have to be seen to be appreciated. They are the authentic rooms of the Old Spanish Santa Fe. Fireplaces abound and window sills show the thickness of the ancient walls. Furniture is heavy and massive, but comfortable, and the lamps would have looked right at home centuries ago, yet they do a good job with modern electricity. Colors, wall hangings, everything speaks of Colonial Mexico—of Neuvo España—when Santa Fe became the oldest capital north of Old Mexico nearly four centuries ago.

Hilton of Santa Fe—$$$-$$$$
Built around the historic Casa de Ortiz, this is a different Hilton. It offers 155 rooms and suites and is close to everything. **100 Sandoval St., 988-2811** or **1-800-445-8667**.

La Posada de Santa Fe—$$$-$$$$
Of the 116 unique adobe guest accommodations, 86 have fireplaces. La Posada is three blocks from the plaza and has its own restaurant. **330 E. Palace Ave., 986-0000** or **1-800-727-5276**.

Best Western Lamplighter Motel—$$–$$$
The Lamplighter has 64 units, a restaurant and a lounge. **2405 Cerillos Rd., 471-8000 or 1-800-528-1234.**

Park Inn—$$–$$$
Has 83 units and an easy-to-reach location on south side. **2900 Cerillos Rd., 473-4281 or 1-800-279-0894.**

Eldorado—$$$$
This is one of the fanciest, biggest and highest priced hotels in town, with 218 rooms. **309 W. San Francisco St., 988-4455 or 1-800-CLARION.**

Hotel St. Francis—$$$–$$$$
Its convenient location makes it walking distance to the central plaza. **210 Don Gaspar, 983-5700 or 1-800-666-5700.**

There are dozens of lower-priced motels in Santa Fe. Take a good look. I'm sure you can find what you want in the price range you seek. But be warned that it might be difficult to find a vacancy in the three school-vacation months. If you are having trouble reserving a room in Santa Fe, call **1-800-982-7669** for Santa Fe's central reservation office. In state, call **1-983-8200**.

As you move away from the historic central plaza of Santa Fe, you move away from the cultural ambience—the Santa Fe Style—that is so heavily ballyhooed. But you also move into an area of excellent motels that are not "in," but which offer good accommodations at good prices, and you're still not too far from the historic part of Santa Fe. Many of these are grouped along Cerillos Rd., which is one of the main avenues entering the city. For good values at a short distance from the "style of Santa Fe," you can't do better than the motels along Cerillos Road.

Alamo Lodge—$
The Alamo Lodge has 19 rooms. **1842 Cerillos Rd., 982-1841.**

Best Western High Mesa Inn—$$$
This is a big one with 213 rooms. **3347 Cerillos Rd., 473-2800 or 1-800-528-1234.**

Santa Fe Budget Inn—$$–$$$
There are 160 rooms at the Budget Inn. **725 Cerillos Rd., 982-5952 or 1-800-552-0070.**

El Rey Inn—$$–$$$
Offers 56 rooms. **1862 Cerillos Rd., 982-1931.**

La Quinta—$$–$$$
Offers 130 rooms. **4298 Cerrillos Rd., 471-1142** or **1-800-531-5900.**

Motel 6—$$
Offers 104 rooms. **3007 Cerrillos Rd., 473-1380.**

Quality Inn—$$$
Offers 100 rooms. **3011 Cerrillos Rd., 471-1211** or **1-800-321-2222.**

Stage Coach—$$–$$$
Offers 14 rooms. **3360 Cerrillos Rd., 471-0707.**

Warren Inn—$–$$
Offers 88 rooms. **3357 Cerrillos Rd., 471-2033.**

Howard Johnson Plaza—$$$–$$$$
Offers 131 rooms. **4048 Cerrillos Rd., 473-4646** or **1-800-654-2000.**

CAMPGROUNDS

COMMERCIAL

Tesuque Pueblo RV Park
Eight miles northwest of Santa Fe on U.S. 84 and 285. Hookups, store, laundry, showers, pool. Used to be known as Camel Rock Campground. Open all year. **455-2661.**

Rancheros de Santa Fe
Seven miles southeast of Santa Fe on Old Las Vegas Highway. Full hookups, store, dump station, pool, rest rooms. Open Mar. 15–Nov. 1. **983-3482.**

Apache Canyon KOA
Eleven miles southeast of Santa Fe on Interstate 25, exit 294 or 290. Store, laundry, rest rooms, showers, game room, full hookups, dump station. Open Mar. 1–Nov. 1. **982-1419.**

PUBLIC

Aspen Basin
Fifteen miles northeast of Santa Fe on N.M. 475. Fifteen units. No water. National forest.

Bandelier National Monument
Forty-five miles northwest of Santa Fe off of N.M. 4. Water, sanitary facilities, store, snack bar, hiking. National Park Service. Open Mar.–Nov. **672-3861**.

Big Tesuque
Twelve miles northeast of Santa Fe on N.M. 475. Only 5 units, fishing, pit toilets, no water. National forest. Open May–Oct.

Black Canyon
Eight miles northeast of Santa Fe on N.M. 475. Fifty-two units, water, okay for trailers. National forest. Open May–Oct.

Hyde Memorial State Park
Eight miles northeast of Santa Fe on Hyde Park Rd. Shelters, water, fireplaces, pit toilets. Check in at ranger station. Call **986-0283** for information.

Cochiti Lake Project
Twenty-five miles south of Santa Fe on Interstate 25, then N.M. 16 to Cochiti Lake. Thirty-seven hookups, with electricity, rest rooms, showers, fireplaces. Offers fishing in lake. On Cochiti Indian lands. Open Apr.–Oct. **242-8302**.

OVERNIGHT RV PARKING

Los Campos, 3574 Cerillos Rd., 473-1949. Ninety-five full hookups. $19.75 per night.

Trailer Ranch, 3471 Cerillos Rd., 471-9970. One-hundred twenty hookups, $12 per night.

City parking lot. On Paseo de Peralta, just west of Scottish Rite Temple. Self-contained vehicles only. A $3 fee is charged.

—————— WHERE TO EAT ——————

Santa Fe offers more than 200 eating places, ranging from familiar fast-food places up to the most luxurious restaurants. Santa Fe cuisine is a mixture of Spanish, Mexican, Indian and a little bit of Anglo. Please don't visit Santa Fe without trying out *chalupas*, burritos, *rellenos*, *flautas* and blue-corn tortillas. Red and green chiles lend a wonderful flavor, but don't overdo the chiles until you've learned how your mouth reacts to fiery—and delicious—food.

You'll want to try more than one restaurant, but here are a few of my favorites.

La Casa Sena—$

Located in historic Sena Plaza, just across Palace Ave. from St. Francis Cathedral, the restaurant is easy to miss but worth seeking out. Excellent New Mexican cuisine, featuring such surprises as blue-corn and chicken enchiladas and smoked *butiffarra* sausages at lunch. And at dinnertime, try rack of lamb and *pollo mole norte*. Classy service, excellent food and a well-stocked bar. **125 E. Palace, 988-9232.**

The Shed—$

At **113 1/2 E. Palace Rd.**, just off the historic plaza. Serves lunch only, but that lunch is one of the city's best bargains. You'll be seated in one of a series of tiny interconnected rooms. Arrive early to avoid a long wait. Try the green chile soup. Credit cards and reservations not accepted. **982-9030.**

La Fonda Hotel Restaurant—$$$

100 E. San Francisco St. Good food and excellent service in an interesting setting. Located inside the famed hotel, at the corner of Central Plaza. **982-5511.**

Bull Ring—$$

414 Old Santa Fe Trail. Continental menu. **983-3328.**

La Tertulia Restaurant—$$

416 Agua Fria. Features the cuisine of northern New Mexico, a favorite of locals. **988-2769.**

Palace Restaurant—$$

1423 West Palace Ave. Offers a varied menu at reasonable prices. **982-9891.**

Pink Adobe—$$

406 Old Santa Fe Trail. One of Santa Fe's most famous eateries, the Pink Adobe features a continental menu along with excellent New Mexican dishes. **983-7712.**

San Francisco Bar and Grille—$$

114 West San Francisco St. Good American food at reasonable prices. **982-2044.**

Coyote Cafe—$$
132 West Water St. One of the more unusual eating places in the Holy City of the Faith of St. Francis of Assissi. Menu contains such surprises as venison meals, duck breast and broiled swordfish. Complete bar and wine list. **983-1615.**

SERVICES

Santa Fe Central Reservations, which can arrange advance booking for nearly everything in the city, is reached at **1-800-982-7669;** in state, call **983-8200.**

Twenty-four-hour **taxi service** is available by calling **989-8888** or **988-2090.** It provides delivery service, a wheelchair-lift van, four-wheel drive vehicles and transportation to the Albuquerque Sunport.

Visitor information is available in summer months from a kiosk in Central Plaza. Even better information can be found at the Chamber of Commerce, one block east of Guadalupe on Montezuma, **PO Box 1298, Santa Fe, NM, 983-7317;** or the **Santa Fe Visitors and Convention Bureau, 201 W. Maray St., Santa Fe, NM 87501, 984-6760** or **1-800-777-2489.**

Pueblo Indians still bake excellent bread in these primitive ovens, called *hornos* in Spanish. A fire is built within to heat the structure, then the fire is pulled out and the bread loaves inserted to bake by residual heat.

Española

Just 25 miles north of Santa Fe—nestled in between the 12,000-foot Jemez Mountains to the west and 13,000-foot Truchas Mountains on the east—the town of Española is the trade center of the Española Valley. It is watered by the Rio Grande, and Rio Chama and the Santa Cruz river add their flow to the big river near Española. There's an airport for small craft, with a 5,000-foot paved runway at 5,800 feet above sea level.

Española has earned some slight fame as the home of many low riders, extra-well-polished cars that have been "chopped" to put them close to the ground. Local aficionados for the low-rider fad are often seen cruising Española, particularly on the weekend.

Why would you choose Española as your headquarters for exploration? Many reasons, but first and foremost is that it is much cheaper than Santa Fe or Taos, its two bigger rivals for the tourist trade. The second-best reason is that Española is the center from which to explore the eight Indian pueblos that almost surround it. Española also is close to the Atomic City of Los Alamos and provides easy access to the Bandelier National Monument and to almost everything you come to the northern New Mexico scenic paradise to see and to do.

Española has been home to man since time beyond knowing. At least 500 years ago the Anasazi lived in Puye, whose ruins are nearby. Española is 86 miles north of Albuquerque, 353 miles south of Denver, 24 miles from Los Alamos and 44 miles from Taos. It is 5,595 feet above sea level, about the same as Albuquerque and Denver, but lower than Santa Fe. With only 10 inches of rainfall a year, it is dry country, and irrigation is important. Española is a good small town, but it is most attractive for what surrounds it.

HISTORY

Although Spanish history in the Española Valley starts with De Onate in 1598, the town of Española didn't exist until the 1880s, when it was built as an important station on the Denver and Rio Grande railroad. The railroad disappeared, but Española is very much with us.

GETTING THERE

Greyhound offers daily transportation to and from the Albuquerque airport. The **bus depot** is at the junction of Onate St. and U.S. 285.

—— FESTIVALS AND EVENTS ——

Fiesta de Onate
   In July. Española honors the first Spanish leader to visit the Española Valley.

Farolitos and Luminaria
   On Christmas Eve, this small town puts on a tremendous display to light the way for the Christ Child—a tradition of hundreds of years ago.

Española Valley Arts Festival
   In Oct. On the campus of the Northern New Mexico Community College to show the arts and crafts produced in the valley.

—— OUTDOOR ACTIVITIES ——

There's lots of **trout fishing** in the mountain streams and lakes of the national forests that surround Española. **Hiking** trails are plentiful. Maps can be obtained from the ranger station in Española.
   There are two public **swimming pools** in the town.
   Using Española as a base, explore the **eight northern pueblos**—Tesuque, Pojoaque, Taos, Santa Clara, San Ildefonso, San Juan, Picuris and Nambe. Islands of Indian culture in the Hispano-Anglo sea, the pueblos have done a remarkable job of preserving their language and their culture against great odds. We can learn much from the people of the pueblos. Each pueblo has its own style and coloring of the native pottery.

—— SEEING AND DOING ——

In Española, visit the **Bond House Museum**. Once the residence of a pioneer businessman, it is now home to interesting historical exhibits and rotating displays of local art. The building itself is a combination of adobe and Victorian architecture. **710 Bond St., 753-2377.**
   Visit **Holy Cross Church** in Santa Cruz, built in 1733, housing some of the best examples of Spanish colonial and religious art. Located at **100 Church St., Santa Cruz, NM 87567, 753-3345.**

NEARBY ATTRACTIONS

Rancho de Chimayo, just a short drive from Española on N.M. 76, called the High Road to Taos, offers a delightful old hacienda and an excellent restaurant. Watch closely for the turnoff onto N.M. 520. Call **351-2222** for information. Right there at the intersection, you'll find the eighth generation of weavers working at the Ortega looms. Another half mile on N.M. 520, and you come to the fascinating **Santuario de Chimayo**. On Good Friday as many as 30,000 people make the pilgrimage to the *santuario,* where many miraculous cures have been reported. Whether or not you believe in miracles, you'll enjoy the peace and quiet of this historic church, which dates from 1819.

If you want to spend just an afternoon, plan to eat at the **Restaurant de Chimayo,** a quarter mile north of Santuario on Hwy. 520, now the refurbished home of Hermenegildo Jaramillo, which is at least a century old. Good food, wonderful atmosphere. Reservations recommended. **351-4444.** And if you want to really experience Chimayo, book yourself into one of the seven guest rooms at the **Hacienda de Chimayo,** PO Box 11, the restored home of Epifanio Jaramillo. **1-800-477-1441.** In state, call **351-2222.**

Santa Cruz Lake, about 6 miles east on N.M. 76, then 4 miles south on N.M. 503, is a man-made reservoir that provides irrigation water to the valley and good fishing for stocked trout. You can continue past the entrance to the lake and find the **Borrego Mesa Campground** on the edge of the Pecos Wilderness.

Truchas, one of the most isolated of the Spanish colonial towns, was the scene for much of Robert Redford's movie, *The Milagro Beanfield War.* Spectacular mountain views and some good art galleries. It is 19 miles east of Española on N.M. 76.

Trampas, 25 miles east on N.M. 76, offers the **San Jose Church,** one of the most beautiful built during the Spanish period.

Chamisal, 4 miles past Trampas on N.M. 76, is a typical little village of the Spanish period.

Picuris Pueblo, reached by taking N.M. 76 from Española to the junction with N.M. 75, then 2 miles west, was once home to an Indian tribe. It now operates a tribal museum, **587-2519,** and offers guided tours through the old pueblo. Special day is Aug. 10, when the devout Picuris people celebrate the feast day of Saint Lorenzo. Call **587-2519** for information.

San Juan Pueblo, 4 miles north on N.M. 68, then a mile west to the river on N.M. 74, was the first Spanish settlement in the area that is now New Mexico. Today the pueblo is the headquarters for the eight northern pueblos. The San Juan Pueblo is known for the interesting designs incised into the brown and red clays of its pottery. Special feast day is June 24. For information, call the pueblo at **852-4265.**

Ojo Caliente, 21 miles north of Española on U.S. 285, offers hot mineral springs—spa, massage, restaurant and lodging. Open all year. **583-2233**.

San Ildefonso Pueblo, 10 miles south on N.M. 30, then 4 miles west on N.M. 502, is one of the larger pueblos of the region and is famed for its black-on-black pottery. This was the home of Maria, the potter of San Ildefonso, about whom a book was written. Call the **San Ildefonso Visitors Center** for information at **455-3549**.

Bandelier National Monument, operated by the National Park Service, protects the interesting ruins of a prehistoric people who lived there in the years 1200 to 1500. Take N.M. 30 southwest of Española to N.M. 4, then follow the signs. It's a 20-minute drive. Call **672-3861** for information.

Santa Clara Pueblo, just south of Española, owns and operates the spectacular Puye Cliffs Historic Area, a national landmark. You can walk about in the 740-room pueblo, which was once home to 1,250 Anasazi. Just 7 miles west of N.M. 30 on an excellent blacktopped road, you come to the Puye Cliff Dwellings. Entry fee is $4, $3 for seniors or children. If the climbing trails up to the primitive cliff dwellings are too much for you, get a permit and drive to the top of the mesa. There you'll see the

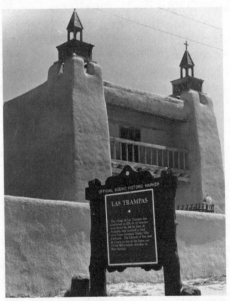

Many Catholic churches dating from the Spanish conquest era are still to be found in the Hispanic Highlands of New Mexico. This one at Las Trampas, east of Española, is a good example.

ruins of adobe dwellings used by the Santa Clara people before they moved down into the Rio Grande Valley.

Four miles farther up the blacktop you'll come to Santa Clara Canyon, which offers good **trout fishing** in three ponds and a fast-running little stream. Be forewarned, however: The prices are high. Costs $10 a day to fish there—no state license needed—and the creel limit is eight trout. There are lovely picnic sites, but the picnicking fee is $8.

For further information contact the **Santa Clara Pueblo Governor's Office** at **753-7330.**

SCENIC DRIVES

The Española Valley offers five excellent scenic tours. Pamphlets at the Chamber of Commerce in the Big Rock Shopping Center will lead you to (1) the Española area tour, (2) the high road to Taos, (3) the river road to Taos, (4) the Ojo Caliente to Chama tour and (5) the Los Alamos and Santa Fe tour. If you move right along, you can combine tours 2 and 3 by taking the high road up to Taos and returning by the river road. But why hurry? This is a serene, restful land where *mañana* is good enough for me.

WILDLIFE

The mountains encircling Española are rich in wildlife, especially mule deer, blue grouse and elk. The many black bears are shy and wary, seldom seen. Check with the national forest people at the ranger station in Española about fishing opportunities, **753-7331.**

———— WHERE TO STAY ————

ACCOMMODATIONS

Western Holiday Motel—$$
Rates are among the lowest in the Española Valley for quality lodging with 24 rooms. A quarter mile south of Española on the Santa Fe Hwy., **753-2491.**

Chamisa Inn Motel—$$–$$$
A lovely adobe-style motel, the Chamisa Inn has 51 units, a restaurant

and a lounge. Discount for seniors or AAA members. Near the junction of N.M. 76 and N.M. 84 at the north end of Española at **920 N. Riverside Dr., 753-7291.**

Super 8 Motel—$$
This is the only motel I know of with room service from the fast-food Sonic restaurant right next door. Brand new, nice, 50 rooms. At **298 S. Riverside Dr.** on the south end of town. **753-5374.**

Bed and Breakfasts—$$$
La Pueblo House, 10 rooms, **753-3981**; La Posada will have four rooms after May 1992, **351-4605**; and Casa del Rio, two rooms accommodate four to five guests, **753-6049.**

CAMPGROUNDS

COMMERCIAL

Chimayo Campground
Eight miles from Española on the high road to Taos; entrance just past the Exxon station in Chimayo. Offers full RV hookups, laundry facilities, showers and a quiet setting. Close to everything. **351-4566.**

Tesuque Pueblo RV Park
Formerly known as the Camel Rock campground, right on U.S. 285 between Española and Santa Fe. Call **455-2661** for information and reservations.

The New Mexico Game and Fish Department, Villagra Building, Santa Fe, NM 87503, 827-7911, will send you an excellent map called "New Mexico Outdoors," which lists all camping sites in the state, with descriptions of facilities and directions to the camping sites.

PUBLIC

Lots of camp sites on the Santa Fe National Forest. Secure maps and directions at the forest service ranger station in Española, **753-7331.**

—————— SERVICES ——————

The **hospital** phone is **753-7111**. The **ambulance-service** phone is **753-3114.**

══════ Pueblo Revolt ══════

The residents of New Mexico's pueblos are a miraculous example of how tenaciously a people can cling to the things that they hold dear. Although surrounded by English- and Spanish-speaking peoples, the Pueblo Indians have kept their own language throughout the centuries.

Raided and pillaged by Navajo, Apache and Comanche for centuries before the Spanish came to add to their troubles, the Indians of the pueblos maintained their integrity in most instances. Some were scared to death (such as those in the salt pueblos east of Mountainair), and a few picked up and joined other pueblos when they were threatened with extinction (for example, the small Rio Grande pueblos joined the Jemez Pueblo for safety reasons).

The peoples who populate the eight northern pueblos of San Juan, Santa Clara, San Ildefonso, Taos, Tesuque, Pojoaque, Nambe and Picuris (also called San Lorenzo) accepted the Roman Catholic faith, which came to them with the conquistadores, but they accepted it in addition to, not instead of, their old-line beliefs. In many cases, the devout people of the pueblos bring statues of the Catholic saints out of the church and put them at a vantage point where they can observe the old beliefs as portrayed in the Corn Dance or other festivals. "We are not ashamed of our old ways," the Pueblo Indians say. "See? We bring the saints out to watch!"

But the rule of the *españoles* was very hard. Indians were generally regarded as a *gente sin razón*, "a people without the ability to reason." They were expected to work long hours for the Spanish and to give up large portions of their crops to tide the Spanish over in winter. But there was a boiling point, even for such calm and peaceful peoples.

The northern pueblos' boiling point was reached in 1680. In 1675, the Spaniards, intolerant of native religious beliefs, had burned kivas and other ceremonial sites, and they had made the mistake of flogging approximately 50 leaders of the native people, claiming that they practiced witchcraft.

One of those flogged was Pope, a member of the San Juan Pueblo. After his punishment, he fled north to the biggest pueblo, the Taos. There, Pope organized the pueblo leaders for a rebellion scheduled for Aug. 13. Then the Indians discovered that the Spaniards had learned of their plans, so they moved the date up three days. On Aug. 10, the northern pueblos rose in unison against their intolerant Spanish masters.

The rebels burned missions and killed priests, soldiers and farmers alike, driving out or killing every Spaniard. The survivors gathered in Santa Fe and withstood a siege by the Indians for nine days. Then the nearly 1,000 Spaniards made a break for it, traveling downriver to El Paso. The Indians watched them go and then moved in to occupy Santa Fe. Once in the capital of New Spain, they ceremoniously eradicated every sign of Spanish occupation.

The Indians held Santa Fe for 12 years, until Aug. 1692. Then the Spanish began a systematic reconquest of the now factionalized Pueblo Indians. Led by Don Diego de Vargas (his full name was Don Diego de Vargas Zapata Lujan Ponce de Leon), they marched up the Rio Grande and easily conquered the first pueblos they encountered. They then laid siege to Santa Fe, convincing the few Indians holed up there that they had no chance against De Vargas's soldiers. The Indians surrendered rather meekly, and De Vargas moved back into his capital city. It took him four years, however, to quell the revolt in the northern pueblos. He attacked them one by one. The Jemez Pueblo fought hard and long, but some of the smallest pueblos, such as Zia and San Felipe, not only surrendered but actually joined the Spaniards in the fight against Jemez.

Nowhere in North America did the native people rebel so long and so successfully against European occupation. This stubbornness has served the Pueblo people well in their struggle to maintain their language and keep their old ways in addition to their devout Catholicism.

Some of the pueblos allow you to take pictures—for a fee—such as Taos; some bar cameras entirely. Others allow cameras for some feast days and bar them for other days. Please respect the wishes of the Pueblo Indians. They signed peace treaties with the United States, and they have lived up to those treaties. Don't try to sneak a couple of photographs where photography is forbidden—it may cost you your camera.

An interesting speculation: What might have happened if the Spaniards had been benevolent occupiers instead of cruel tyrants? Would the tremendous expanse of New Mexico, along with part of Colorado, all of Texas and all of Mexico, still be New Spain? Surely the course of history would have been different.

═══════ Taos ═══════

One of the oldest continuously occupied locations in North America, Taos Pueblo has existed, in one form or another, since 3000 B.C. The town of Taos is small, but it packs much of interest. Almost everything is within walking distance for the tourist. Taos is only 70 miles from Santa Fe, sitting up against the beautiful Taos Mountain, part of the Sangre de Cristo (Blood of Christ) Mountains. They got their name when Spanish explorers saw the snow-clad slopes gleaming a dull red in the late-afternoon sun. Taos is renowned for three things: (1) the Taos Pueblo, (2) art colonies and galleries, among the best in the world, and (3) skiing.

─────── HISTORY ───────

If history is among your main interests, you'll be fascinated by the three Taoses. The Taos Pueblo, a five-story apartment dwelling–cum–fort, has been inhabited by Indians since time immemorial, certainly since the year A.D. 300. The City of Taos is a relative newcomer, as it was founded in 1598 by Don Juan de Onate, the official colonizer of New Spain. That means that the town is almost 400 years old (and then there's Ranchos de Taos, a relatively new development). Taos is the home of Kit Carson and the terminus of one branch of the Santa Fe Trail.

Spanish settlers in Taos had a rough time of it. To avoid starvation, they were forced to battle the Taos Indians to steal some of their corn. Naturally, this did little to bring about good relations with the Taoseños. The Pueblo Revolt of 1680 killed or drove away all of the Spanish settlers and their priests. That rebellion, the only one in North America that reclaimed land for the native Indians, was started in Taos. In 1692, Don Diego de Vargas led a reconquest of the region and brought all of the pueblos back under Spanish rule. De Vargas did little to win a popularity contest. He raided the Taos Pueblo again in 1694 to get corn for the starving settlers. The Taos Pueblo rebelled again in 1696, and again De Vargas came to quell the rebellion. From that date forward, the people of the Taos Pueblo were allies of the Spanish and, later on, allies of the Mexicans when the Indians won their independence from Spain.

Starting back in the last decade of the seventeenth century and continuing into modern times, Taos trade fairs were important business and social events on the Spanish frontier. Even during the 1760s, when the Comanches raided the pueblos and drove away some of the settlers, the trade fairs grew in importance. In 1779 Colonel Juan Baptista de Anza whipped the Comanche and put a stop to their raids against Taos.

The famed frontiersman Kit Carson made his home in Taos from 1826 until 1868. He married Josefa Jaramillo and built a house for his bride. He's buried in Taos, where a beautiful park is named for him.

When American troops under General Stepehn W. Kearney occupied Taos, the Pueblo Indians decided that they didn't care for this group of palefaces either. They killed Governor Charles Bent in his home in Taos in 1847.

During the Civil War, when the Confederate flag flew over Sante Fe, frontiersmen flew the American flag over Taos. Kit Carson, Smith Simpson and Ceran St. Vrain guarded that American flag. Because of their bravery, Taos is granted the privilege of flying the American flag both day and night.

Gold was discovered in the nearby Moreno Valley in 1866, which brought another invasion of people. But the most lasting invasion started in 1898, when artists flocked to Taos, attracted by the clear light and majestic scenery. That invasion is ongoing, and many famous artists live and work in Taos, making its galleries some of the most important in the entire art world.

The latest invasion consists of skiers, and they come by the thousands to enjoy both downhill and cross-country runs. As a vacation spot, Taos has something to offer everyone, every day of the year.

Taos is two and a half hours from Albuquerque's Sunport. Regular shuttle service is provided by **Faust Transportation**, at **758-3410**. Rental cars are available in Albuquerque, Taos and the Taos Ski Valley. Taos has a municipal airport, **758-4995**. Angel Fire Airport also serves Taos, **377-3160**.

—— FESTIVALS AND EVENTS ——

Fiestas de Santiago y de Santa Anna
   In July.

Taos Pueblo's Annual Powwow
   In July.

International Chili Cook-off
   On Labor Day.

Turtle Dance and the Deer or Buffalo Dance
   In Jan. At Taos Pueblo. Dates vary from year to year.

Santa Cruz Corn Dance
   In May. At Taos Pueblo.

San Antonio Day Corn Dance and San Juan Day Corn Dance
In June. At Taos Pueblo.

Matachines Dance
In Dec. At Taos Pueblo.

San Geronimo Day
In Sept. Trade fair and dances at Taos Pueblo.

Contact the Taos County Chamber of Commerce for dates and other information, **758-3873** or **1-800-732-8267, Drawer I, Taos, NM 87571.**

────── **OUTDOOR ACTIVITIES** ──────

During the winter, you can take your family or friends on a **sleigh ride** in 10-person Russian-type sleighs, complete with hot beverages, Indian chili and storytelling! Call **758-3212** or **1-800-659-3210,** and talk to the folks at the Taos Indian Horse Ranch for an appointment and information on rates.

For information on cycling in Taos, contact **Taos Sports Company, 312 S. Santa Fe Rd., 758-9831.**

Horseback riding is available May–Oct. at Shadow Mountain Guest Ranch, **758-7732,** and the Taos Indian Horse Ranch, **753-3212.**

You'll find many trails to ride in an **off-road vehicle,** whether it be a snowmobile in the winter or a four-wheel drive all year long. Best bets are on the Camino Real Ranger District of the Carson National Forest, which is in Penasco. Call **758-8268,** or write **PO Box 68, Penasco, NM 87553.**

Fishing is available at many places on the three units of the Carson National Forest and in the Rio Grande Gorge, all described in a publication (with map) offered by the Carson National Forest on Cruz Alta Road in Taos. For an advance copy, telephone the national forest at **758-6200,** or the Bureau of Land Management, **758-8857.** Some of my favorite spots close to Taos include Cabresto Lake, 9 miles from Questa. This 15-acre lake is kept well stocked with rainbow trout. Camping is allowed at the lake, but don't try to drive a big motor coach over that road. The Shuree Lakes provide five small ponds in a majestic mountain locale—excellent for young anglers learning the art of fishing.

The Red River trout waters at Eagle Rock Lake and Fawn Lakes offer lots of good trout fishing. They are described in the Red River chapter. Hopewell and Lagunitas lakes, on the west side of the Rio Grande gorge, are also excellent possibilities. The Chama River, one of the state's best trout streams, and the El Vado-Heron Lake complex are described in **Chama.**

Mountain biking is popular in the Taos area, with the best routes being in the Carson National Forest. A good mountain biking pamphlet is obtainable from the national forest headquarters in Taos. There are trails for different degrees of difficulty, so check with the forest rangers, **587-2255**, about the trip you plan before you set out. You can even bike to Gallegos Peak, at an elevation of 10,500 feet. The best bet of all is a 5-mile loop, the Devisadero, right at Taos. It has much to offer, but it is for experts only.

Whitewater rafting is available from May through Aug. depending on the flow of the Rio Grande gorge area. Taos Central Reservations will be glad to give you the latest information and arrange a rafting trip for you. Call **1-800-821-2437,** or in state, **758-9767.**

SKIING NEAR TAOS

The Taos Ski Valley is famous for its powder snows, bright winter sunshine and slopes to challenge all comers. The valley offers 71 slopes, and the vertical drop is 2,612 feet!

Forty-five minutes from downtown, the valley averages about 325 inches of snowfall every winter. The town of Taos is 7,000 feet above sea level, but Taos Mountain towers up to 11,819 feet. During the long ski season (Thanksgiving to Easter), the weather is generally good, with temperatures dropping to about 10 degrees in the morning and warming into the 50s most afternoons. Ernie Blake, a Swiss ski enthusiast, envisioned the famous Taos ski resort and made his dream come true. Skis and equipment can be purchased or rented, and expert instructors can get you started right. Buy your lift tickets at the Olympic Ski Shop in town or the ticket office in the ski valley for $12 per half day for kids 12 and under, up to $32 for adults for full days. A mogul medical clinic is open daily during ski season.

Excellent cross-country skiing can be had in the Carson National Forest. For information, call **587-2255** For information about snow conditions in the area, call **776-2916** for the latest 24-hour snow information.

——— SEEING AND DOING ———

Taos offers even more than just skiing, perusing art galleries and visiting Indian Pueblos. Before setting out to explore this interesting old town, pick up a map at the local Chamber of Commerce and talk to the folks in that office. The office is on Pueblo Sun, next to Indian Hills Inn,

758-3873 or 1-800-732-8267. They'll answer most of your questions and steer you right. Here are some "don't miss!" places to visit.

Taos Pueblo is a 900-year-old Indian community still inhabited by the Taos Indians. Go north on Paseo del Pueblo Norte. There's an entrance charge of $5 per person and an additional $5 per camera. It's worth it! They'll give you a map of the Pueblo and show you where you can and cannot go. Write the Visitors Center, Box 1846, Taos Pueblo, NM 87571, or call 758-9593.

Millicent Rogers Museum, 4 miles north of Taos on N.M. 68, features excellent exhibits of Hispanic and Native American art. Open daily, 9–5 (closed Mondays in winter). Call 758-2462.

Kit Carson's Home and Historical Museum, on E. Kit Carson Rd. at Taos Plaza, will teach you a lot about the history of the real Old West and this historic figure from our pioneer past. 758-4741.

Ernest L. Blumenschein Memorial Home, on Ledoux St. west of Taos Plaza, is a reminder of the art and adobe charm of old-time Taos, blended with European culture. Ernest L. Blumenschein was one of the early artists who established the city as an important art colony. His restored home contains both examples of his art and that of other early Taos artists, but also artifacts of the period when Indian, Spanish and European cultures were blending in this city, which has been attracting artists for nearly 400 years. 758-0330.

Governor Bent House and Museum, on Bent St. one block north of the plaza, displays lots of artifacts of Taos history and culture. Unlucky Governor Bent was named to the post and took over, but his term was shortened because he was killed by the Pueblo Indians.

Nicolai Fechin Institute, on Paseo del Pueblo Norte (N. Pueblo Rd.), is the home of Russian artist Nicolai Fechin. 758-1710. Closed holidays.

Martinez Hacienda, a magnificent home of 21 rooms, built around two courtyards, was fortified against Indian attack. It is more than 200 years old. Located 2 miles from the plaza on Ranchitos Rd., 758-1000.

St. Francis de Assis Church is the one painted by Georgia O'Keeffe and others. It is 6 miles south of Taos on Hwy 68. Very photogenic.

Stables Art Center, 133 Paseo del Pueblo Norte, in the heart of Taos, has as many as 14 shows each year, the finest art of Taos and all of New Mexico. 758-2052.

Rio Grande Gorge Bridge, which won numerous design awards, spans the 650-foot-deep gorge carved by the Rio Grande. Go north on N.M. 68 to the junction with U.S. 64, then go west. Fifteen-minute drive.

Stop in at the Taos Chamber of Commerce on Pueblo Sun (758-3873), and pick up a free pamphlet for a self-guided walking tour of historic Taos. It outlines things you would otherwise miss, such as the oldest building in the city, which now houses the El Patio restaurant, and the famed Taos Murals, upstairs in Burke Armstrong's gallery.

Kit Carson Park, just two blocks north of the plaza, is a lovely place of shade and greenery, and a nice spot to rest your tired feet before setting out again to explore this fascinating city.

NIGHTLIFE

Sagebrush Inn
The favorite gathering place in Taos, with nightly live entertainment. S. Santa Fe Rd., **758-2254**.

Adobe Bar
Just north of the plaza on N. Pueblo Rd. at the Taos Inn, features complete bar service, famous margaritas (take it easy—they sneak up on you) and an excellent restaurant. **758-2233**.

El Patio
Just off the plaza in the northwest alley, offers classical guitar worth hearing. Call **758-2121** for more information.

———— WHERE TO STAY ————

ACCOMMODATIONS

Taos Inn—$$$
Just steps off of the plaza on N. Pueblo Rd., the Taos Inn is a museum in its own right. The comfortable rooms have fireplaces, antiques, hand-loomed Indian bedspreads and original artwork. **1-800-TAOS-INN** or **758-2233**.

Ramada Inn Taos—$$$
One mile from the plaza, the Ramada offers 124 rooms, a restaurant and a lounge. **758-2900** or **1-800-228-2828**.

Kachina Lodge—$$–$$$
Located on N. Pueblo Rd. five blocks north of the plaza, this Best Western motel has 122 rooms with entertainment, a restaurant and a bar. **758-2275** or **1-800-528-1234**.

Shadow Mountain Guest Ranch—$$$
Surrounded by the national forest, this ranch is open all year, offering

rooms, cabins, family-style meals, horseback riding, fishing and hiking. **758-7732.**

Quail Ridge Inn Resort—$$$–$$$$
Four miles north of Taos on Hwy 150 to Taos Ski Valley. The resort offers 110 suites and rooms, fireplaces, color TV, a heated pool open all year, saunas, a restaurant, lounge and a fitness center. **1-800-624-4448** or **776-2211.**

Quality Inn—$$$
Just 2 miles south of the plaza on N.M. 68, the Quality Inn is decorated in the Southwestern style, with a good restaurant, lounge and hot tubs. **1-800-228-5151** or **758-2200.**

Sagebrush Inn—$$$
This inn has been a landmark in Taos since 1929. It is 2 miles south of the plaza on N.M. 68 at S. Santa Fe Rd. Good restaurant and lounge. **1-800-428-3626** or **758-2254.**

El Monte Lodge—$$$
Located on E. Kit Carson Rd., this lodge boasts a history of 50 years. Lots of personality. **1-800-828-TAOS** or **758-3171.**

El Pueblo Lodge and Condominiums—$$$
The lodge, on Paseo del Pueblo Norte, has 46 units, a heated pool and a spa. Three two- and three-bedroom condos also on site. **1-800-433-9612** or **758-8700.**

Hotel La Fonda de Taos—$$$
Quiet yet right on the south side of the historic plaza. **758-2211.**

San Geronimo Lodge—$$$
At corner of Witt and San Geronimo roads, the lodge offers 18 units in century-old adobe, mountain views and saunas. **758-7117.**

There are several dozen motels in lower price ranges, with rates all the way down to $32 per night. The Taos Chamber of Commerce can furnish a complete listing, and **Taos Accommodations Unlimited** can book you into a motel in your price range. The phone is **1-800-548-2146.**

At last count there were over 30 bed and breakfasts in Taos, at prices from $25 to $75. The **Taos Bed and Breakfast Association** will gladly mail you a list, **1-800-876-7857** or **758-4747** or **758-5648.**

CAMPGROUNDS

COMMERCIAL

Sierra Village Campground and Mobile Home Park
Eight miles east of Taos. Offers fishing, hiking and peace and quiet.
Priced from $8 per night. **758-3660.**

Taos RV Park and Campground
About 3 miles south of town on Hwy. 68. Has 30 spaces and laundromat.
Priced from $12. **758-1327.**

Taos RV Park
Open all year. **1-800-323-6009** or **758-2524.**

Taos Valley RV Park
Two and a half miles south of Taos. Has 92 spaces, including 60-foot pull-
throughs. Priced from $10.75 per night. Also spaces for tenters. **758-4469.**

PUBLIC

Camping opportunities are everywhere in the Taos area. The Camino
Real Ranger District alone offers 15 forest service campgrounds, with fees
charged at the three campgrounds that offer potable water (there's running
water next to all the camping sites, but it is not potable). Bring your own
beverages, and camp free. You can also camp anywhere in the national
forest, and pick your own site. For information and a good map of the camping
areas, write to the **Carson National Forest, Taos, NM,** or call **758-6200.**

————— WHERE TO EAT —————

Doc Martin's—$$$
125 Paseo del Norte in the Taos Inn. Excellent food and good service.
Call **758-1977** for reservations.

Casa de Valdez—$$
Paseo del Pueblo Sur. Casual atmosphere and good food—especially
steaks and barbecued meats. **758-8777.**

Don Pedro's—$$$
On S. Santa Fe Rd. Serves fine sopaipillas and *chile rellenos*—the real
thing. Closed Mon. **758-9281.**

El Patio—$$

Right behind the plaza. Offers good classical guitar with your dining by the indoor fountain. The food is as good as the ambience, and that's a compliment. **758-2121**.

Northtown Restaurant

North on U.S. 64. Another local favorite. Try the green chile! **758-2374**.

Montes Chowchat

On Paseo del Pueblo Sur. Offers good Spanish and American foods in the lower price range. **758-9317**.

El Taoseño—$

On Paseo del Pueblo Sur. Favored by locals for good Mexican food— a good recommendation. **758-9511**.

Michael's Kitchen—$

On Paseo del Pueblo Norte. Offers both Spanish and American meals at excellent low prices. **758-4178**.

Roberto's Restaurant—$

On Kit Carson Rd. Featuring local-flavor Spanish cuisine. **758-2434**.

——————— SERVICES ———————

Taos has only one taxi service, but this one is enough. Call **Faust's Transportation** at **758-3410** or **758-7359** no matter where or when you want to move. Faust's provides a daily shuttle service from Taos Ski Valley, Angel Fire and Red River to the Albuquerque airport and also furnishes the ski valley shuttle from Taos on convenient schedules.

Pride of Taos provides daily shuttle service from Taos to the Albuquerque airport. Call **758-8340**.

Taos Accommodations Unlimited will make reservations for almost everything offered in Taos, including all lodgings and rentals. Call **1-800-548-2146** or **758-8899**.

Taos Central Reservations can also make your reservations. Call **1-800-821-2437** or **758-9767**. Office hours are Mon.–Fri. 9 A.M.–6 P.M., Sat. noon–5 P.M.

Angel Fire

Half an hour and 22 miles east of Taos on scenic U.S. 64, you'll come to Angel Fire, clearly marked by big signs. Start watching for it after you top out over 9,100-foot-high Palo Flechado pass. Angel Fire is a tastefully designed total community, built around the famed ski slopes and the world's highest 18-hole championship golf course. If you are looking for permanent residence, you can find it here. If you are looking for golf or skiing—not in the same month, however—Angel Fire is the place. Angel Fire ski areas offer six lifts to get you up there and 41 runs to challenge you on the way down.

The **Inn at Angel Fire** ($$) is a lovely place to stay, offering 33 rooms with a private bath and color TV in every room **(377-2504)**. A continental breakfast is included. There are eight restaurants, six tennis courts, hiking and golfing packages. The **Legends Hotel**, right at the ski area, has 157 rooms and two fine restaurants to serve you. For current prices and all information on Angel Fire, call Jimmy Linton at **377-6401**.

Snow Smoke: All but hidden by the rising spume of powder, this skier powers a turn to catch the next mogul as he eases down Hell's Bells, one of the most challenging slopes at Angel Fire Ski Resort in the high Rocky Mountains of Northern New Mexico.

Vietnam
Veterans Memorial

A few miles northeast of Angel Fire on the west side of U.S. 64, you'll see the sweeping lines of the Vietnam Veterans Memorial. In simple eloquence, the chapel forms a curving line to a slender peak. It was built by a grieving father for his son lost in Vietnam and has been taken over by the Disabled American Veterans. This monument really looks like it belongs there and may bring a lump to your throat. But it will also give you a feeling of peace—for the once forgotten and now remembered veterans who served their country in Vietnam. Admission to the chapel and visitors center is free. You really should stop to see this memorial. Then head north to Eagle Nest Lake and on to Red River.

The Vietnam Veterans Memorial near Angel Fire was built by a father who lost his son in the Vietnam war. (Photo by Mark Nohl, New Mexico Economic and Tourism Department.)

Eagle Nest
Lake and Town

Continuing northeast from the Vietnam Veterans Memorial, you'll see the shining expanse of Eagle Nest Lake, a prime trout-fishing spot in the Hispanic Highlands. The lake is leased from its cattle-ranching owners by the game and fish department, and access is free. All you need is a New Mexico fishing license, and you can catch rainbow trout from the shore or from your boat.

The lake was built by Charles Springer to provide irrigation for the Moreno Valley. The dam was built in 1916, but the town of Eagle Nest wasn't established until 1920. It is still a mighty small town, and there's no high-priced, high-pressure recreation area—only a beautiful spot to enjoy windsurfing and fishing in the summer, and snowmobiling, ice fishing and cross-country skiing in the winter. To really take advantage of the lake and its fishing for rainbow, cutthroat and kokanee salmon, rent a pontoon boat ($70 for a half day, $120 for a full day; 7 A.M.–8 P.M.). In Eagle Nest call **377-6813**. If you're making Red River your headquarters, call **754-2441** in that town for reservations and information.

Looking for a motel in Eagle Nest? Try the **Moore Rest Inn** ($$) on the highway at the east edge of town. **377-6813**.

Golden Eagle RV Park, right in town and close to everything, is operated by Ray and Margie Mott from Apr. 15 through the end of Oct. **377-6188** or **1-800-388-6188**, reservations only. The price is $14.50 for two people.

Weather's Store on U.S. 64 just east of town has 10 spaces with hookups and a big overflow area **(377-2276)**. A very economical price of $7.50 with all hookups, $5 with electricity and water. But if you require nothing, the charge is only $2.50. You'll never find the overflow area filled, the owner told me, because "there's a lot of room in that pasture."

══════ Red River ══════

Red River is only two and a half blocks wide, but it stretches for 2 miles along the edge of the river for which it is named. The town is walled in by mountains on both sides. It is cool in the summer and snow-clad in the winter. One of the three top ski areas in New Mexico, Red River has worked hard to promote itself as a summer destination—the ski slopes take care of winter visitation. Square dancing is a favorite pastime year-round, and the nation's top callers work the square dances in the community center.

HISTORY

The first white men to roam through Red River were thought to be fur trappers. Apache and Navajo had traveled through the scenic canyon for a century before the coming of the white man, usually on their way to raid the pueblos nearby. Miners came to this area in 1860, spurred on by small gold strikes. Gold fever brought a lot of colorful characters, including the infamous Black Jack Ketchum, who relieved several miners of their gold pokes.

In 1905, Red River boasted 3,000 residents, with 15 saloons, 4 hotels, 2 newspapers, a barbershop, a hospital, a sawmill and an active red-light district.

Gold, silver and copper mines operated here until 1925; now molybdenum is still mined west of the town. Later, the real treasures of Red River were appreciated—wonderful ski slopes and 155 inches of snowfall annually in cool mountain air and beautiful scenery.

GETTING THERE

Red River is the northernmost station on New Mexico's Enchanted Circle, which includes Taos and Angel Fire. The nearest commercial airport is in Albuquerque, 125 miles away. Rental cars are available in Albuquerque, Santa Fe and Taos. There's a hard-surfaced airfield at nearby Angle Fire for private planes.

Driving from Albuquerque, you'll go north on Interstate 25 to the junction of U.S. 84 in Santa Fe. Go north on U.S. 84 to Española, switch to N.M. 68 to Taos, then go east on U.S. 64 to junction with N.M. 38. Go north to Red River, climbing over the 9,000-plus-foot Bobcat Pass. Beautiful scenery all the way. Driving south from Denver, you'll be on Interstate 25 to 10 miles south of Raton, then on U.S. 64 west to junction with N.M. 38, then north to Red River.

—— FESTIVALS AND EVENTS ——

Father's Day Mountain Bike Race
  In June. **754-2366.**

Red River–Cimarron Team-Roping Contest
  In June. **754-2366.**

Fourth of July Parade
  In July. **754-2366.**

Cowboy New Year Rodeo
  In July. **754-2366.**

Mountain Man Rendezvous
  In Aug. Muzzle-loader events. **754-2366.**

Top of the World Mountain Bike Race
  In Sept. Call **754-2366.**

Century Bike Tour
  In Sept.

Top of New Mexico Trail Ride
  In Sept. **754-2366.**

Aspencade
  In Sept. You'll see the fall foliage in all of its glory. Call **754-2366.**

Skiing
  After Oct. skiing takes over, and you'll need to make your reservations early. Call **754-2382.**

——— OUTDOOR ACTIVITIES ———

Red River means fine **skiing**. Of the 33 trails, half are intermediate and the other half are divided evenly between beginner and expert. There are two tows and five chair lifts, with a capacity of 7,400 happy skiers per hour. Elevations from 10,274 feet down to 8,750. Most accommodations are ski in, ski out. Excellent snow-making machines to fill in where nature fails—but with 155 inches of natural snow per winter, there's lots of powder. Bar and restaurants are right on the slopes. For information, call **1-800-348-6444**. For the snow report, call **754-2382**. Day care and kiddie lessons available.

Rent a **mountain bike**, and try the mountain trails. There are many opportunities for the cyclist, ranging from very easy to very difficult.

Cross-country ski on the groomed trails of Red River's Enchanted Forest area. Rental equipment, lessons and guides are all available in Red River.

Snowmobiling along groomed trails is available close to Red River, with all necessary equipment for rent in town.

Four-wheel-drive vehicles can be rented in Red River, and there are hundreds of miles of mountain roads and trails for you to enjoy. **Four-wheeling** hits its peak in October, when hundreds take to the mountain trails to enjoy the fall colors during Aspencade.

Jeeps rent for $85 per eight-hour day. Contact **Gold Rush Rentals** on Main St. to line up a jeep rental, or arrange a jeep tour at $15 for a three-hour tour, which starts at 9 A.M., 1 P.M. and 3 P.M. For more information, call **754-2441**. **Roadrunner Tours** offers jeep tours and rentals, moped rentals, horseback riding and guided fishing trips via jeep. There's lots of variety—try the Middlefork Lake jeep ride, the Old Red River Pass ride or the trip to the midnight ghost town. Scenery is unbelievable, so bring a camera. Call **754-6649** for reservations.

Ride the **chair lift** in the summer to the top of the mountain, where you can see forever. It's a one-hour round-trip, but you can stay on top of the world (10,274 feet above sea level) for as long as you like. There's a fast-food restaurant on top of the mountain. The chair lift operates from Memorial Day through Labor Day, 10 A.M.–4 P.M. The price is $7 for adults, $5 for seniors and $4 for kids under 12. Take your camera along. There's a leaflet to guide you on the nature walk. If you're the rugged type, you can walk down to Red River.

Backpacking is popular in this mountainous area. If you're ambitious, hike to the top of Mount Wheeler. At 13,161 feet above sea level, it's the highest spot in New Mexico. And there are one million acres of national forest for your hiking pleasure, with 138 miles of marked trails for hikers! Stop at the Chamber of Commerce on Main St. to pick up a free map of the hiking, cycling and jeep trails around Red River.

Red River is the **square-dancing** capital of the Southwest, with dancing in the community center on Main Street five days a week. If you don't know how, they'll teach you. Hoedowns in the evenings are fun for all, whether you do-si-do or just watch.

Float trips on the Rio Grande—there's an outfitter right in Red River.

Fun for the kids is always available at the **Black Mountain Playhouse**, right in town, with a pool, video games, roller skating, miniature golf, whatever your pleasure.

Trout are the main attraction at more than 20 lakes in the immediate vicinity of Red River, along with a lot of beautiful trout streams. A one-day license costs $8.50, a five-day license is $15 and a seasonal license for out-of-staters is only $25.

——— SEEING AND DOING ———

Mine Shaft Theater in the Red River Inn presents the real old-time meller-drammer theater, Wed. and Sat. in June and Wed., Thurs., Sat. and Sun. in July and Aug. at 8 P.M. Sometimes there are shows in winter too.

Elk like this fine young bull are common in the high forestlands of northern New Mexico. (W.M. Rush, U.S. Fish and Wildlife Service photo.)

Boo the villain, clap for the hero—have fun, and put yourself into the act! It is reserved seating, so call **754-2930** early.

Red River Jubilee presents bluegrass music Tues. and Sat. at the Red River Theater. No alcohol but lots of fun.

Don't miss the **Shoot-out at Fryes Old Town** every Tues., Thurs. and Sat. at 4 P.M. during July and Aug.

Play **Bingo** at the Black Mountain Playhouse during July and Aug. Check at the Chamber of Commerce for times. **754-2366**.

NEARBY ATTRACTIONS

It's less than a half-hour drive to the **18-hole championship golf course** at Angel Fire.

The **Rio Grande Wild and Scenic River Area** is less than an hour away. Follow N.M. 38 west to Questa, then go 4 miles north on N.M. **522** to the well-marked entrance of this Bureau of Land Management attraction. It's a U.S. fee area—$6 for overnight camping. Drive out to the end of the area at the junction of the Rio Grande and the Red River. Over the centuries, both rivers have carved deep gorges. You may see the eagles soaring over the canyon depths. For the *very* rugged hiker types, there's a trail to the bottom of the gorge. See Wild Rivers Scenic Area section.

SCENIC DRIVES

Take the entire Enchanted Circle from Red River to Eagle Nest Lake, to Angel Fire and on to Taos. Return by a different road. Lovely trip.

———— WHERE TO STAY ————

Red River is a popular vacation destination, winter and summer, so it is a good idea to secure lodging before you leave home. For information of all kinds, call **1-800-348-6444** or **754-2366**. For the snow report, call **754-2223**.

ACCOMMODATIONS

Golden Eagle Lodge—$$–$$$
Rooms, apartments and condos for rent at the east end of Main St. **754-2223**.

El Western Lodge—$$–$$$
Offers 15 rooms. **1-800-548-5713**.

Lifts West Condos—$$$–$$$$
Offers 75 apartments and/or condos, 10 rooms and a restaurant right on Main St. toward the west end. **1-800-221-1859**.

Riverside Lodge—$$–$$$
Like many other operators in this resort city, the lodge handles all kinds of accommodations: apartments, rooms and cabins. Call **1-800-432-9999**, and they'll describe what they have, ask what you want and tell you what it costs.

Caribel Condos—$$–$$$$
Sixteen apartments and 32 rooms, priced according to size and season. **1-800-237-7310**.

Sportsman Lodge—$$–$$$
Offers 16 apartments and 4 rooms. **754-2273**.

CAMPGROUNDS

COMMERCIAL
Roadrunner Campground
Has all hookups for RVs, plus tent camping and cable TV. Very convenient to all that Red River offers. **PO Box 808, Red River, NM 87558**. Reservations are a good idea. Rates from $14 to $18. **754-2286**.

PUBLIC
Five campgrounds are along the Red River, on N.M. 38 west of Red River town, on the Carson National Forest.

Elephant Rock and Junebug campgrounds
Fire rings, picnic tables and bathrooms but no running water. $6 per night.

Columbine and Fawn Lakes campgrounds
Running water, fire rings, picnic tables and bathrooms. $8 per night. For reservations, call **1-800-283-CAMP**.

Goat Hill
By the molybdenum mine, has picnic tables. No fees. For more information, call the Questa Ranger District at **586-0520**.

—————— WHERE TO EAT ——————

Sundance Mexican Restaurant—$-$$
At the corner of High St. and Copper King. Serves a lot of good food to high country appetites. **754-2971.**

Alpine Lodge—$$
On the corner of Main and Pioneer near the bottom of the ski lifts. Serves Bavarian food and American standards. **754-2952.**

Texas Red's—$$-$$$
Right on the main street. Known for good steaks and cocktails. **754-2964.**

—————— SERVICES ——————

Red River has no taxi service, but you can walk to all parts of this compact but fun town.

Church services are offered for Catholic, Episcopal and Church of Christ, along with a nondenominational service. Places and times will show on local TV channel 2.

Rio Grande
Wild Rivers Scenic Area

Drive west out of Red River along the scenic Red River Canyon; it's just 15 minutes to the town of Questa. There turn north on N.M. 522. Three miles north of Questa you'll see the signs for the Rio Grande Wild River Recreation Area. Turn left (west) onto that road through the tiny settlement of Cerro, and follow the signs 3 more miles to the recreation area.

Here the Red River canyon slices into the deep gorge of the Rio Grande at La Junta (the junction) Point. It is a rugged area, carved by the two rampaging rivers, but the level mesa top provides a point from which you can look down into the awesome canyons. There are no motels or hotels, but RVers enjoy river-view camp sites right on the canyon rim, with water and toilets but no hookups, for $6 a night. Hardy backpackers revel in the five trails leading down to the river: El Aquaje is .75 miles long, La Junta is one and a quarter miles long, Little Arsenic is exactly 1 mile long, Big Arsenic is .8 miles long and Chifloi is only .4 miles down to the river. Once on the river level, you can hike a 3-mile trail connecting Big Arsenic to La Junta.

When you are driving south toward La Junta Point, the road divides. Take the left-hand fork to reach the visitors center, which tells you a lot about the area. It is really two very different areas—the arid mesa top, where it may take piñon trees 300 years to mature, and the lush green of cool pines and sparkling waters down below. Don't overestimate your own physical ability. Remember that when you walk down any of the trails, you have to walk back up too.

There's a fine publication on sale at the visitors center for 50 cents. It will answer your questions about the geology, history and plant and animal life of the area. If you are lucky, you may see the eagles soaring on the updrafts along the canyon walls, and if you camp there, you probably will hear the eerie night song of the coyote. One man described the sound thusly: "The coyote lets out a long, quavering high note, then chases after it, biting it into pieces." The wild rivers area is well worth your visit. If all you want to do is look, you can make it a day trip from either Red River or Taos.

Chama

Chama has one of the loveliest locations in all of the Land of Enchantment. It is about 8,000 feet above sea level, which helps to explain why the tiny town had 22 feet of snow the first time I visited. Southern and western terminus of the Cumbres and Toltec Scenic Railroad, Chama is now a popular spot for summer vacationers. It is just 8 miles below the Colorado border, on U.S. 64/84, and about a dozen miles east of the Continental Divide. Chama residents can look out at 11,403-foot Brazos Mountain. The Azotea Tunnel diverts Colorado water into the Rio Chama, which is one of the state's best trout streams.

Chama was once an important mining town, which accounts for the narrow-gauge railroad winding its scenic way from Antonito, Colorado. The Denver and Rio Grande Western Railroad began construction of a rail extension in 1880, which ran from Alamosa, Colorado, to Durango, Colorado, by way of Chama. The first rail travel in Chama happened in February 1881, and for the next 30 years, Chama was a roisterous little place, complete with honest-to-goodness holdups of the payroll train, lots of saloons and a great influx of good and bad individuals. The Charles Allison gang robbed and stole at will for a time.

At the same time, loggers clear-cut the dense forests and formed the grasslands you see today—they did not replant the forests. Because of the grasslands, sheep and cattle ranching flourished and are still important here.

The catastrophic winter of 1932 almost wiped out livestock in the Chama Valley, a blow from which this frontier town never really recovered.

Today Chama is a major tourist town with much to offer.

SEEING AND DOING

The **Cumbres and Toltec Scenic Railroad** is the longest (64 miles) and the highest (Cumbres Pass is 10,015 feet above sea level) narrow-gauge steam railroad in North America.

Everyone should ride the Cumbres and Toltec at least once in a lifetime; I've ridden it at least a dozen times. Colorado and New Mexico state governments bought the line many years ago as a prime historic sight. Now they operate it as a prime tourist attraction. You start your trip at Chama or Antonito, ride to the halfway point (Osier) and change trains. Or you can ride halfway and return on the same train. If you go all the way, buses will bring you back to your starting point. The wood-burning and coal-burning engines huff and puff and spin drivers occasionally; black smoke belches from the stacks as the train winds back and forth over the state boundary. The train schedule for tourist season is late May through Oct. 14, and the price for the interesting ride is $29 for the round-trip to Osier for adults, $11 for children under 11. There's a snack bar aboard, but you won't want to spoil your appetite, because a really filling meal is served at the halfway point. For more information, call the Chama depot at **756-2151** or the Antonito depot at **(719) 376-5483**, or write to **PO Box 789, Chama, NM 87520**.

Chama can be the jumping-off place for many **fishing excursions**. For the very hardy, ride the scenic railroad to the halfway point, then hike down into the depths of Toltec Gorge to enjoy some relatively unspoiled trout fishing. The crystal clear waters make for tough fishing in sunlit hours, but it can be much easier to entice a brown or rainbow once the long shadows reach the water.

Another trout spot is in the Carson National Forest. Drive north of Chama on N.M. 17, cross the border into Colorado, then look for an exit on the right side leading back into the Land of Enchantment and the national forest. There you'll find some scenic drives into the high country, and you'll probably see blue grouse, mule deer and elk. Or descend to the level of Apache Creek, and have a go at stocked rainbows. None of them are very big, but they are willing—and very tasty. For most of its northern half, the Chama River is prime rainbow-trout habitat.

It's only a short drive to the **El Vado–Heron Lake** complex on the Chama River. Heron Lake has broken the state record for lake trout for the past four years. But that's not surprising. Heron Lake is the only water in the state containing lakers. In both lakes, there are plenty of rainbows and kokanee salmon. During the special snagging season for kokanee, in Dec., hundreds of anglers fill their freezers with the tasty salmon.

It's a short drive west of Chama to the **Jicarilla Apache Indian Reservation** and the town of **Dulce**. The Apache Reservation is managed intensively for elk, mule deer and trout, so hunters and anglers seek it out. For many years, the 850,000-acre reservation had a deserved reputation for producing trophy-class mule deer. For full information about hunting and fishing on the reservation, write to **Jicarilla Natural Resources, PO Box 546, Dulce, NM 87528**.

Many outfitters will cater deluxe **hunting trips** for elk, deer, bear and mountain lion—for a price. The average cost of an elk rifle hunt is $3,500 per person, for example.

Although there are lots of mountains in the area, there is no downhill skiing to be had. However, **cross-country skiing** on the groomed and maintained 6.4-kilometer Chama Community Trail north of town is very popular, with snow conditions more predictable than anywhere else that I know of. The trail is 12.5 miles north of town on N.M. 17. Instruction available on weekends.

Just north of Chama you can hike the trails of the **Sergeant Wildlife Preserve**. Excellent for bird-watching and botany study.

Western Outdoor Adventures in Chama will arrange for you to add a horseback trail ride to the scenic railway trip, meeting you at Osier (the midpoint) with your horses and leading you on an overnight or half-day ride across the high country of Osier Mesa. Design your own trip, if you wish. Trail ride prices begin at $95 per day. **756-2653**.

The Stockyards in Chama will provide horseback rides from one hour to all day, hay rides and hunting trips both on private land and in the national forest. It also caters pack trips and services drop camps. **756-2685**.

Corkin's Lodge on the Brazos River on N.M. 542 (turn off just before crossing the Brazos River north of Tierra Amarilla), offers private access to two and a half miles of the Brazos River for trout fishing, plus a small well-stocked lake of rainbows. There's a heated swimming pool, 758 miles of hiking trails, lots of activities . . . or just peace and quiet. Rates from $99 to $155 per day. **588-7261**.

WILDLIFE

The Carson National Forest, which surrounds Chama, is home to countless mule deer and elk, black bear and mountain lions. Use a forest-service map for guidance, and drive slowly along forest roads. You'll see deer and elk for sure, along with blue grouse and many other bird species. Bear and lions are common, but both species are very wary and mainly nocturnal. You can catch a glimpse of deer from the scenic narrow-gauge railroad.

——————— WHERE TO STAY ———————

ACCOMMODATIONS

Branding Iron Motel—$$
Right on the highway through Chama. **756-2162**. The restaurant is also recommended. A cheeseburger and fries here is not a snack; it's a full meal. **756-2808**.

Fosters Hotel—$-$$

Offers nostalgia and the old frontier ambience, right on the main drag in Chama, across from the railroad station. **756-2296.**

Jones House—$$

A bed and breakfast in Chama. **756-2908.**

River Bend Lodge—$$-$$$

In Chama. **756-2264.**

Shamrock Hotel—$$

In Chama. **756-2416.**

Little Creel Lodge—$$

Offers cabins near the river on the southern edge of town. **756-2382.**

Jicarilla Inn—$$-$$$

West of Chama, on the Jicarilla Apache Indian Reservation, you'll find top-notch accommodations at the Jicarilla Inn, operated by the tribe. If you're willing to admit to being a senior citizen, like me, there's a 10 percent senior-citizen discount. This is a Best Western motel; call **759-3663** or **1-800-528-1234** for reservations. Oh, yes. Jicarilla is pronounced "hick-a-ree-ah."

Chevez Creek Lodge—$$$

It calls itself a bed and breakfast, but the lodge has much more than that. Log cabins, yes, but modern log cabins with hot tubs. Private pond and stream fishing, guided fishing on the Chama and on the lakes. The DeMasters can be reached at **756-2653.** Located 8 miles south of Chama. Reservations required.

CAMPGROUNDS

Twin Rivers Campground

At the junction of U.S. 64/84 and N.M. 17 as it continues north. Has 36 spaces with all hookups, at $13 per night, and lots of tenting spaces at $11 per night, which includes rest rooms and hot showers for the tenters. **756-2218.**

River Bend Lodge

Offers both RV camping and motellike lodging. **756-2264.**

Also, there is lots of camping in the Carson National Forest, at El Vado Lake State Park and at Heron Lake State Park.

Carson National Forest Compgrounds

There's no ranger station in Chama, so you'll have to pick up your forest map at the Canjilon ranger station, 2 miles east of U.S. 84. The exit is about 7 miles south of Tierra Amarilla. It's plainly marked.

Once armed with your forest map and the free pamphlet "Summer Fun," you can pick and choose from the Canjilon district campgrounds. **Canjilon Lakes**, at 9,900 feet, is 12 miles northeast of the village of Canjilon. Forty camping units, at $5 per day; tables, grills, drinking water (not hookups), toilets and garbage removal are provided.

Trout Lakes is almost as high at 9,300 feet. Tent camping is all that is provided, as narrow access limits vehicles to 16 feet or less. Primitive peace and quiet but no drinking water. These camp sites are in ponderosa pine, clean and lovely, high country. Enjoy it!

Echo Amphitheater campground, just 500 yards west of U.S. 64/84, 14 miles or so south of the Canjilon exit, and just 3 miles north of the Ghost Ranch, with its Living Museum. Ten spaces at 6,600 feet, for $4. Drinking water, garbage removal, toilets, tables and grills are provided. Camping is free.

———— WHERE TO EAT ————

Branding Iron Restaurant—$$

This is my favorite spot to eat in this town; prices are reasonable in winter and summer, and the food is good. What more can you ask? On the west side of the highway, southern edge of Chama. **756-2162.**

Vera's Mexican Kitchen—$

Turning out authentic New Mexican food since 1963. It's just north of the junction of N.M. 17 and U.S. 64/84. Call Vera Alcon at **756-2557.**

———— SERVICES ————

There are no taxi cabs in Chama, but distances are not great and traffic can hardly be called heavy. The nearest hospital on the New Mexico side is in Española. Grocery stores and sporting-goods stores are easy to find in Chama, with almost everything you need.

══ Tierra Amarilla ══

Tierra Amarilla means "yellow earth" in Spanish. The town is a mile or so off of U.S. 64 and N.M. 4, just north of their junction. Tierra Amarilla is one of the most Spanish towns in New Mexico, and although it is just off the main highway, it is 200 years back in the Spanish colonial past. Tierra Amarilla is definitely not tourist oriented. But it is worth a drive-through of 15 minutes, just to see the sagging walls and homes of 100 years ago.

This is the county seat of Rio Arriba County. Its wide valley and fertile land was home to the Jicarilla Apache (who had forced more-sedentary Indian tribes off of it) before they were forced off by the Spanish. Starry-eyed dreamers maintain that the land granted to them by Spanish kings in 1832 is still theirs. A violent struggle over this point occurred a couple of decades ago, when Reyes Lopez Tijerina and his followers attempted to take back their ancestral lands. There was a march on Tierra Amarilla in 1967, with a lot of shooting and one death. Hard feelings linger to this day. An Indian friend of mine once told me that he hoped the Tijerina group won. In amazement, I asked why. "Because they stole it from us Indians," he replied. "Maybe we could get it back from them."

You can take a lovely drive east on U.S. 64 from T.A., as it is called locally, in the summertime. In the winter, heavy snows keep this scenic drive closed. The road will take you across the mountains to Tres Piedras and continue southeast across the Rio Grande Gorge to Taos.

While in this part of northern New Mexico, you may hear of *los penitentes*, more properly called Los Hermanos de Luz, the "Brothers of Light." The members of this unauthorized sect within the Roman Catholic church felt that their imitation of Christ included the imitation of his sufferings. During Lent and Holy Week, the *penitentes* punished themselves by self-flagellation with whips made of the native yucca plant while carrying a cross long distances.

Legends says that they even crucified one of their members—and I do mean crucifixion to death—during Good Friday rites. These *penitentes* were found all the way from northern Mexico into Colorado. A similar religious sect is found in southern Mexico, where crucifixion unto death is still carried out in remote areas.

In 1828 the Catholic church banned membership in the *penitentes*, citing the extreme nature of its rites. But this did not stop all the *penitentes* from their own method of following Christ. By 1948 the Catholic church gave its blessing to a more moderate *penitentes*, without the ritual cruelty. Remote villages in the Hispanic Highlands still witness the ceremonies of *los penitentes*, but the rituals are kept secret and the casual tourist has very little chance of seeing one.

Abiquiu

Nineteen miles north of Española on U.S. 84, we come to Abiquiu (pronounced "ah-bee-kew"), right where the road crosses the Chama River flowing out from under Abiquiu Dam. Here we find the shaded pastel cliffs and the deep-red sandstone bluffs that inspired famed artist Georgia O'Keeffe to make her home here. This is the center of "O'Keeffe Country." After her days of living in and near Taos, she discovered Abiquiu and moved to the Rancho de los Burros, a part of what is now called the Ghost Ranch. Then she moved to her own home atop a ridge in the village of Abiquiu. She said that she was fascinated by the view back toward Española from her house. If she were to look out from that same house today, she'd get another landscape to paint—a landscape that includes a Muslim mosque! The old ivory painted mosque and buildings are across the river and high on the bluffs. It houses a Muslim community, which once was so prosperous that it maintained its own elementary school. In December 1989, however, the school was closed and the children redistributed to public elementary schools in the vicinity. The Muslim community, named Dar al Islam, welcomes visitors.

I would like to tell you how to find the mosque and Georgia O'Keeffe's house, but it is of no permanent value to tell you to turn to the right after the trailer home with the satellite dish. The trailer might be moved. Just ask anyone. They'll tell you.

A good source of information is the **Abiquiu Inn** ($$–$$$), a well-recommended hostelry on the right as you go north on U.S. 84. The lodge is open all year, but the nice little restaurant closes in the winter. There's also a gift shop, offering such diverse wares as African baskets, Pueblo pottery, Turkish rugs and Navajo dolls. **685-4378.**

Ask at the Abiquiu Inn how to find the Monastery of Christ in the Desert, run by the Benedictine order. It is located deep in Chama Canyon. You exit U.S. 84, north of the Ghost Ranch exits.

The Anasazi settled here about A.D. 1000, after drought forced them out of Mesa Verde and Chaco Canyon. They prospered here until A.D. 1500, when the Spanish influence was felt. The *españoles* began Santa Rose de Lima de Abiquiu down on the level of the Chama River, but floods occurred and the spot was impossible to defend against Indian raids. So they moved to the fortresslike location of the old Abiquiu pueblo.

Abiquiu Dam and Reservoir, built by the U.S. Army Corps of Engineers, provides a 12,000-acre lake, known for tremendous populations of crappie, black bass and catfish. Rainbow and cutthroat trout are also found in the reservoir and brown trout in the waters below the spillway. There are 54 camp sites but no hookups; drinking water and showers are provided. There are also 15 tent pads in the Riana area. Two launching ramps allow easy access to the lake for fishing and boating. Call the Corps of Engineers for more information at **685-4371**.

Leaving Abiquiu north on U.S. 84, you'll come to the Ghost Ranch Conference Center exit. Skip that, and go on another 2 miles to the entrance to the **Living Museum of the Ghost Ranch**, which is operated by the forest service. The museum has artifacts of the area and excellent educational walks that teach of the local geology and conservation of soil and water. Bears, elk, mule deer, wolves, coyotes and many birds are held in pens here—leaving a bad taste in the mouth. Roadside zoos are a pet peeve of mine, and these caged critters are a good argument against them. The Living Museum is currently engaged in raising enough money to upgrade the facilities. Admission is free, but a donation is requested. Perhaps your donation will help provide modern conditions for the birds and animals and help get rid of the cages.

From the high point at the Living Museum, you can just make out the house where Georgia O'Keeffe lived. She was a very private person, and no access is allowed to any of the homes she once lived in.

No camping is allowed on the Ghost Ranch, but at the **Echo Canyon Amphitheater**, just 3 miles north of the Ghost Ranch, there are 10 primitive sites, plus water.

If you want to see what this country looked like 100 or 300 years ago, take the drive over N.M. 96 (turn off north of Abiquiu), which crosses the dam and then goes to the tiny towns of Youngsville, Coyote, Gallina and La Jara, connecting with N.M. 44 2 miles north of Cuba. From Cuba (which has stores, restaurants and gas stations galore), you can continue the circle on N.M. 126 and N.M. 4 to the Valle Grande, to the atomic city of Los Alamos and on through Española to return to Abiquiu.

The Mosque of Dar al Islam, near Abiquiu.

=========== Los Alamos ===========

Sitting high on the volcanic cliffs and pine forests 20 miles southwest of Española, Los Alamos—the Atomic City—is the birthplace of the atomic bomb, the site of the secret work in 1942–1945 that brought the end of World War II in two mighty explosions at Hiroshima and Nagasaki.

Los Alamos has more Ph.D.s per capita than any other city in the world. It also boasts the best public school system in the state, perhaps in the nation, because those Ph.D.s make sure their children do their homework. As one high school junior told me recently, "It's not easy being a kid in Los Alamos." Until 1962, the federal government owned everything in the city, but the Disposal Act of 1962 began the process of selling off the government buildings and creating a more usual city.

The people of Los Alamos don't seem to want tourism. Who can blame them? They have an idyllic uncrowded location in the tall pines and a lot of peace and quiet. The government laboratories, which are still engaged in hush-hush work, are off-limits and protected by barbed wire and security guards: You can't go see them. But two excellent free museums, the **Los Alamos Historical Museum** and the **Bradbury Science Museum**, have a lot of fascinating stuff about the first atomic bombs. Get your self-guided walking tour of the town at the historical museum.

The Los Alamos Golf Course is an 18-hole municipal golf course right in town, and is open to the public. **662-8139.**

Of the two hotel/motels in Los Alamos, try the **Hilltop House** ($$$), at the corner of Trinity and Central. There's a restaurant and lounge and a great view of the Sangre de Cristo Mountains. **662-2441.**

Limited camping facilities are available on the edge of the town— inquire at the Chamber of Commerce. A better bet is to camp at the Bandelier National Monument.

Bandelier
National Monument

Ten miles farther along N.M. 4 from Los Alamos is the entrance to the Bandelier National Monument (you leave Los Alamos on N.M. 501 but soon run into N.M. 4). Now we need to take time out for a short bit of geology. About a million years ago, give or take a few millennia, several volcanoes in the Jemez area erupted, covering some 400 square miles with tuff, volcanic ash squeezed into a denser shape by its own weight. Some of the deposits were 1,000 feet thick and formed a tremendous plateau. But when the volcanoes stopped grumbling and roaring, they cooled and shrank away under the lava roof and no longer supported the mesa. The huge roof of this once fiery region collapsed with a roar that must have been audible for 100 miles. The caldera that was formed has been called the largest in the world. Part of that caldera is what we now call the Valle Grande, which is on N.M. 4, your road west of Bandelier.

The monument is named in honor of Adolf Bandelier, the eminent explorer who mapped the Bandelier ruins from 1880 to 1886. Its 54 square miles of soft rock and pines is cut by creeks that bring snow melt down from the higher mountains. The most accessible part of these important pre-Columbian ruins lies in Frijoles Canyon. It's a short walk along macadam trails from the interesting visitors center to the well-preserved ruins of Tyuonyi, with its big house and ceremonial kiva. Within 200 yards of these ruins, you can climb to far more primitive dwellings carved into the soft tuff by harder stone implements. Safe railings and stairs give you a vantage point from which to take pictures of the ruins.

You can spend a day in Bandelier, or a year—you won't see it all. The original inhabitants were farmers who raised corn, beans and squash in this beautiful ribbon of green beneath the red-and-beige cliffs of Frijoles Creek. Oral histories of some of the Rio Grande pueblos claim descent from Bandelier, and it is possible that the people who lived here from the 1200s until 1550 came from Chaco Canyon, an area killed by drought from A.D. 1275 to A.D. 1300.

Most of the many walking trails—ranging from half a mile to 20 minutes—are on fairly level mesa top, and the only serious climbs are easily negotiated by stairs and ladders.

Close to the visitors center, be sure to stop and see the stone lions. Although they are not heroic in size, they may be the only statues produced by these primitive people. The ambitious Stone Lions Shrine is more remote, reached by 12 miles of walking, an estimated eight-hour round-trip.

The visitors center has excellent exhibits of the archaeology of the fascinating area, a small gift shop and a really good collection of the paintings of Helmut Naumer. Included are 14 fine pastel paintings of the Indian pueblos nearby. Also on exhibit are many photographs taken by Laura Gilpin, a pioneer photographer of the Indians of the Southwest.

There are 98 camp sites at **Juniper Campground** just inside the entry road to the monument. If you intend to camp here in the summer months—drinking water and dump stations are available but no hookups—pick your site early because the campground usually fills up by midday.

For more information on the Bandelier National Monument, telephone the superintendent at **672-3861.**

Personally, I rank Bandelier in the top 10 attractions in the entire state, along with such crowd-pleasers as Carlsbad Caverns, the most beautiful in the world.

Bandelier National Monument. (Photo by Mark Nohl, New Mexico Economic Development and Tourism Department.)

Cuba

Cuba is the only town of any size on the long stretch of N.M. 44 between Albuquerque and Bloomfield. Most people think of it as a gas and coffee stop enroute to Farmington and the Navajo River and Reservoir, one of the state's best fisheries.

Cuba was established by a Spanish land grant in the 1700s and has been a farming-and-ranching center for 200 years. Today it is the best gateway to the San Pedro Wilderness Area in the Santa Fe National Forest. Get a forest map at the ranger station on the south side of town, half a block off the highway. The map will guide you to San Gregorio Lake and many good trout stream spots, to campgrounds and the serenity of the undeveloped high country. There are several campgrounds on the western half of the Santa Fe National Forest. You reach them via N.M. 126 out of Cuba, which connects with N.M. 4. But, and this is a huge BUT, if you're herding a motor coach or trailer, check with the ranger station in Cuba before heading for a campground. Roads are usually well maintained, but some are not suited for big vehicles. Only in the very best of conditions can you take a motor coach or trailer over N.M. 126. I won't do it, ever. For a beautiful drive with car or pickup, follow the route on your forest service map out of Cuba on N.M. 126, and then across the mountains to Los Alamos. On that route, you turn to the left on N.M. 4. If you take a right turn onto N.M. 4, you're headed for Jemez Springs, Jemez Soda Dam and Jemez Pueblo.

There's really nothing to do in Cuba itself but eat and rest up.

WHERE TO STAY

Cuban Motel—$
Has 18 units. **289-3269**.

Del Prado Motel—$$
Has 15 units and a cafe in connection with it. **289-3475**.

Frontier Motel—$$
Has 20 units and a cafe in connection with it. **289-3474**.

—————— WHERE TO EAT ——————

El Brunos Ristorante and Cantina—$

Right on the highway going through Cuba. The best place to eat in Cuba. Excellent selection of Mexican and New Mexican dishes in quiet, dignified atmosphere. Not everything on the menu is Hispanic. Last time I was there I enjoyed reasonably priced all-you-can-eat beef ribs. **289-9429.**

Scenic area north of Cuba. (Photo by Mark Nohl, New Mexico Economic Development and Tourism Department.)

===== Jemez Country =====

When the first *españoles* came to this country and the south end of the Jemez Mountains, they asked the Indians what they were called. The Indians replied that they were "H'emish." "H'emish" simply meant "people." Remember, the Indians had no written language, so this is a phonetic rendition of their word. Now remember that the Spanish *J* is pronounced like our *H*. So the Franciscan friars named the people the "Jemez," and the name was later attached to the mountain range, to the springs north of the pueblo and to the pueblo itself.

When the pueblos revolted in 1680, the Jemez Pueblo was one of the fiercest in driving out the Spaniards. During the reconquest of 1682, the Jemez people again fought long and hard. Zia, a neighboring pueblo, gave up easily. To this day, 300 years later, the Jemez people look down on the Zia for just that reason.

Turn north on N.M. 4 at San Ysidro, leaving N.M. 44, and you'll find yourself moving through the green oasis that the Jemez Creek carved out of these blood-red mountainous cliffs. Red was the symbolic color during the bloody reconquest of the pueblos. The road leads to the **Soda Dam**, where the mineral-laden waters formed their own dam, and to the mother house of a Catholic order of nuns, called the Handmaidens of the Precious Blood. A little farther along the red-walled canyon you'll come to the retreat house of the Servants of the Paraclete, another Catholic order. Right across the street from the beautiful spired church of the Servants of the Paraclete, you'll find **Jemez State Monument Park**. The entrance fee is $2 (children 15 and under are free) and allows you to stroll through the ruins of the church and the convent, built by the Jemez Indians under the direction of Franciscan padre Alonzo de Luga in 1620. The Indians got along fairly well with the religious authorities but rebelled against the harsh civilian rule of the Spaniards. The interesting set of exhibits will give you a feel for the area. **829-3530**.

The Jemez Indians, who formerly lived at the site of the church, were moved to the present location of **Jemez Pueblo**, south of Jemez Springs, when the Spanish gave up this mission in 1696. Today the Indians still don't look favorably on intruders. Don't pull out your camera at the pueblo without getting permission first.

Snack food and sandwiches are available in **Jemez Springs**, and if you're lucky, you'll see Jemez Pueblo women selling Indian bread (highly recommended) alongside N.M. 4. Incidentally, N.M. 4 goes on north through some gorgeous mountain country to **Fenton Lake**, where there are camp sites below the **Fenton Lake Dam**, at $7 per night. This is a popular area for us locals and is crowded on weekends and on national holidays. You'll have fair to good fishing for rainbow trout in Fenton Lake and some of the nearby streams.

Ski Areas
of New Mexico

Skiing is one of America's favorite outdoor sports. There is hardly anything more exhilarating than a flashing run down a steep slope covered with knee-deep powder that plumes in great white clouds in the bright sunlight. Bright sunlight is what makes a day on the slopes memorable. Skiing is no fun when you are frozen stiff. New Mexico recognizes these facts and combines the most days of sunlight of any skiing state with some of the world's finest skiing snows. Our high mountain elevations provide the snow; the famed New Mexico sunshine provides the beautiful warm days on the slopes. New Mexico is a great skiing state! Come try it! Here are the nine best downhill ski areas in New Mexico. For basic information, call **982-5300**. For ski conditions, call **984-0606**.

Angel Fire is where the ski areas, high, wide and challenging, are just part of a year-round development. Peak elevation, 10,608 feet. Base elevation, 8,500 feet. Vertical drop, 2,180 feet. Fifty-four runs, three triple chair lifts, four double chair lifts. Has snow-making equipment covering 115 acres. For information and reservations, call **1-800-633-7463**.

Ski Apache, operated by the Mescalero Apache Indian Tribe, is located on the slopes of 12,000-foot Sierra Blanca, near the town of Ruidoso. Peak elevation, 11,500 feet. Base elevation, 9,700 feet. Vertical drop, 1,800 feet. This is the farthest south of any ski area in the Rocky Mountains. Forty runs, five triple chair lifts, two double chair lifts and one surface lift, plus a gondola. For information, call **336-4356**.

Red River Ski Area, right in the town of Red River, is one of New Mexico's most beautiful and challenging areas. The ski runs are located between two of New Mexico's highest peaks. Ski lifts begin right in town, within walking distance of most resorts or motels. Peak elevation, 10,350 feet. Base elevation, 8,750 feet. Vertical drop, 1,600 feet. Runs two triple chair lifts, three double chair lifts and one surface lift. For reservations and information, call **1-800-331-SNOW** or **754-2366**.

Sandia, on the outskirts of Albuquerque, can be reached by car, but why do something so tame. Why not zip up on the world's longest aerial tramway. The tram will whisk you from 6,000 feet above sea level on the eastern edges of Albuquerque to the top, 10,387 feet, in just 15 minutes. Peak elevation, 10,387 feet. Base elevation, 8,600 feet. Vertical drop, 1,778 feet. Twenty-five runs. Four double chair lifts and two surface lifts provide quick return to the heights after each run. Fully certified instruction available. You'll be amazed at the change from the arid semidesert western slope of the Sandias to the pine-clad, snow-covered eastern slopes. And before your day ends, why not have a lovely meal at one of the restaurants up on top, where the skies are clear and you can almost reach out and touch the stars? For information, call **296-9585**.

Santa Fe Ski Basin is 16 miles from downtown Santa Fe. Peak elevation, 12,000 feet. Base elevation, 10,350 feet. Vertical drop, 1,650 feet. Thirty-eight runs, one quadruple chair lift, one triple chair lift, two double chair lifts and two surface lifts. Full food and lounge services in the area. Features the high speed Super Chief Lift, which whisks you from base camp to 12,000 feet. For information, call **982-4429**; for reservations, call **1-800-982-SNOW**.

Sipapu ski area is located in the Sangre de Cristo Mountains to the east of Española, halfway between Taos and Santa Fe ski areas. This is a small but complete facility. Peak elevation, 9,065 feet. Base elevation, 8,200 feet. Vertical drop, 865 feet. Eighteen runs, one triple chair lift, and two surface lifts. Accommodations at the ski area range from dormitory to cabins and suites. Lounge, restaurant and cafeteria. For information, call **587-2240**.

Sugarite Ski Basin, 12 miles east of Raton on N.M. 72, offers skiing in the state park. For information, call **445-5607**. Accommodations in nearby Raton.

Taos Ski Basin, the result of a vision of the perfect ski area on the part of veteran ski instructor and developer Ernie Blake, has more skiers every winter than its two nearest competitors in the Land of Enchantment. Just 19 miles from downtown Taos. Peak elevation, 11, 819 feet. Base elevation, 9,207 feet. Vertical drop, 2,612 feet. Seventy-one runs, one quadruple chair lift, one triple chair lift, five double chair lifts and two surface lifts. For information, call **776-2291**; for reservations, call **1-800-992-SNOW**. Lots of accommodations in the immediate area.

—————— NORDIC SKIING ——————

The **Enchanted Forest** area offers 30 kilometers of groomed track on 600 acres of mountains and meadows, located 3.5 miles east of the town of Red River, just below the summit of 9,850 foot Bobcat Pass. This full-service center has equipment for rent, professional instruction and special race clinics. For information, call **754-2374** or **754-2240**. Accommodations available in nearby Red River.

Rio Chama Trail, five and a half miles long, connects Heron Lake and El Vado Lake, providing excellent cross-country skiing in Heron Lake State Park, which is near Chama and Tierra Amarilla (11 miles west of Tierra Amarilla on U.S. 64 and N.M. 95). For information, call **588-7470**.

THE NORTHEAST REGION

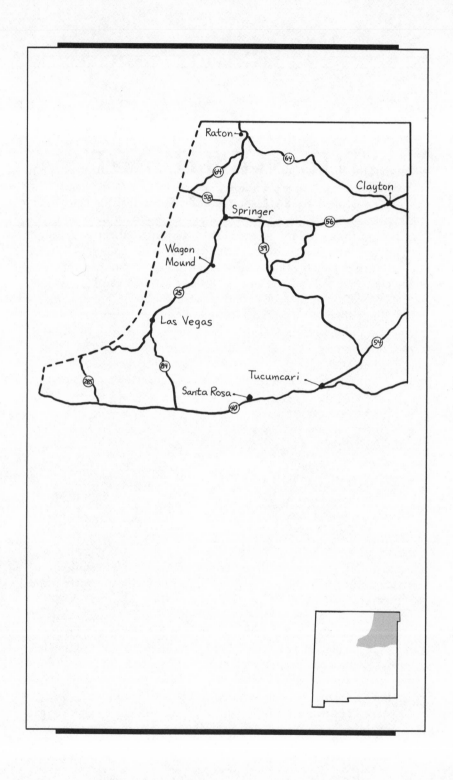

═══ Raton ═══

─── HISTORY ───

Raton is the first city south of Raton Pass on Interstate 25. Its position at the southern end of rugged Raton Pass is its reason for existence. The Santa Fe Trail followed the Indian footpaths through Raton Pass, but it was mighty rough on the wagons. So Uncle Dick Wootton dynamited a pass through the mountains' worst parts and set up a toll station to collect from anyone who wanted to go through and on to Santa Fe. The only alternative to paying the toll was a detour around the mountains, which added about 125 miles to the trip. In 1879 the Santa Fe Railroad bought the toll road from Uncle Dick and pushed the rails through. Raton quickly flourished as a railroad, coal-mining and ranching center. It's a fascinating place, with lots of pioneer history still visible. My biggest peeve with this city is that the inhabitants pronounce the name of their town wrong. They say "rat-tone," just as if the word had two t's in it. It should be pronounced "rah-tóne." The word means mouse in Spanish.

─── SEEING AND DOING ───

Shuler Theater on Second St. was once just one of five opera houses in booming Raton. Opened in 1915, it had its glory days. Today it supports a varied calendar of events, ranging from local historic tableaux to the Queen City Dixieland Jazz Band. The theater may present *The Wizard of Oz* one month and Rene Heredia, a master of flamenco and classical guitar, the next. With something new every week through the summer months, it is well worth an inquiry. For further information and play dates, call **445-5520**.

Sugarite State Park is 10 miles northeast of Raton in a heavily wooded area with three lakes, a stream and the ruins of a historical coal-mine camp. Lots of wildlife, including rainbow trout, is best reached by boat on Lake Maloya. No gasoline motors are allowed on lakes, because Lake Maloya provides Raton's water supply. Lake Alice also has trout. Overnight camping is allowed at Lake Alice and at Soda Pocket. See Campgrounds section.

La Mesa Park offers pari-mutuel betting on the horses year-round. Live races from late May into early Sept., but when no horses are running locally, there's intertrack racing via television simulcasts. This is the oldest privately owned race track in New Mexico. Easy to find, it's 1 mile south of Raton right alongside of Interstate 25. General admission is free, $3 for grandstand seating and parking is free. For information, call **445-2301**, or call the Chamber of Commerce, at **445-3689**.

Antiques Trail. Stop in at the Chamber of Commerce (Second St. and Clayton Rd.) to pick up a map that will lead you to the shops along the Antiques Trail.

A short drive to Cimarron will take you to the **Old Mill Museum**, built in 1864 by Lucien Maxwell, and the historic **St. James Hotel, 376-2664**. Frederick Remington painted in this hotel, and Zane Grey wrote a novel here. Much of the hotel has been restored to the look of the early days. In the summer Cimarron operates an information center to help you find your way.

Walking tours of Raton lead you to 29 buildings, each one an exhibit of Raton's checkered past. Pick up the free guide to the walking tour at the Chamber of Commerce, **445-3689**.

If you've had enough walking, try one of the **driving tours** described on the brochure, "Raton's One-Day Trips," available at the Chamber of Commerce. I especially recommend tour number 7, which takes you to Folsom and the Capulin Monument. There's a problem, however. If you want to see deer, elk and antelope along N.M. 72, you should embark early—best right after sunrise. But that will put you in the tiny town of Folsom too early to get into the interesting museum of pioneer days and some archaeological stuff. (This is where the Folsom point was found. Its discovery pushed back the date of man's arrival in North America by 10,000 years.) The museum doesn't open until 10 A.M. After Folsom go on to the Capulin Monument.

Capulin Mountain National Monument is a full-scale (Mother Nature's scale) exhibit of volcanism. It's located on N.M. 325, which connects U.S. 64/84 with N.M. 72 at Folsom. Excellent exhibits, movies and slide shows complement the exhibits at the visitors center. If you've ever wanted to walk right into the center of a volcanic crater, here's your chance. After viewing the visitors center exhibits, drive 2 miles spiraling around the mountain to the parking lot. If you're up to it and the day is cool enough, take the mile-long hiking trail that circles the caldera itself, with lots of explanatory exhibits along the way. The views from several spots along the trail are magnificent—on a clear day you can see parts of five states. The monument comprises 790 acres, all of it an exhibit in volcanoes.

Philmont Boy Scout Ranch, just 5 miles south of Cimarron, is the home of the Boy Scouts around the world, but it also offers three museums of great interest to the general public. Waite Phillips donated to the Boy Scouts of America the first parcel of what is now 137,493 acres of scenic mountains and mesas, ranging in elevation from 6,600 feet above sea level all the way up to 12,441 feet, at the top of Baldy Mountain. Phillips also donated a 23-story office building in Tulsa to help pay the upkeep. All summer long the ranch is overrun with scouts on the adventure of their lives. It's a working cow ranch, with more than 250 head of Herefords, and maintains 100 burros and 250 riding horses for the summer trail-ride programs. More than 550,500 scouts have passed through the programs at Philmont. The Villa Philmont, which Waite Phillips built to house his family, was completed in 1927. The villa and the Seton Memorial Library are other attractions at the ranch. Seven miles south of Philmont headquarters is Rayado, first European settlement on this land. Rayado is the site of Kit Carson's home before he moved to Taos and married Josefa Jaramillo. Daily tours are conducted June through Aug.

Dorsey Mansion, perhaps one of the most isolated places in the entire state, is reached by driving Interstate 25 to Springer, then U.S. 56 east 23 miles. Then turn north on a dirt road for 12 miles to reach the place where Senator Stephen Dorsey built his fabulous home back in 1878. Using oiled logs and red sandstone, Dorsey built a magnificent 36-room home for his beloved wife, Helen, complete with a rose garden that spelled out her name, a swimming pool with three islands in it and angry gargoyles carved from stone glaring out at all comers. Always involved in questionable schemes, Dorsey left the state in 1892, leaving bad debts and angry partners. Since he left, the mansion has been at times a tuberculosis sanatorium, a post office and a private residence. For a while it offered a bed and breakfast out in the middle of nowhere, but that is no longer true. Now the mansion is owned by a Californian, who employs a caretaker to look after the building and grounds. Considerable renovation work has been completed, and more is planned, but local residents tell me that complete restoration has been forecast many times before, starting in 1971, and little came of those plans. Don't just drive out to see the Dorsey Mansion, because locked gates will keep you a mile away. Always call ahead to see if and when you can visit. The phone is **375-2222**. If no one answers, don't be too surprised.

In the fall and winter, great numbers of ducks and geese congregate on the **Maxwell National Wildlife Refuge** near the town of Maxwell, 25 miles south of Raton on Interstate 25. There's really not much to see there in the spring and summer after the migratory waterfowl are gone, unless, of course, you are a dedicated birder. There is camping allowed on this refuge.

Raton Rodeo, held in late June each year at the Raton Rodeo Grounds on York Canyon Road, is a Professional Rodeo Cowboys Association approved stop on the road to the national finals. Authentic bucking, bulldogging and bull riding. For dates and other information, call the Chamber of Commerce at **445-3689**.

Skiing at Sugarite. Twelve miles from Raton and up on the slopes of Waltons Mountain are runs suited to beginner and expert. The natives call it "Sugar-eet," not "Sugar-ite." For information and dates, call **445-3689**.

WILDLIFE

Excellent mule-deer and wild-turkey hunting is found all over this northeastern region of the Land of Enchantment. Most of it is on private land, with permission of the landowner needed. But the great expanse of national forest provides good hunting, free for all. Merriam turkeys are the top game bird in the nation, and they are present here in goodly numbers. Elk are present in small numbers. New Mexico requires that a hunter under the age of 18 have completed a hunter safety course. For information on seasons, rules and regulations, contact the game and fish department office on N.M. 555, going south out of town, just past La Mesa Park. For information about hunting on private lands, try the **Kiowa Hunting Service**. Contact T. J. Barrclough, **403 Hill St., Raton; 445-5294**.

B & A Outfitters, at **226 Uracca in Raton**, offers complete outfitting and guiding service to ensure memorable, quality big-game hunts for elk, deer, antelope, black bear, cougar and wild turkey. For information and prices, call **445-9225**.

Raton Museum, at **218 S. First St.**, exhibits Santa Fe Trail artifacts, along with memorabilia of railroading and coal-mining days. Open 10 A.M.–4 P.M., Tues.–Sat. in summer. **445-8979**.

———— WHERE TO STAY ————

ACCOMMODATIONS

We counted no less than 20 motels in Raton, which points up its strategic location, halfway between Denver and Albuquerque. Here are a few that you can't go wrong in choosing:

Village Inn—$$
Located at **1207 S. Second St.** 20 units. **445-3617**.

Motel 6—$$
Offers 103 rooms, with a restaurant, a swimming pool and television. At junction of Interstate 25 and U.S. 87. **445-2777**.

Sands Motel—$$$
Offers 50 rooms, with a restaurant, a swimming pool and television.
300 Clayton Rd. 445-2737.

CAMPGROUNDS

COMMERCIAL

Hi-Lo Campground
Conveniently located at **1330 S. Second St.** Offers 92 units, with hookups and all the usual amenities. Prices from $14.24, including tax, for two people. **445-3488.**

Summerlan Park
Yes, that's right: There's no *d* on the end of Summerlan. At the junction of Interstate 15 and U.S. 87. Has 42 spaces with all amenities. Rates start at $13 for two campers. Air-conditioning will cost you a buck extra. **445-9536.**

PUBLIC

Sugarite Canyon State Park
Ten miles northeast of Raton on Hwy. 72 going to Folsom. Lake Alice and Soda Pocket offer 25 semiprimitive spaces in a rustic setting and six walk-in sites for campers who want privacy. Fee is $7 for developed camp sites. **445-5607.**

——————— WHERE TO EAT ———————

All of the fast-food chains are represented in Raton, along with family restaurants and fine dining spots. I recommend:

Sweet Shop—$$
At **1201 S. Second.** Has a varied menu. **445-9811.**

All Seasons—$$
At the junction of U.S. 87 and Interstate 25. **445-9889.**

The Oasis—$$
1445 S. Second. 445-2766.

Springer

Forty miles south of Raton on Interstate 25, you come to the pioneer town of Springer, where you find the junction with U.S. 56, which runs east for an interminable 83 miles to Clayton. That road, incidentally, crosses the flattest, driest, most featureless part of New Mexico. Please remind yourself that this part of New Mexico represents some of the best cattle pastures in the nation. This is the ranch country of the Land of Enchantment, and fortunes have been made and lost on these broad plains.

There's a business route of Interstate 25 that gives you easy-off, easy-on access to Springer. On this main street through the town, you'll see the information center. Located in a hundred-year-old building that houses a surprisingly interesting museum, the Chamber of Commerce operation is supervised by a fascinating lady named Bertha Chavez. She will tell you more intriguing things about this pioneer town than you would believe possible. For example, the century-old building has been at one time or another a county courthouse (before unprincipled rascals came with guns in the night, stole the courthouse records and took them away to Raton), a reform school, a library, city offices and the sheriff's jail.

For today's tourist, Springer is famous mostly for being the site of **Springer Lake**, arguably the state's best fishing for big northern pike and for rainbow trout. It's just 5 miles west of Springer, on the road that goes past the State Reform School for Boys. Fishing from the shore is productive here, especially in early spring and late fall, when aquatic weed growth is least. Springer Lake produced the coholder of the state record for northern pike, with a 36-pounder. The other coholder, with another 36-pounder, came from nearby **Miami Lake**, which is about 21 miles west of Springer on N.M. 21.

Eight miles south of Springer on Interstate 25, you turn to the west on N.M. 569 to **Charette Lakes**, a prime trout-fishing lake. The lake originally was built for irrigation purposes, but that didn't work out—wrong soil type, they tell me. The state game and fish department leases the access to the lake for fishing purposes, an arrangement that works out well. You have to want to go to Charette Lakes; you can't just happen by. N.M. 569 runs to the lake and back again, no place else. There are toilets at Charette Lake State Park, but nothing else, except trout and privacy. Camping is free.

Twenty-two miles east of Springer on U.S. 56, you'll find the turnoff to the north, which leads you across 12 miles of dirt road to the famed **Dorsey Mansion**, described in the Seeing and Doing section of Raton.

Twenty miles east of Springer on U.S. 56 is N.M. 39, which goes south through the **Kiowa National Grasslands** and on to **Chicosa Lake State**

Park. Although this tiny state park is quite popular with the local people, the lake was completely dried up when I last visited. It's a good idea to call ahead for information. **485-2424**.

Springer offers gasoline, several good restaurants, good grocery stores and three motels. Be aware that the State Reform School for Boys is here at Springer and do not pick up hitchhikers in the vicinity.

———— WHERE TO STAY ————

ACCOMMODATIONS

The Oasis Motel—$
On the north edge of Springer. Offers 17 units. AARP discount. **483-2777**.

Broken Arrow—$
Has seven units. **483-5555**.

CAMPGROUNDS

There's also a **campground**, offering 15 sites with full hookups and cable TV, priced at $10.55 (including tax) per night. The campground is behind the **Sportsmen's Supply store**, which is also a good source of information about local fishing. **483-5020**.

Pronghorned antelope are often seen from Interstate 25, both south and north of Springer, New Mexico. Fawns, like this one, are dropped in spring and can run as fast as the adults in one week's time.

Fort Union
National Monument

Twenty-six miles north of Las Vegas on Interstate 25, you'll come to the well-marked exit to Fort Union. It's N.M. 161. Eight miles west on black-topped N.M. 161, you come to Fort Union itself. It's worth a look. The area is open daily 8 A.M.–5 P.M., except for Christmas and New Year's Day.

There have been three forts, starting with the first in 1851, which was built to help defend travelers on the Santa Fe Trail from marauding Indians. Nothing visible remains. The second fort, built in 1861, was intended to defend the Union against the expected Confederate invasion (Civil War, remember). The Confederates did invade in 1862 and were repulsed by the Colorado Volunteers from Fort Union at the Battle of Glorieta Pass, which is 25 miles southeast of Santa Fe. That was the last Confederate attack on New Mexico. Very little remains of the hastily constructed second fort, where living conditions were so bad that most troopers preferred to camp outside in tents. Then the third Fort Union was begun in 1863 and completed in 1869. It is this fort you visit today. Although it was abandoned in 1891 as no longer necessary, it is a reminder of the days of both the Indian War and the Civil War. Fort Union was easily the most important fort in New Mexico.

Today you can stand in the central plaza of the crumbling ruins and hear the bugle of 140 years ago. Thanks to an excellent recording system, you can listen to the commands given and the horses hooves on the parade ground. Meanwhile your mind recreates the sights of long ago.

Along the northern edge of the hospital ruins, you'll find the ruts of the old Santa Fe Trail—still visible after 170 years!

No camping is allowed at Fort Union. This is a national-fee area, so it costs $3 to get in, unless you carry the biggest bargain in America today, the Golden Age Passport, which is free to senior citizens and admits you to almost all federal installations. **425-8025.**

The stark ruins of historic Fort Union, north of Watrous, New Mexico, just 8 miles off of Interstate 25.

Las Vegas

Las Vegas—New Mexico, not Nevada—is a city of paradoxes. It's a sleepy little village of 16,000 souls, steeped in Spanish and pioneer lore, but it is also the home of Highlands University, the location of the Luna Vocational-Technical Institute and the place chosen by magnate Armand Hammer for his United World College. It sits on the edge of the eastern plains, a semiarid land of hot winds and driving snows, but it also sits at the edge of the Sangre de Cristo Mountains and looks up at snow-clad peaks about eight months of the year. Las Vegas' eastern horizon stretches flat endlessly, all the way into Texas; its western horizon soars abruptly upward to the sparkling tips of the Rockies.

HISTORY

Las Vegas got its start in 1822, when Captain William Becknell rode into Arrow Rock, Missouri, with tales of riches to be made by trading with the Spanish in faraway Santa Fe. The Santa Fe Trail was pushed through 900 miles of hostile Indian territory so American traders could meet up with the Camino Real. The "Royal Road" stretched more than 2,000 miles from gold-and-silver rich Mexico, along the banks of the Rio Grande and to the capital of New Spain in Santa Fe.

Despite Indian attacks, thousands of merchants took to the three months of toil that was the Trail, and in 1835, Las Vegas had started to become an important way station. It thrived as a center for Spanish pioneers, but in 1860 the Anglos started coming in numbers, including a lot of French Canadians and German Jews, most of whom became successful merchants in "Vegas." The French influence was strong from 1849 through 1894, when the Des Marias family lived in a big house on the east side of the plaza.

In 1846 the United States declared war on Mexico, and American armies, led by General S. W. Kearney, moved west to consolidate the new territories. Las Vegas was the first town of any size encountered by Kearney in what had been Mexican territory. There was little or no opposition to the American invasion of Las Vegas; after all, it was a long, long way to Mexico City. Another reason for the lack of resistance was General Kearney's promise, "I shall not expect you to take up arms and help me fight against your countrymen. But he who is found in arms against me, I will hang."

———— GETTING THERE ————

It's easy to find Las Vegas. Just stay on Interstate 25 for 110 miles north from Albuquerque, and you're there. Or stay on Interstate 25 for 110 miles south from the Colorado border, and you'll see it.

—— FESTIVALS AND EVENTS——

Kiwanis Ice Carnival
In Jan. **425-8631**.

Storrie Lake Fishing Derby
Sat. before Easter. **425-8631**.

Rails and Trails
In May. Memorial Day weekend. **425-8631**.

Early Years of the Santa Fe Trail.
In mid-June. At Fort Union. **425-8025**.

Fourth of July Fiesta
In July. At Plaza Park. **425-1401**.

Sailboard Regatta
In mid-July. On Storrie Lake. **425-8829**.

An Evening at Old Fort Union
In July. **425-8025**.

Southwest Culture Festival
In mid-July. **425-3745**.

San Miguel County Fair
In Aug. **425-8829**.

Tour of Historic Homes
Sat. in late Aug. For tickets and information, call **425-8829**.

Piedras Golf Classic
In Sept. On the New Mexico Highlands University course. **425-8829**.

——— OUTDOOR ACTIVITIES ———

There's lots of good **fishing** near Las Vegas. For example, **Storrie Lake State Park**, just 6 miles north of the city on N.M. 3, offers rainbow trout. Another 24 miles north on that same highway you come to the **Morphy Lake State Park**. There's no drinking water at Morphy Lake State Park, so bring along your own. **McAllister Lake**, 8 miles east on N.M. 104, has a well-deserved reputation for both northern pike and trout.

Stream anglers will find action with rainbow trout in the **Gallinas** and **El Porvenir rivers** in the canyon above Montezuma, which is reached by driving north of Las Vegas on N.M. 65. You'll be going that way, anyhow, to see Montezuma's Castle.

Above Mora, north of Las Vegas on N.M. 518, both the **Rio La Casa** and **Coyote Creek** offer rainbows and brown trout.

At 40 miles west on Interstate 25, you'll come to the **Rio Pecos**, which offers a different kind of trout fishing, with a much larger stream but the same rainbows. Work your way up into the wilderness area along the Pecos, and you'll have excellent populations of trout in beautiful surroundings.

Llama trekking? You bet! You can trek the Pecos Wilderness, west of Las Vegas, with the llama doing all of the load-toting. Call the **Shining Star Ranch** in Las Vegas, **425-1072**. Some llama treks go all the way to the top of Hermit's Peak, at just over 10,000 feet. Typical cost is $750 for a six-day operation, including two nights in Las Vegas hotels, on the first and last days, and four days in the wilderness, just you and your llama, on a free-and-easy, unhurried vacation, with your guides doing all the work. Everything included.

——— SEEING AND DOING ———

Cleveland Roller Mill, a few miles north of Las Vegas on N.M. 518, between Mora and Cleveland, was built in 1900 by a transplanted Pennsylvanian named Joseph Fuss. The two-story adobe mill has a checkered history and was used intermittently until 1954. It is currently being restored.

A walking tour of the famous stone homes of Las Vegas, guided by a free brochure obtained from the Chamber of Commerce, is a look into the past of this city, an authentic history written in stone. The fortunes made along the Santa Fe Trail, added to the sudden riches that accompanied the arrival of the railroad, led to the construction of elegant stone homes by carvers brought from faraway Italy.

Library Park Historic District is also easily reached by a self-guided walking tour. Pick up your free guide at the Chamber of Commerce, and take another look back into the glorious past of nineteenth-century Las Vegas.

Residences of Las Vegas Tour is for those who don't want to walk. Pick up your brochure at the Chamber of Commerce. It will guide you—in your auto—to 24 mansions out of the past. The oldest, the Rheus Pearce house, dates back to 1846.

There are two or more self-guided walking tours, and if you've covered these, you'll know where to find them.

Montezuma's Castle and Armand Hammer United World College. Just off N.M. 65, at the town of Montezuma, you'll be surprised at the gigantic building known as Montezuma's Castle. It was built by the Santa Fe Railroad in hopes of making this beautiful spot into a prime vacation spot. That failed, perhaps because the location was too isolated from great numbers of vacationing people. It later became a Baptist seminary, and after that failed, it was a Catholic seminary. Next it was a tuberculosis sanatorium and finally was condemned as unsafe. However, Armand Hammer had lots of money and a hankering for world peace. He financed the United World College of North America, one of seven such institutions worldwide. The United World College recruits about 200 students a year from as many as 68 different countries and enrolls them in a two-year course that stresses world peace. Armand Hammer also purchased the condemned Montezuma's Castle and planned to restore it. The cost of restoration is estimated at $2 million or so. Now that Armand Hammer has passed on, no one seems to know what the future of the United World College will be.

Madison vineyards. Drive south 20 miles on Interstate 25 to the junction with N.M. 3. Go 6 miles south on N.M. 3 to see a good New Mexico vineyard and winery. **421-8028.** To reach Madison vineyards wine-tasting room, go north on N.M. 3 and follow the signs. **421-2299.**

Castenada Hotel, an excellent example of Spanish Mission architecture, stands at the side of the railroad tracks, just three blocks from the town square. Once a luxury stopover on the railroad, it was the scene of Teddy Roosevelt's reunion with his famed "Rough Riders," heroes of the Spanish-American War. Today, a few rooms are rented out upstairs, and there's a beer parlor on the main floor. Visitors can walk the spacious veranda and look at it from the outside, but there is nothing left of the glory that was yesteryear.

—————— WHERE TO STAY ——————

ACCOMMODATIONS

A few suggestions:

Carriage House Bed and Breakfast—$$
This 95-year-old house is full of antiques. There are only five units, but it might be worth a phone call. **925 6th St., 454-1784.**

Inn of Las Vegas—$-$$
Swimming pool, restaurant and 56 units. **2401 N. Grand Ave., 425-6707.**

El Fidel Hotel—$-$$
Has 52 units. At the corner of Grand and Douglas. **425-6761.**

If you have any trouble finding the kind of accommodations you want, please contact the Chamber of Commerce, **729 Grand Ave., 425-8631.** The folks there are very friendly.

CAMPGROUNDS

KOA
Visible on the east side of Interstate 25, south of Las Vegas. Big, clean and easy to reach. **454-0180.**

Storrie Lake State Park
On the northern outskirts of Las Vegas on N.M. 3. Has 19 sites with electricity and water and an additional 22 shelters without hookups. There are hot showers, toilets and a dump station. **425-9231.**

Morphy Lake State Park
About 35 miles north of Las Vegas on N.M. 94. Camping and trout fishing. **387-2328.**

Coyote Creek State Park
About 40 miles north of Las Vegas, near the tiny town of Guadalupita. **387-2328.**

Important: Information about all state parks can be gained by calling **1-800-451-2541** only in New Mexico. State park camping fees are $7.

Pecos River RV Camp
Twenty-five miles west of Las Vegas on Interstate 25. Take exit 319 off

of the interstate. Has 35 sites with all hookups and another 30 that are pull-throughs. Hot showers, rec room, small store, lots of space everywhere. Rates are $12.50 for two; $1 for each extra person. **421-2211.**

——— WHERE TO EAT ———

There are many restaurants in Las Vegas, ranging from the fast-food variety all the way up to some really fine dining.

El Alto Supper Club—$
On Sapello Street. I enjoy eating here; opens at 6 P.M. for dinner only. **454-0808.**

El Rialto Restaurant—$
141 Bridge St. Also recommended; good New Mexican cuisine plus steaks and seafood. **454-0037.**

Plaza Hotel Restaurant—$
230 Old Town Plaza. Elegant atmosphere, plus good food, continental and New Mexican. **425-3591.**

——— SERVICES ———

Las Vegas' full-care medical facility, **Northeastern Regional Hospital,** is located at **1235 8th St., 425-6751.**

Greyhound services Las Vegas, as does **Amtrak,** with two passenger trains daily.

There are even two chambers of commerce in Las Vegas. The Chamber of Commerce is at **PO Box 148, Las Vegas, NM 87701; 425-8631.** The Hispanic Chamber of Commerce is at **PO Box 1416, Las Vegas, NM 87701; 425-8829.**

Pecos
National Historical Park

The newest national park in New Mexico, Pecos National Historical Park, protects and preserves one of the oldest sites in New Mexico. You leave Interstate 25 at exit 307, just east of Glorieta Baptist Assembly turnoff. The sign may still read "Pecos National Monument," but this area became a full-fledged national park in July 1990. A grant from the Andrew Mellon Foundation enabled the turnover of the 5,500-acre Greer Garson Fogelson Ranch to the monument.

The enlarged park is a microcosm of the history of New Mexico. It is one of the top attractions of the state.

In 1540 the 2,000 Pueblo Indians who had lived at Pecos for several centuries heard of Coronado's expedition to search for the fabled (and nonexistent) Seven Cities of Cibola. In their naiveté the Pueblos invited Coronado to visit them. He did, and their troubles began. The *españoles* returned in 1598 to settle in this beautiful valley and to Christianize the Indians. Although the Pecos Indians were happy to add Roman Catholicism to their old-way belief, they were unhappy with the hardships inflicted on them by the Spanish civil authorities. Resentment continued to fester for almost a century, when the Pecos joined the other Pueblos in the bloody Pueblo Revolt of 1680, which killed off the priests and most of the Spanish settlers and destroyed the first church that had been built in Pecos, circa 1622. The Indians lived in relative peace and quiet for a dozen years, taking advantage of their trading-post position on the Pecos River, near the best pass through the Sangre de Cristo Mountains to the many pueblos of the Rio Grande. But the Spanish returned with a vengeance in 1692. Led by Don Diego de Vargas, the Spanish quickly subdued the southern pueblos, and life returned to the way it had been before the revolt. Pecos men fought with the Spaniards against the raiding Comanches. The church built in the years following 1717 is the church whose ruins tower over the plain today.

Spain did not consolidate its holdings in what is now New Mexico, and the total number of Spanish settlers was never great. Usually, the tax collector was the only representative of the distant Spanish king who was ever noticed in New Spain.

Pecos was now an imposing pueblo and the hub in trade for the Indians of the Plains, who brought meat, hides and other goods to exchange for the more sophisticated wares of the Pueblos along the Rio Grande.

In 1821 an enterprising Yankee trader opened the Santa Fe Trail, and merchandise from the young United States arrived in Pecos on its way to Santa Fe, where it would meet up with the Camino Real. The "Royal Road" stretched, somewhat tenuously, all the way to Mexico City.

In 1948, when the United States declared war on Mexico, General S. W. Kearney led an expeditionary force against the resident Spanish forces. Spanish Governor Armijo organized his forces in Pecos to resist the oncoming Americans. But at the last moment, he withdrew to prepare another stand at Glorieta Pass and at Apache Canyon. Kearney bivouacked a few days at the pleasant site of Pecos before continuing to crush the tiny bit of Spanish resistance and incorporate New Mexico into the United States.

Free of the Spanish conquerors, Pecos flourished for a while by catering to trade on the Santa Fe Trail. But Pecos's fortunes suffered, and the number of residents continued to decline. Constant raids by the Plains tribes decimated the population. No longer a viable population, the Pecos survivors fled across the Rio Grande to join the friendly tribe at Jemez Pueblo. Pecos Pueblo was dead.

Here at Pecos National Historical Park, you can see the remains of the primitive (and peaceful) Pueblo Indians, whose city was once the most magnificent of all the pueblos. You can walk into the ruins of the Spanish Mission Church and learn of the history of Spanish rule—which failed to succeed, by reason of its cruelty. You can see the ruts of the old Santa Fe Trail, one of the most important routes of American history. In the excellent visitors center, you can see the story of American victory over Spain and the conversion of New Spain into the Land of Enchantment in the United States.

It is hoped that with its promotion from national monument, the Pecos National Historical Park will transcend the shameful neglect of the National Park Service that occurred through the eighties. Possibly the park will receive sufficient funding and manpower to get a start on the great job that lies before it. The main pueblo of the Pecos people lies on a ridge to the west of mission ruins. One can guess its outlines under centuries of drifting sand that covers it. The pueblo should be excavated carefully by trained archaeologists, and this is surely a priority for the National Park Service. As I write this, only three employees are engaged in restoration and excavation work at Pecos National Historical Park. Ten people couldn't keep up with the work of safeguarding the fragile reminder of our storied past. Today, these three employees spend most of their time making adobe bricks to replace those eroded by wind and rain. The ruins of the last church, mixed adobe and stone, have withstood the elements since 1717—59 years before our Declaration of Independence. Surely we can preserve them for the education of future generations.

Pecos National Historical Park has an excellent visitors center, with entertaining and informative exhibits. It features a 10-minute movie about the area, narrated by that classic red-headed beauty Greer Garson Fogleson. After your orientation in the visitors center, plan on an hour or two to walk slowly along the blacktopped paths, guided by a tour leaflet, and enjoy this reminder of New Mexico's turbulent past.

A self-guided tour leads one to the ruins of a church, built in 1717, at Pecos National Historical Park.

Villanueva

The picturesque Spanish colonial village of Villanueva is located on the Pecos River, about a dozen miles south of interstate 25 on N.M. 3. As soon as you leave the interstate, you enter a different world, where houses are still being built of adobe and where tiny villages, each dominated by a church, line this road into the past. Once in Villanueva, please seek out the church of **Nuestra Señora de Guadalupe**. It contains a tapestry—265 feet long—made by 36 local ladies during the years of 1974 to 1976, and it is a striking bit of primitive art. If the parish priest is in, he'll show you the interior of the church and its tapestry. If he is out on his parochial duties, inquire at the small store across the street from the church. Someone there will open the church for you and tell you about the tapestry. The tiny village is worth a second look. It's a typical example of rustic Spanish culture still living in New Mexico.

Just over a quarter of a mile out of town, the **Villanueva State Park** is well worth your visit or extended stay. It has camping accommodations, whether for tents or big motor homes. The 22 sites have water hookups but no electricity. There is no dump station or sewer hookup, because of the proximity to the Pecos River, which carved this lovely canyon out of the red-sandstone cliffs. There are rest rooms with showers. Investigate the walking trails if you want to see the area in depth. In the days of the Spanish conquistadores, this was one of the routes of conquest, following the Pecos River north into the Sangre de Cristo Mountains, and old Spanish ruins can be found in the state park. As in all of New Mexico's state parks, camping fee is $7 for developed sites. **421-2957**.

The church of Nuestra Señora de Guadalupe in Villanueva. The stone structure is unusual for a Spanish Colonial church.

=== Roadside Crosses ===
and Flowers

In many parts of New Mexico you will see a cross in the ditch or alongside the right-of-way. The cross may attract your attention by being decorated with fresh-cut flowers.

First-time visitors often ask if there is really a grave there. The answer, of course, is no. The Mexican tradition is to place a cross where a death occurred, to mark the spot where the soul left the body and began its trip into the hereafter. Family devotion is strong in Mexico and all of the Hispanic American countries. It is not unusual for families to return to the location of a loved one's death to replace the flowers on the anniversary of the death and to continue the practice for as long as 20 years.

These roadside shrines are more common the farther south you travel in our lovely state. Some may feature statuary and votive lights and be protected by an elaborate concrete structure. I've seen votive lights fashioned from empty beer cans. Other shrines may be crude wooden crosses. So rest assured that there's no body buried there, just solid evidence of the devotion of these people and their ingrained habit of praying for the dead. *Familia* means much to New Mexicans, who trace their roots into Old Mexico.

Montezuma's Castle, built in the 1880s as a resort, looms over the campus of Armand L. Hammer's United World College, just north of Las Vegas.

Clayton

Nine miles from Texas on U.S. 87 and 10 miles from Oklahoma on U.S. 56/64, Clayton is the first town of any size encountered by many newcomers to New Mexico. Clayton is the trade center of a large and sparsely populated area. The number one attraction here is located in **Clayton Lake State Park**, 12 miles to the north, where one of the world's best collections of dinosaur tracks (or traces) is found. More than 500 dinosaur tracks are plotted in the fossil area, including a rare set of handprints of the pterodactyl, a winged reptile. The pterodactyl was evidently taxiing for a take off, because it left a series of prints where its wing's knuckle hit the mud of some prehistoric lake as it fought to get airborne.

These tracks are 100 million years old! When they were made, this area was probably along the northern shore of the Gulf of Mexico. The dinosaur tracks were discovered when a small dam was built on Seneca Creek in 1956.

There is a campground in Clayton Lake State Park, with drinking water and toilets. There's also a boat-launching ramp to allow you to go fishing on the lake. Camping costs $7 for developed sites. **374-8808.**

Camping is also available at the **KOA**, a few miles north of the highway through the town. Rates start at $19.50 for two people with all hookups. Winter rates are $18.95. **296-2729**.

You'll want to visit the small **Union County Historical Museum**, the **Eklund Dining Room and Saloon** and the **grave of Black Jack Ketchum**. Folks in Clayton hanged ol' Black Jack back in 1901. The hanging didn't go well. Did you know about that? And if you know where to look, you can find the ruts of the Santa Fe Trail nearby, but they're more discernible at Fort Union.

Clayton has lots of motels and restaurants, a hospital and many of the conveniences found only in larger cities. There's a nine-hole golf course, tennis courts and a swimming pool.

This tremendous expanse of grassland was the scene of historical travels. The Santa Fe Trail passed to the west of present-day Clayton during the time that most of the traffic used the original path over Raton Pass. Rabbit Ear—a distinctive rock formation—was one of the most sought-for landmarks on the trail, for it meant that two more days' travel would bring the security and comfort of Fort Union. When most of the traffic began using the Cimarron cutoff, the new trail again was within easy reach of present-day Clayton.

When this nation was building westward, the cattle herds of Texas pastures were trailed to railheads in the north, for eventual delivery to eastern markets. But enterprising trail drivers also brought great herds north and west, beyond the railheads and sold them to mining communities and the U.S. Army forts that dotted the new frontier. The Goodnight-Loving Trail brought thousands of longhorns north to New Mexico and to Colorado. The herds were so large that one drive lost nearly 1,000 cattle to raiding Comanche, and the drive still showed a handsome profit for the long trip and the hard work. The trail drivers used several different routes because of the necessity of avoiding Indian ambushes. Goodnight said that he preferred the trail that led him across the endless grasslands to Chicosa Lake, because it was a certain supply of water for his thirsty herds. He would have to change his route today, for Chicosa Lake is often dry now. Chicosa Lake lies southwest of Clayton, almost surrounded by the Kiowa National Grasslands.

For further information about Clayton, call the Chamber of Commerce at **374-9253.**

Dinosaur tracks are clearly visible at Clayton Lake State Park. (Photo by Mark Nohl, *New Mexico Magazine.*)

Conchas Lake

Located 34 miles northwest of Tucumcari on N.M. 104, Conchas Lake State Park consists of a 9,000-acre lake surrounded by 1,160 acres of recreational opportunity. It is also reached by taking N.M. 129 from Newkirk, which is on Interstate 40. Conchas Reservoir is formed by a dam built by the Corps of Engineers on the Canadian River. With Ute Lake, which is upstream, Conchas Reservoir once shared the title of being New Mexico's best walleye and crappie fishing water. The long, narrow lake stretched for 25 miles through scenic red-sandstone cliffs, which made for wonderful water skiing and windsurfing. Waterfowl hunting is popular here in winter months.

This was one of the most developed of all the state parks, featuring rental cabins, marinas, a nine-hole golf course, a 4,800-foot-long airstrip and a 38-room lodge complete with a lounge and a restaurant.

Did you notice that I said it *was* one of the best developed?

Conchas Lake justifies its existence by being a source of irrigation water for 41,400 acres near Tucumari. Because irrigation gets first claim on the water, Conchas is vulnerable to extreme drawdowns. In 1990 there was virtually no snowmelt in the Sangre de Cristo Mountains, and Conchas was in trouble. The level went 28 feet below normal, which exposed mud banks and rocky shelves that hadn't seen the light of day for quite a spell.

For lack of water, the lake was almost lost. For lack of a lake, the tourist visitation was lost. For lack of the tourists, the lodge concessionaire went bankrupt. In the late summer of 1990, the lovely lodge was closed and tumbleweeds were growing in every crack of the concrete.

Fishing remained fair despite the lowered water levels. Perhaps the drawdown served to concentrate the fish in a smaller volume of water. **Camping** is excellent regardless of the water level. There are two main campgrounds. **Electric Point** with 28 sites, with hookups (electricity and water, but no drains), and **Bell Point**, with 33 more spaces with hookups. Halfway between the two RV campsites is a large tenting area. There are two marinas and one more under construction, all with good launching ramps. At the north-side area is a store, a lounge and restaurant and a bait shop. As is usual with the state parks, camping costs $7 for a developed site.

There's a **nine-hole golf course** ($3.50 per round) close to the park entrance. There's no phone, but there is a self-pay collection box at the first tee.

I hope I haven't discouraged the use of Conchas Lake State Park too much, for it is still a lovely place and popular with local people. Let's hope the snowmelt is excellent next spring, that the lake level comes flooding back and that the lodge is opened and running smoothly. To find out if our hopes come true, call ahead, **868-2270**.

Ute Lake

Just 3 miles west of Logan on N.M. 540, Ute Lake State Park lies on the shores of Ute Lake, which impounds the waters of the Canadian River and Ute Creek. With its twin lake (Conchas) upstream on Canadian, Ute Lake claimed the title of best walleye and crappie lake in New Mexico. In addition to the walleyes and crappies, the lake provides good sport and good eating with black bass and channel catfish. Walleyes and catfish are best caught after dark, especially during the summer. To locate walleyes, troll slowly with a bottom-bumping lure in 20 to 40 feet of water. There are many places to try your luck, for Ute Lake has a surface area of more than 8,000 acres. Evidence of good fishing is the fact that no less than nine bass fishing tournaments are held here each year, including one or two of the big regional contests.

Ute Lake has one tremendous advantage over its former twin, Conchas. Ute Lake is the only large body of water in New Mexico that is not used for irrigation. As a result, it enjoys a much more stable water level. The state raised the dam structures about five years ago, and that has helped immensely. When Conchas Lake was 28 feet below its level, Ute was only 5 feet down. Ute is now the second largest body of water in the state. Windsurfing is an increasingly popular sport here and on all the larger lakes of New Mexico. Without reservations, I recommend Ute Lake for a vacation destination.

Five miles away, Logan claims Ute Lake as its own, and even the Chamber of Commerce represents both Ute Lake and Logan. Logan is an old town, dating back to 1901, but had fallen on hard times when Ute Lake was built on the Canadian River. Businesses have made quite a comeback since the waters piled up in the reservoir. Now you can find almost everything you want in Logan. Among its many attractions is a saloon that labels itself "The Road to Ruin."

Close to the Fourth of July, Logan stages its biggest deal of the year, a **Beef and Beans Barbecue**, which attracts as many as 1,100 people. A car or pickup or boat—winner's choice—is raffled off. There's also a big fireworks display and a full-fledged rodeo.

WHERE TO STAY

ACCOMMODATIONS

Ute Lake Inn—$$
This motel nearest the water offers 12 rooms and 5 apartments with

full amenities. In addition, there are kitchenettes. At the north park area, **487-2245.**

Yucca Motel—$$
Has nine rooms. In Logan. **487-2272.**

Fireside Motel—$$
Has eight rooms. In Logan. **487-2247.**

B.J.'s—$$
And finally, there's a tiny three-room motel. In Logan, **487-2354.**

The motels in Logan are definitely not four-star accommodations, but they are used when fishing is good at Ute Lake and when Logan has its celebrations. Call ahead and ask questions.

CAMPGROUNDS

The state park offers camping and picnicking and is a favorite spot for eastern New Mexicans and vacationing Texans. There are full hookups, showers, a dump station, electricity, a playground, a marina and all the amenities you expect in a trailer park. The park and its facilities have been clean and well kept every time I've been there. As always, developed sites cost $7.

Don't be surprised at the absence of sewer drains in these excellent RV facilities, for the ground is solid red sandstone, and it is difficult to dig sewer lines. Dump stations are well laid out and easy to access. Launching ramps are wide enough for ease in launching any boat. Picnic shelters are numerous. From the tourist's viewpoint, Ute Lake has the advantage of being isolated enough to receive light usage. Last July, we parked our motorcoach in Logan Park, and we had the entire state park to ourselves and no competition for the best fishing spots. State park telephone is **487-2284.**

Logan Park
Twenty-four sites near the state park office.

North Area
Another twenty-four sites.

—————— WHERE TO EAT ——————

Fireside Cafe—$$

Looking for a place to eat in Logan? Best bet is this cafe in the Fireside Motel, right on U.S. 54 going through town. It's very old but well-frequented by truckers. **487-2247**.

If you can't find the goods or services you want in Logan, it is only 22 miles to Tucumcari, which claims to have 2,000 motel rooms, lots of stores, banks, services and the reputation for travelers' services dating back to the days of old Route 66.

Truth In Advertising, the sign of a saloon in Logan, New Mexico.

Tucumcari

Back in the days when Nat King Cole urged America to "get your kicks on Route 66," Tucumcari was the main stopping point on this Chicago-to-Los Angeles route. Because it was halfway between Amarillo and Albuquerque, it was an overnight stop for auto travelers who felt that 250 miles per day was a long run. Now the cars and roads have improved so much, there is not the big need for a stopover point—you just make the trip in one day.

Then the second shoe fell. Route 66 was widened into a divided highway named Interstate 40, and the concrete slabs bypassed Tucumcari, curving along the southern edge of the city. Tucumcari began having trouble filling its 2,000 motel rooms every night in tourist season. In addition, the big chain motels moved in, locating nearer to the exits off Interstate 40. As the tourists began using the bigger, newer, closer motels, the little old ones back in town began to fade. That process is still continuing.

HISTORY

Whence the name "Tucumcari"?

Well, it really was an Indian word for the flat-topped "mountain" that is the big landmark in the vicinity. The Indians claimed that Tucumcari meant "land of the buffalo hunts," and there is plenty of evidence that Indians hunted great herds of buffalo in this area. But Tucumcari is only the latest name. It was once called, "Liberty," because it was the liberty town for soldiers from nearby Fort Bascom. It was once called "Cactus Flats," and once it was called "Six-Shooter Siding," for obvious reasons. You'll hear the silly tale about the name coming from the murders and suicides of a quartet of Indians named Tucum, Kari, Tonopath, etc. If you believe that so-called legend, please call me. I'd like to sell you the Brooklyn Bridge. Since its incorporation in 1903, the city where you got your kicks on Route 66 has come a long way. Now it boasts a full-service airport with 7,100-foot runways, a fine 56-bed hospital, 27 churches, a branch campus of Eastern New Mexico University, six city parks and a big swimming pool, a nine-hole golf course and a historical museum. There are two local newspapers and a radio station, two UHF television outlets and a progressive attitude. In addition to its fame as an overnight stop, Tucumcari is actually becoming a vacation destination.

The famed **Bell Ranch** is nearby, still conducting its cattle drives with horses and using a chuck wagon to feed the cowboys who rope calves and drag them to the branding iron each year. The brand was registered in 1875.

The **Ladd S. Gordon Wildlife Area**, right on the city limits, is an excellent bird-watching spot and attracts many birders during bird migration time.

Its nearness to both **Conchas and Ute lakes** is a definite plus, and many fishermen ply those waters by day and eat and sleep in Tucumcari.

There's a **nine-hole golf course** just west of Tucumcari on Interstate 40. No tee time required; rental carts and clubs available. **461-1849**.

Horses are still a big part of life here, and the **Tucumcari Trailriders Association** dates from 1972, its members participating in many community events.

The **Tucumcari Museum** is one of many in the dry east plains of New Mexico, housing a varied collection of Indian artifacts, pioneer memorabilia, rocks and a display of petrified wood. It also houses an authentic moonshiner still. Hours are 9 A.M.—6 P.M. in summer, and there is a small admission charge. It's just four blocks off of old 66, now called **Tucumcari Boulevard**.

—— FESTIVALS AND EVENTS ——

Quay County Jamboree
In Mar. or Apr. Call the Chamber of Commerce for information at **461-1694**.

Craft Fair
In June and Dec. For information, phone **461-1694**.

Piñata Festival
The last full week in June brings the top event of the year, nonstop fun and games, including athletic contests, dances, election of a king and queen, a Tucumcari pageant, food booths, sidewalk sales and combined choirs of the churches joining into one grand songfest. For information, call **461-1694**.

Cutting Horse Association Show
In July at the fairgrounds. Ever seen a horse and rider seemingly controlled by one mind? That's a cutting horse. There's also a 4-H horse show and rodeo. For information about these horsey events, call Jim Duncan at **461-1694**.

Billy the Kid Pageant

All summer long at the Caprock Ampitheater. The show lasts an hour and a half, and there's a barbecue before the performance. Tickets cost $6 for adults, but seniors over 64 get in for $5. Children 5 to 12 years of age are only $1 apiece. There is no reserved seat in the house; everything is general admission. Come early, and enjoy looking around the natural ampitheater, located in San Jon, 27 miles east of Tucumcari on the superslab Interstate 40. Allow 30 minutes for driving. The show starts at 8 P.M. every Thurs., Fri. and Sat. from June 14 through Aug. 18. For information, call **576-2455** or the Chamber of Commerce, **461-1694**.

Quay County Fair

In Aug. For information call **461-1694**.

Apache Wells Lions Club Bar-B-Q and Rattler Reunion

Held in Aug. at the park 5 miles west of Tucumcari on—you guessed it—Route 66. Costs $4 for adults, $2 for children under 12. Lots of fun for all.

———— WHERE TO STAY ————

ACCOMMODATIONS

As you might expect in a town overbuilt with motels, rates are the lowest along Interstate 40. Competition is rough for the traveler's lodging dollar. Motels refused to be quoted about rates because there is almost always a price war going on. Please take my word for it, motels are inexpensive. Even the major chains are cheaper here than elsewhere. Here are a few recommendations.

Americana Motel—$$

On old Hwy. 66. **461-0431**.

Ramada Inn—$$$

Sixty-one units. On Tucumcari Blvd. (Route 66), **461-3140**.

Holiday Inn—$$$

One hundred units on the east edge of town, **461-3780**.

Palomino Motel—$$

Thirty units on East Tucumcari Blvd., **461-3622**.

Pow Wow Inn—$$

Ninety-two units on the west side of town, **461-0500**.

Discovery Inn—$$
One hundred units (a Best Western motel), **461-4884.**

Motel 6—$$
One hundred and twenty-two units at **2900 E. Tucumcari Blvd., 461-4791.**

CAMPGROUNDS

KOA
Located on old Route 66, just on the east edge of Tucumcari. A lovely park where I've stayed often. Shady sites and all the usual KOA amenities. Has 45 units with all hookups and another 75 with water and electricity. Best of the crop, by far. **461-1841.**

Hunts Campground
Located right on the main drag, in town, at **501 W. Tucumcari Blvd.** Phone is not listed, evidently out of operation. I found no one at home on two different days, but the campground is in use.

Red Arrow Campground
At **1316 E. Tucumcari Blvd., 461-2501.**

———— WHERE TO EAT ————

My top choices for restaurants in Tucumcari include:

Pow Wow Restaurant and Lodge—$$
At **801 W. Tucumcari Blvd.** Varied menu; drinks available. **461-2587.**

Ramada Inn Restaurant—$$-$$$
At **1302 W. Tucumcari Blvd., 461-3140.**

Golden Corral—$$
At **1324 W. Tucumcari Blvd.** This chain is famous for filling up a hungry teenager at a reasonable price. Featuring "super bars" and all-you-can-eat deals. **461-0299.**

Golden Dragon—$$
At **1006 E. Tucumcari Blvd.** Well-prepared typical Chinese food. **461-2853.**

Santa Rosa

A place chronicled in tales of Route 66, Santa Rosa is a surprisingly interesting spot. It is located on Interstate 40, 59 miles west of Tucumcari and 114 miles east of Albuquerque.

Although Indians had known about the Blue Hole and the natural lakes of this city for centuries before the white man, Santa Rosa was not really on the map until 1879, when one of the earliest Spanish settlers, named Don Celso Baca, built a small chapel in honor of his mother. He named the chapel for Saint Rose of Lima, which accounts for the town's name—Santa Rosa. The remains of the chapel still stand. The ruin is located on N.M. 91, which leads out of the city toward Puerto de Luna.

FESTIVALS AND EVENTS

Santa Rosa Days

Over Memorial Day, the town features its Memorial Day Tournament, along with parades, raft races, softball and food booths. A three-day celebration. For more information, call the Chamber of Commerce at **472-3763**.

Fourth of July

The celebration brings a big aerial display of fireworks, free to the public.

Annual Custom Car Show

In Aug. The show features a scenic hot-rod run to Puerto de Luna, street dances, and the car show at the football field. Call **472-3763** for dates and times.

Santa Rosa Fiestas

Also in Aug. Features entertainment, food booths, a duck drop (you mean to tell me you don't know about duck drops?), a dance and crowning of the Fiesta queen.

SEEING AND DOING

Don't think of Santa Rosa as just another wide spot on the fabled road. It is now a vacation destination, and there are a lot of things going on out there. For starters there are seven natural lakes in the area, the Pecos River flows through the city almost unnoticed, and it is one of the most interesting **scuba diving** destinations.

Scuba diving? No, I am not kidding. Five minutes from downtown Santa Rosa is the famous **Blue Hole**, an artesian-fed hole in the sandstone. The water, a constant 64° F, is clear as bathtub gin, and visibility extends down to 80 feet. Divers come here all year long, but they need wet suits in the winter. The hole is about 80 feet in diameter, and expert divers have penetrated to 160 feet, called the second chamber.

The city of Santa Rosa has provided steps and platforms for easier entry. Expert divers know that they must change the calibrations on their equipment to compensate for the fact that the surface of Blue Hole is nearly 5,000 feet above sea level. Camping is allowed right at the site, and there are numerous motels and restaurants in Santa Rosa.

Scuba diving in the high desert is certainly unusual, but Santa Rosa is not your usual small town. Population is about 3,300 and holding fairly steady.

Santa Rosa Lake State Park is another of the area's big attractions. The Corps of Engineers built this impoundment on the Pecos River in 1980 and justified its existence by offering irrigation water. As a result, extreme drawdowns are the rule rather than the exception. However, a big drawdown in lake level doesn't seem to hurt the park so much, because it exposes the sides of steep rock-walled canyons, not wide mud banks. In 1990 I would list the small lake as one of the top fishing spots in the entire state. Huge catfish, fished at night, usually taken on water dogs for bait, run to 40 pounds. Walleyes, black bass, crappie and bluegills are found in abundance. It is quite possible to fish from shore and earn a tasty meal. See Campgrounds section.

Puerto de Luna (moon gate) is an old-timey village 10 miles south of Santa Rosa—signs on the main street start you off on N.M. 91—where tiny irrigated farms and adobe homes reflect the New Mexico of two hundred years ago. The road is good, and the red rock formations along the way contrast beautifully with the emerald green of irrigated crops. Puerto de Luna is the end of the road. When you reach it, ask for directions to see **Coronado's Bridge** site, and take a look at the lovely Catholic church that overlooks the calm, peaceful village.

—————— WHERE TO STAY ——————

ACCOMMODATIONS

Just as in Tucumcari, motel owners are engaged in a price war most of the time, competing for the traveler's dollar. They are reluctant to quote prices, but I can vouch for the fact that Santa Rosa motels are almost as cheap as those in Tucumcari. You'll find a huge variety of accommodations. Let me recommend a few of the 16 motels in this town.

Holiday Santa Rosa—$$
Reached on east exit 277. Has 100 rooms. **472-5411.**

Scottish Inn—$$
Has 47 units. At **860 Will Rogers Dr., 472-3466.**

Super 8 Motel—$$
Has 52 units. At **1201 Will Rogers Dr., 472-5388.**

CAMPGROUNDS

COMMERCIAL

KOA
On Will Rogers Dr., convenient to downtown, offering 96 units. **472-3126.**

Santa Rosa Lake State Park
An excellent family camping area, with 50 camp sites at Rocky Point— 15 of them have electricity and water. All have picnic grills and shelters. To show you how up-to-date things are, there are solar-heated showers at this camp site. **472-3110.**

Juniper Park
There's a primitive camping area with 25 sites. A modern comfort station has rest rooms and everything you'd want except showers. There is a good launching ramp in the Juniper Park area. Because it is too expensive to dig drains in the solid rock, the park provides an excellent dump station for RV use.

There is more camping opportunity in the city. Please call the Chamber of Commerce at **472-3763** for details.

───────── WHERE TO EAT ─────────

Club Cafe—$
561 Parker Ave. In 1990 Michael Wallis published the book *Route 66*, and in it he mentioned Club Cafe, which has been doing business at the

same location since 1935. I didn't know it was famous. I just knew that I had stopped there many times and had always enjoyed the food, whether Mexican or standard American. My wife has enjoyed a fine, inexpensive chicken enchilada with guacamole salad.

In addition to the food at Club Cafe, there is an interesting gift shop, with lots of memorabilia for the growing cult of folks interested in 66. **472-3631.**

Joseph's Restaurant and Cantina—$$

At **865 Will Rogers Dr.** Serves some excellent Mexican meals, along with lots of the food you are accustomed to. **472-3361.**

Sun and Sand Restaurant—$$

At **1120 Will Rogers Dr.** Offers a good menu featuring both Mexican and American dishes. **472-3092.**

The Land of Enchantment is known for its Mexican food. (Photo by Mark Nohl, *New Mexico Magazine*.)

THE NORTHWEST REGION

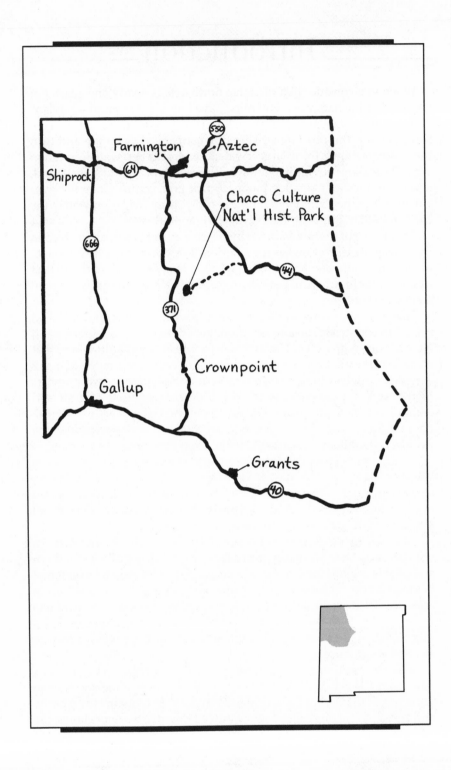

Introduction

When you consider that the huge northwest is nearly one quarter of the Land of Enchantment, you must have one word in mind—Navajo!

The Navajo Dam and the Navajo Reservoir impound the waters of the San Juan and the Los Piños rivers downstream of Colorado and turn them into the state's third-largest water area and its best water recreation area. The waters provide irrigation for thousands of acres of Navajo land, and the miracle of irrigation paints a great green stripe along the river valley below the dam. Even on mesa tops, spray irrigation waters the corn and other grains for the Navajo Irrigation Project.

The stretch of the San Juan fed by the cold waters from down deep in the Navajo Reservoir makes for wonderful trout fishing. Wise management of this tailwater has resulted in what many call one of the 10 best trout streams in America! To many Americans, Navajo means wonderful fishing and boating.

To many other Americans, Navajo means the nation's largest Indian tribe (215,000 strong) on a reservation that stretches across Arizona and New Mexico with a bit of Utah thrown in. The Navajo Nation—and that is the term they use often—has many self-governing attributes. In many ways it resembles our federal government, complete with corruption, its own brand of Watergate, with its top officials accused of graft and embroiled in lawsuits. Nevertheless, the Navajo people are wonderful. Laura Gilpin, one of the earliest to write about and photograph the people, called them "enduring Navajo," and they certainly are that.

Navajos govern themselves from their reservation headquarters in Window Rock, Arizona. Most of their chapter houses are in New Mexico, along with much of their past. I'll tell you how to see the Navajo and how to enjoy the beauties of their land, from the harsh rock canyons to the cool pines, from the dry arroyos to the trout streams.

This Northwest Region is bordered on the south by Interstate 40, which bisects New Mexico, going east to west. Even here, at the southern end of this region, the Navajo presence is big. The Indian Ceremonial held at Gallup, on Interstate 40, is one of the largest Indian festivals in America. To the eternal shame of the Navajo, the town of Gallup admits to being the "drunken Indian" capital of America; its mayor led a pilgrimage to the state capitol last year to ask for help with his Navajo alcoholism problem.

Before we continue with our description of the Northwest Region, let's talk about the Navajo. Insofar as we are able to determine, the Navajo came across the Bering Land Bridge from Asia. At that time the Apache and Navajo were one tribe. As they moved down to warmer climes, the two tribes became separated, and there are now great differences between them. Many characteristics of the Navajo language evidence the people's Asian origin, and they do possess the epicanthic fold in the corner of their eyes, somewhat like the Chinese and Indochinese. The Navajo are a short people, lean and brown and capable of great feats of endurance. To this day, the Navajo walk great distances and think nothing of it, although the white man's pickup truck is now their preferred method of transportation.

Many Navajos still want nothing to do with the white man. They tend their sheep and small garden plots in the interior of the reservation and avoid the city man and his ways. Other Navajo have become almost completely westernized and have adopted the ways of the cities, becoming college graduates and professional workers.

Most Navajo do not want their picture taken, so it is wise to ask permission first. If the answer is no, don't argue. Accept their right to their own beliefs. A Navajo friend of mine explained it this way: "After you take the picture, you have something in your camera that it didn't have before. Right? Well, the only way you can add to what is yours this way is to take away something that is mine. Right?" I tried to talk him out of it, but I had to give up or lose a friend.

Navajo beliefs may be hard for us to understand, but then the Navajo don't understand us very often either. In the old belief, when a person died in a hogan (the round or octagonal house preferred by the Navajo), the traditionalist burned the house down. At a minimum, he would pull part of the house apart to show it was abandoned. He also said that this damaged house was "chin-dee," which means that it was taboo and that the Navajo people should avoid it. It is easy to see that this custom was designed to prevent the spread of disease by avoiding the source of infection.

Some of the more traditional Navajo refuse to speak English or Spanish. They feel that they are Din-nee, which translates as "the people," and they want nothing to do with outsiders. They are a pastoral people who shepherd their sheep across what seems to us to be a vast emptiness, but it is the Navajo Nation.

They are expert weavers, and Navajo blankets and rugs have earned prices as high as $10,000 in recent years. Each vicinity of the sprawling Navajo Nation produces its own recognizable style in weaving, such as the Two Grey Hills and the Ganado Red styles, which fetch the highest prices. Navajo are also skilled silversmiths, creating excellent jewelry of silver and turquoise. In the last few decades, they have also become good potters, turning out excellent jugs, jars and trays. We'll tell you where to look for their products and how to buy them as we go along on our journey through the Navajo Nation. We'll also tell you about Navajo tacos and the standby item of diet, mutton stew and fried bread.

Almost every religious sect known to man has a mission somewhere on the Navajo reservation, or just off of it. They are all busy teaching the Navajo how to quit sinning—while forgetting that the Navajo didn't even know that those sins existed before the white man came.

I have a lot of respect for the Navajo. The Navajo are a people of dignity. Although they are a dignified people, Navajos laugh easily and love to share a common joke. For example, when an infant first laughs out loud, it is cause for celebration and feasting among the traditional Navajo people.

During World War II, many Navajo fought for their country. Some of them used their spoken language on the radio to function as a code. The Japanese never broke that code!

Yes, the word "Navajo" should always be in our minds when in northwestern New Mexico. If you want to study up ahead of your visit, write to **Navajoland Tourism, PO Box 663, Window Rock, AZ 86515, (602) 871-6436**. Ask for the fine four-color publication *Explore the Navajo Nation*.

Navajo potter signs her work at Four Corners National Monument.

Farmington

It's easy to find Farmington. It's the biggest city (more than 45,000 citizens) in the northwest corner of the state, astraddle of U.S. 64, which runs east and west across the north edge of New Mexico, and U.S. 666, which runs north and south through the Navajo Nation from Colorado down to Gallup.

Farmington is the supply center for the oil and gas industry, which has many operations in this part of New Mexico and on into Arizona and Utah. Farmington has prospered and regressed along with the oil and gas industry. It's the biggest trading center for the huge Navajo Nation and the store of choice for the irrigated farming area nourished by the Navajo Reservoir.

The Farmington area is underlaid with coal, and its controversial (with environmentalists) Four Corners Power Plant is one of the nation's biggest users of soft coal for power generation.

FESTIVALS AND EVENTS

There's always something going on in Farmington.

Charity Ball
In mid-March. For information, call **1-800-448-1240**.

Pro-Rodeo Roundup
In Apr.

Horse Racing
Starts at San Juan Downs in Apr. and runs through Labor Day. Post time is 1 P.M. Sat. and Sun.

Memorial Day Balloon Festival
Balloon launches at 6 A.M. Sat. and Sun. For more information, call the Chamber of Commerce, **1-800-448-1240**.

Riverfest
In May, a festival of music, arts and crafts, river raft rides and so forth.

Sheriff Posse Rodeo
In June. The largest open rodeo in the state. It's on the County Rodeo Grounds on U.S. 550, east of Farmington.

The Anasazi Pageant

Celebrating the multicultural heritage of this area, the pageant is presented in a dinner-theater setting at the outdoor amphitheater at Lions Wilderness Park in Farmington. Starts each year about June 20 and continues through Labor Day, Wed.–Sat. at 8 P.M., with dinner at 6 P.M. One of the better outdoor dramas. Tickets are $16 for adults and $10 for children under 12 for both dinner and the drama.

Farmington Trade Days

In June, with arts and crafts for everyone and a merchants trade show. For more information, call the Chamber of Commerce, **1-800-448-1240.**

Dave Thomas Charity San Juan Golf Tournament

Last weekend in June.

Freedom Days Celebration

Fourth of July weekend, with fireworks, outdoor concert, food fair, street dance, parade and triathlon and sailboat races. The Chamber of Commerce will answer your questions.

Connie Mack World Series Baseball Tournament

In Aug. This is the big one, seven days of baseball—17 games—featuring top amateur players from all over the U.S. and Puerto Rico. The pro scouts are always there. Call **327-9673 or 327-7701, ext. 1197** for information.

San Juan County Fair

In Aug. Loyal boosters call it the biggest county fair in New Mexico. They just might be right.

Totah Festival

Labor Day. Features a juried fine arts and craft show, highlighted with an Indian rug auction. For more on the value of Indian rugs, see the Introduction to The Northwest Region. For more information, call **327-7701, ext. 1145.**

Shrine Circus

Sept. 9. Call **1-800-448-1240** for information.

Road Apple Rally

In mid-Sept., bikers from all over the country assemble for the annual mountain-bike race and tour. Men and women, pros and amateurs, young and old ride an 18-mile-loop course through canyons and arroyos and around Farmington Lake.

Shiprock Fair
In Oct. The top celebration for the northern half of the Navajo Nation. Parade, rodeo, crafts, along with traditional songs and dances.

Festival de los Farolitos
In Dec. a display of traditional Spanish lanterns is held at the Aztec Ruins at dusk. This is a beautiful sight. For information, call the Chamber of Commerce at **1-800-448-1240**.

—— SEEING AND DOING ——

Farmington Museum at **302 North Orchard** has good displays of historic and environmental subjects. Appropriate for kids because of its hands-on exhibits. Admission is free. Phone is **327-7701, ext. 1179.**

Aztec Ruins and National Monument in the town of Aztec, just 15 minutes from Farmington. The name "Aztec" was certainly not well-chosen, for we find no link between this site and the Aztec Empire 2,000 miles to the south. Well-preserved Anasazi ruins and the world's largest reconstructed kiva. Occupied from about A.D. 1100 to about A.D. 1250. Much of this important archaeological site has not yet been excavated. Other parts have been excavated and then back-filled to protect them from falling down. They await further archaeological work. Well worth your time and effort. Phone at the monument is **334-6174.**

Salmon Ruins and the San Juan Research Center is on U.S. 64 a dozen miles east of Farmington. Here you can see the remains of Chaco culture Indian buildings, along with the remains of the pioneer homestead of a man named Salmon, for whom the site is named. Very good museum collection of artifacts and extensive Chacoan ruins. Salmon was built by Chacoan ancestors and then abandoned after only 60 years of use. In fact, it was abandoned three times. Why? Phone is **632-2013.**

Bisti Badlands, about 40 miles south of Farmington on N.M. 371, is a good example of erosion, and the end result is a lunar landscape, desolate and unfriendly. I was disappointed in this spot and do not consider it worthy of a side trip. Angel Peaks tells the same story but better. Incidentally, a few words of caution about roads on the Navajo lands. There's a unimproved road shown on the highway map, leading from Bisti (pronounced "Bist-eye") eastward to Chaco Canyon. Don't try it. I couldn't find my way across. There are no road signs because the Navajo already know where they're going.

De-Na-Zin wilderness is managed by the Bureau of Land Management to preserve its unique wilderness values. Solitude is its best attribute, and isolation is its best protection. You can find it by going south on N.M. 371 from Farmington to the intersection of County Road 7500, going east. This is only for the rugged hiker who enjoys desolation and wilderness. The Navajo name means "tall crane," which is explained by a Navajo tale that long ago many cranes stopped here on their annual migration. Too dry for cranes these days. For further information, contact the B.L.M. in Farmington at **1235 La Plata Hwy**, call **327-5344**.

Ship Rock is a huge rock formation, towering 1,700 feet above the plain, southwest of the town of Shiprock. In Navajo it is called Tse be dahi, which I can't pronounce, but I know it means "rock with wings." About an hour's drive from Farmington. While you are over that way, investigate the shopping mall Tse-bit-a-i, where the Navajo Nation shops.

Then continue west from Shiprock on U.S. 64 and U.S. 160 to the **Four Corners National Monument**. Consider that the "national" in that title refers to the Navajo Nation, so don't expect the National Park Service to have an interest here. This is the only spot in our country where four states meet at a common point. Pose the kids with one foot in Colorado, another in Utah, and their hands in Arizona and New Mexico. Follow the curving road northeast, and you'll drive through parts of Arizona, Utah, Colorado and New Mexico in 10 minutes time. Lots of curios for sale in booths at the Four Corners Monument and *some* of them are very good.

WILDLIFE

One of Farmington's biggest drawing cards is the excellent **fishing** to be had in **Navajo, Jackson and Morgan lakes and in the San Juan River**

Shiprock—the rock with wings—juts 1,700 feet into the New Mexico sky.

flowing out from under the Navajo Dam. Navajo Lake offers 200 miles of shoreline around a 15,160-acre lake, famed for rainbow trout, kokanee salmon and black bass. Three full-service marinas cater to the boating fisherman.

The San Juan River offers the best chance of taking a trout longer than 20 inches of any water in America! That's a proud boast, but the San Juan has been backing it up for a decade. In the waters closest to the dam itself, you find fast fishing for rainbows, but this is catch and release water—barbless hooks and you keep nothing but a quick picture of the fish. That's the stretch, about a quarter of a mile, reaching down to the cable crossing.

Then you come to the quality fishing area, 3.5 miles of wonderful fishing, where you are allowed to keep only one fish per day and that fish must be more than 20 inches long! Again, you must use barbless hooks and artificial lures only. No worm dunkers allowed here.

Fishing licenses are available at sporting goods stores in the area, and at the eight guide and outfitter services working this area. They are:

Complete Fly Shop, run by Chuck Rizuto, at **4251 E. Main** in Farmington. **326-0664**.

Four Corners Guide Service, run by Tim Jimerson at the tiny community of Navajo Dam. **632-3569**.

Heath Guide Service, run by Ric Heath, at **6209 Doe St.** in Farmington. **325-1635**.

Rocky Mountain Anglers, run by Paul Faust, at **Navajo Dam. 632-0445**. Two experienced guides, and a complete fly tying service. The guides have been fishing the river since they could walk, and they do give the angler his money's worth.

San Juan Troutfitters, run by Harry Lane, in Farmington. **327-9550**.

Sportsman Inn, run by Louie Vaughn, at **Navajo Dam. 632-3271**. The inn also provides a restaurant and lounge. His green chile cheeseburger is a meal in itself.

Born and Raised on the San Juan River, Inc., run by Tim Chavez out of **Abe's Motel**, at Navajo Dam, **632-2194**. Tim really was born and raised on the river, and his reputation for putting anglers on to big trout is well known.

Duranglers, at Navajo Dam, **632-5952**. Complete guide service and flyfishing supplies. A Durango, Colorado, based outfit.

Guiding fees are fairly uniform, ranging from $125 to $200 for a half day of either guided wade fishing or float trips. It pays to shop around.

New Mexico offers a short-term fishing license—$8.50 for one day and $15 for five days. A season long license is $24.50. You'll also need habitat stamps. For licensing information, call **827-7880**.

—— WHERE TO STAY ——

ACCOMMODATIONS

I counted more than 22 motels in Farmington. Here are a few recommendations that add up to 940 rooms, so you ought to find what you want.

Apple Tree Inn—$$
Has 32 rooms. **5915 E. Main, 326-1555.**

Encore Motel—$$
Has 36 units. **1900 E. Main, 325-5008.**

Motel 6—$$
Has 134 rooms. **1600 Bloomfield Hwy., 326-4501.**

Super 8—$$
Offers 59 units. **1601 Bloomfield Hwy., 325-4564.**

Anasazi Inn—$$
Has 68 units. **903 W. Main, 325-4564.**

Farmington Lodge—$$
Has 34 units. **1510 W. Main, 325-0233.**

La Quinta—$$
Has 106 units. **675 Scott Ave., 327-4706 or 1-800-531-5900.**

Motel 6—$$
Has 98 units. **510 Scott Ave., 327-0242.**

Executive Inn—$$$
Has 15 rooms and 26 suites. On the Bloomfield Hwy., **327-4433.**

Holiday Inn—$$$
Has 150 units. **600 E. Broadway, 327-9811 or 1-800-HOLIDAY.**

The Inn, Best Western—$$$
Has 194 units. **700 Scott Ave., 327-5221 or 1-800-528-1234.**

CAMPGROUNDS

COMMERCIAL

Crabtree RV Park

In Kirtland, which is a few miles west of Farmington on U.S. 64. Has 12 spaces with all hookups. $7.50 per night. **598-6180**.

KOA Bloomfield

At **1900 E. Blanco Blvd. in Bloomfield**, which is 14 miles east of Farmington on U.S. 64. Offers 70 spaces with full hookups, swimming pool and all the other things you expect in a KOA. Convenient to the lake and to the stream fishing below Navajo Dam. Prices start at $12 per night. **632-8339**.

Mom and Pops

At **901 Illinois**, just off of Bloomfield Hwy., right in Farmington. Thirty-three spaces with full hookups, shower and rest rooms. Nice, friendly place but completely lacking in shade trees. Prices start at $12 per night. I stayed there recently and really enjoyed the park and the people. **327-3200**.

River Grove Trailer Park

At **801 E. Broadway**, in Farmington. Twenty-eight spaces with full hookups, including cable TV and telephone hookups. Ten bucks per night. I got good TV reception without the cable, using the motor coach's antenna. **327-0974**.

Riverside Park

On Light Plant Rd., in Aztec, which is 15 miles northeast of Farmington on U.S. 550. There's a well-stocked fishing pond and a dump station. Cost is only $6 per night. Very convenient if you want to visit the Aztec Ruins. There is no phone at the park, but you can call the Public Works **at 334-6725** for information.

San Juan Mobile Home Park

On Light Plant Rd. in Aztec. Offers 13 spaces with full hookups, at $9 per night. **334-9532**.

The Beach at Bloomfield

Offers 13 spaces with full hookups at $12 per night. **632-1677**.

PUBLIC

Navajo Lake State Park

Offers a total of 200 camping spaces—50 with water and electricity and eight with full hookups. Campground fee is $7 for developed camp sites. Right on Navajo Lake, close to fishing and boating opportunities. **632-2278.**

Angel Peak

About an hour southeast of Farmington, just off N.M. 44. A campground and picnic site, administered by the Bureau of Land Management, is reached by a washboard gravel road 6 miles from the blacktop. If you have the urge to camp in a silent land, with land and rock carved into weird shapes by the eroding fingers of wind and water, this is the place. Picnic shelters and rest rooms are available, along with peace and quiet and sometimes the howling of coyotes. I like the place.

———————— WHERE TO EAT ————————

Coyote's Restaurant—$$
903 W. Main. Steaks and seafood. **325-4564.**

K.B. Dillons—$$
101 W. Broadway. Steaks and seafood. **325-0222.**

Chef Bernies—$$
910 W. Main. Family dining. **325-1361.**

Kettle Restaurant—$$
685 Scott Ave. Family dining. **326-0824.**

Village Inn—$$
514 Scott Ave. Family dining. **325-3498.**

El Charro—$$
737 W. Main. Mexican food. **327-2464.**

La Fiesta Grande—$$
1916 E. Main. Mexican food. **326-6476.**

Los Rios—$$
915 Farmington Ave. Mexican food. **325-5699.**

Beijing Restaurant—$$
San Juan Plaza. Oriental food; lunch and dinner only. **326-2129.**

Golden Dragon—$$
2324 E. Main. Oriental food; lunch and dinner only. **325-5100.**

───────── SERVICES ─────────

Two commuter airlines serve Farmington: **United Express, 1-800-525-0256,** and **Mesa Air Lines, 327-0271** or **1-800-545-5119.** Both are officed at the airport.

In addition, **Four Corners Aviation** offers chartered air tours from the Farmington airport. Contact owner Morris Wilson at **325-2867.**

Rental Cars are available from no less than six companies in Farmington. **Avis, 327-9864; Budget, 327-7304; Hertz, 327-6093;** and **National, 327-0215.**

Inside the reconstructed kiva at Aztec Ruins, Aztec, New Mexico. Said to be the largest kiva ever reconstructed by archaeologists.

Chaco Culture
National Historical Park

It used to be called Chaco Canyon, but the National Park Service upgraded it to a historical park and enlarged its area of interest, which necessitated a new name. No matter what you call it, this spectacular grouping of stone ruins, dating from the period A.D. 900 to A.D. 1300 is one of the premier attractions in the entire state.

Despite three quarters of a century of study, we really know very little about the people who built these grand buildings. We think that there were as many as 10,000 Anasazi living here about 900 years ago. That means that Chaco was once probably the biggest city in North America.

The Anasazi were peaceful farming and gathering people who eked out a living in this arid land. Their life-style must have been fairly easy, however, for they found time to construct great roads leading to outlying towns, and they built kivas for religious purposes. The Anasazi had a good knowledge of irrigation and raised crops in alluvial fans of sand washed down from the sandstone cliffs. Chaco was settled once, abandoned and then resettled, maybe more than twice. About A.D.1300 the Anasazi gave up the struggle here—for reasons still not understood—and moved in with pueblo communities. We used to think that the great drought of A.D. 1275–1300 "dried" them out, but later research has shown that the canyon was near desert even before the Anasazi began to build there. There is no evidence that they were driven out by other marauding people. Some of them went southwest and joined forces with Zuni and Acoma pueblos while others went to the Rio Grande pueblos—such as Santo Domingo and Pojoaque. True descendants of the Anasazi are found in the pueblos. The Navajo came on the scene after the great buildings of Chaco Canyon had stood empty for centuries.

In the national park, you drive on blacktopped loop roads that lead you up close to the 600-room building known to us as **Pueblo Bonito**. You can also get up close to **Chetro Ketl, Casa Rinconada, Pueblo Arroyo** and **Casa Chiquita**. Travel at your own pace, or take scheduled walking tours led by park rangers. There's an excellent visitors center and a gift shop with a good collection of books and pamphlets about this mysterious people and their great civilization. Take time to stand and wonder at the achievements of these "ancient ones"; look at the three-story stone buildings they put up without benefit of machinery. Ask yourself why the Anasazi built wide, rock-surfaced level roads—roads that were carefully oriented with true north in some cases (and remember that they did not have the wheel, the compass or the clock). Look down into their religious kivas, and envision the meeting of leaders there, perhaps trying to figure out how to feed their growing population on the scant supply of arable lands. Remember that the Anasazi traded for shells with the people of Baja California, for turquoise with Cerillos in New Mexico, even perhaps with far-off Mexican peoples. Scientists have studied Chaco culture for many decades, and each answer they dig up brings five new questions.

If you're camping or RVing, you are in luck, for there's a good campground near the visitors center. The Golden Eagle Passport will get you free entry into the park and will also bring a 50 percent discount off the $5-per-night charge for using the campground. Where else can you find petroglyphs and pre-Columbian ruins right in the campground?

But if you are not self-contained enough for an overnight stay, you've got a small problem. Chaco is out in the middle of nowhere, and there are no motels for your convenience. Best bet is to stay in Farmington or Bloomfield and drive the sixty miles down to Chaco to arrive before 10 A.M. This will give you time to explore the wonderful ruins and still drive home in the daylight.

According to the road maps, there are three roads leading into the park. The best is N.M. 45, which leads to the park from N.M. 44 (the main road from Albuquerque to Farmington) at Nageezi for 25 miles of rough gravel.

The second is almost the same, for it features N.M. 57 south from Blanco at N.M. 44 to join up with N.M. 45, halfway to Chaco. This is a smoother road, but it is slippery and dangerous after a rain. True, it doesn't rain very often, but we still recommend the road through Nageezi.

The third entry to the park is NOT recommended in any weather nor for any vehicle less than a four-wheel-drive pickup with strong springs and shock absorbers. This is N.M. 57 on state highway maps, leading off of N.M. 371 north of Crownpoint. There's no N.M. 57 sign, but there is a Navajo (arrowhead-shaped) sign calling it Navajo 9. It's not too bad for the first 10 miles, but then you have to turn north on Navajo 14 to the park. That road is solid rock and still manages to be a washboard to the ultimate degree. I made it one summer in a 31-foot motor coach, but we didn't arrive in one piece. The inside rearview mirror rattled loose and fell in my lap, and my CB radio jiggled loose and fell on my foot. When I was safely in the fine campground at Chaco, I found that one of the overhead cabinets was loose and hanging by one bolt! Don't try the road south of Chaco to Crownpoint. Please, don't try it!

But don't let bad roads keep you from visiting Chaco Canyon. It is one of New Mexico's top attractions.

Gallup

Unlike Denver and Albuquerque, Gallup doesn't call itself the "Mile High City." Gallup stands at 6,515 feet above sea level, which makes it a mile and a quarter high.

Gallup is just 22 miles from Arizona, on Interstate 40 (the historic Route 66). It's well supplied with 42, count 'em 42, restaurants and more than 1,700 motel rooms. Gallup is the shopping town for the huge Navajo Reservation to the north and to the Zuni and Ramah Navajo reservations to the south. It is the junction for U.S. 666, which goes straight north to Shiprock and on into Colorado. Gallup continues to be an important stop on the railroad, as it has been for decades.

With Grants, Gallup shares the privilege of being the gateway to the **Zuni Pueblo**, the **El Morro National Monument** and **Bandera Volcano and the Ice Caves**. It is only a 15-minute drive out to Red Rock State Park, which is the site of much of the **Intertribal Indian Ceremonial**, the biggest event in Gallup, in the first half of Aug. each year. During the Indian ceremonial, there are daily performances each evening at 7:30 P.M. In addition, market-places are filled with Navajo rugs, kachinas, jewelry, pottery, basketry and beadwork, paintings, sculpture and other Indian arts and crafts. And, of course, the competition is held for Miss Indian America and Little Miss Indian.

For me the biggest attractions are two evenings of ceremonial dances, resplendent with the most beautiful costumes and offering greater variety than you can expect to see anywhere else in the world. In addition, afternoon performances give the amateur photographer a better chance to record the dances and the costumes by natural light. To my mind, this Gallup ceremonial is the most authentic Indian happening in the world. Famed western author Zane Grey was at the first ceremonial in Gallup, and it has gotten better every year of its 69 years.

HISTORY

A fairly young city, Gallup was the pay station for construction workers on the Atlantic and Pacific Railroad. It got its name from the paymaster David L. Gallup. People talked about going to Gallup to get paid, hence the name. It was organized as a village in 1881, but the Western Overland Stage stopped here even before 1880. In this quiet frontier village, most residents wore their "shooting irons"—until a municipal ordinance stopped that in 1896.

The railroad was a mainstay of the economy for decades, along with the mining of the huge coal deposits that underlay so much of this country. Today, the big sheep-processing facility, oil refineries, and lumbering provide a solid base for Gallup, in addition to the growing tourism industry.

Many tourists come to Gallup solely for the silver and turquoise jewelry. Here a word of advice might be worthwhile. The genuine Old Pawn turquoise and silver is the most valuable. It was made for and by the Navajos. It usually features larger pieces and heavier silver mountings and got its name from the fact that the Navajos pawned their jewelry when they were short of cash. When it wasn't redeemed, it was put up for sale. Thus Old Pawn means the most authentic. The modern stuff, made to sell to tourists, may be even more beautiful, but it lacks the collector's value of Old Pawn. But remember that a piece of jewelry doesn't become Old Pawn just because some trader says it is. You might look first at **Richardson's Cash Pawn**, and ask the Richardsons to show you the difference. They are reliable and located at **222 W. 66**. Been there since 1913!

——— GETTING THERE ———

Amtrak serves Gallup, as do two transcontinental bus lines and Mesa Airlines. Gallup is on Interstate 40. Charter service is available at the Gallup Airport.

——— OUTDOOR ACTIVITIES ———

Fishing

The sprawling Navajo Indian Reservation ends just 9 miles north of Gallup, and the southern part of the reservation holds some of its most scenic areas. In addition, there is good **fishing** for trout and other species on several waters of the reservation. Follow **U.S. 666** north past Yah-tah-hey and past the turn off to Route 9. You'll find three fishing **lakes—Chuska, Asaayi** and **Whiskey**—that offer good rainbow-trout fishing. The waters of the Navajo reservation are kept well stocked with trout from federal fish hatcheries.

The Navajo Nation charges $12 for a seasonlong permit; a one-day permit goes for $5, and a two-day permit costs $8. The Navajos also put out a regular fishing report, which gives an accurate picture of the current fishing chances. They tell it like it is. If fishing is slow at a particular lake, or if the lake level is too low, they'll tell you so. For further information, contact the **Navajo Fish and Wildlife Department in Window Rock, Arizona**, at **(602) 871-6451**. Remember, if you are not a Navajo, you'll also need a New Mexico fishing license.

Indian Markets

At the downtown walkway, between Second and Third streets, the markets display authentic Navajo and Zuni arts and crafts. You buy from the artists themselves. Native food and native entertainment make the market a big success with visitors. Sat. from 10 A.M.–4 P.M. For more information, call Elmo Baca at City Hall, **863-1234.**

Historic Building Tour

A self-guided walking or driving tour of historic Gallup. Pick up your free guide, which contains a map, at the Chamber of Commerce, on the north side of old Route 66 downtown. Watch for the big sign. If you can't find it, call **863-3841**.

Red Rock Balloon Rally

Held the first weekend of Dec. every year, and this attraction is growing yearly. For more information, call the Chamber of Commerce, **722-2228**, or write to the chamber at **PO Box 1395, Gallup, NM 87305**.

Golf

This is a challenging **18-hole municipal course**, 6,644 yards, with a rating of 70.0. There's a complete pro shop, and rental carts and equipment are available. Tee times are recommended in the summer months.

——— WHERE TO STAY ———

ACCOMMODATIONS

Along with every other major town on Interstate 40, Gallup has a plethora of motel accommodations. No need to worry; you'll find a room. In Gallup, all you have to do is get your kicks on Route 66, and you'll find a good motel. Get your rest on Historic Route 66. If you want my recommendations, so that you can play it safe and call ahead, here they are.

Holiday Inn—$$$

Offers 212 rooms. Swimming pool. **2915 W. Hwy. 66, 722-2201.**

The Inn Best Western—$$
Has 124 rooms. Swimming pool. **3009 W. Hwy. 66, 722-2221** or **1-800-528-1234**.

El Rancho—$$
A historic inn. Because so many movies have been made in the Gallup area, many famous movie stars have signed the register here, including Spencer Tracy, Katherine Hepburn and Kirk Douglas. A B-movie actor named Ronald Reagan also signed in here. Arts and crafts on display here are among the very best. **1000 E. 66 Ave., 863-9311**.

Rodeway Inn—$$
Offers 94 rooms. Swimming pool. **2003 W. Hwy. 66, 863-9385** or **1-800-228-2000**.

Travelers Inn—$$
Offers 108 rooms. Swimming pool. **3304 W. Hwy. 66, 722-7765**.

Motel 6—$$
Offers 80 rooms. Swimming pool. **3306 W. Hwy. 66, 863-4492**.

Shalimar Inn—$
Offers 118 rooms. **2618 W. Hwy. 66, 722-4493**.

Days Inn—$$
Offers 77 rooms. Swimming pool. **1000 W. Hwy. 66, 863-3891**.

Thunderbird Motel—$
Offers 61 rooms. Swimming pool. **1811 W. Hwy. 66, 863-3888**.

Zia Motel—$
Offers 24 rooms. **915 E. Hwy. 66, 863-4952**.

Golden Desert Motel—$$
Offers 40 rooms. **1400 W. Hwy. 66, 722-6606**.

Cactus Motel—$
Offers 33 rooms. **809 W. Coal Ave., 863-6112**.

Desert Skies Motel—$$
Offers 34 rooms. **1703 W. Hwy. 66, 863-4485**.

Redwood Lodge—$$
Offers 15 rooms. **907 E. Hwy. 66, 863-5411**.

CAMPGROUNDS

COMMERCIAL

KOA

Located just south of Old Route 66, reached by exit 16 off of Interstate 40, KOA is more than just a campground. It's a happening, including Indian dances on summer evenings, a barbecue restaurant, pancake breakfasts, Kamping Kabins, a swimming pool, a playground, a grocery store, a gift shop, a game room, cable TV and laundry facilities. Ninety-one sites with full hookups, plus another 30 tent sites. All hookups for two people cost $19.95 (minus sewer saves you $2), and there is a dump station. Call **863-5021**.

Chaparal RV Park

Exit 20 off Interstate 40. Offers 24 spaces with full hookups, rest rooms and shower facilities. **863-6717**.

PUBLIC

Red Rock State Park

Take exit 26 or 31 off Interstate 40 onto N.M. 566. Has 130 spaces, some with all hookups. There is also a large tenting area, a dump station, a laundry, a general store and a post office. Priced at $7, as with all New Mexico state parks. Be warned that this is the site of the Intertribal Indian Ceremonial doings in Aug., and spaces are at a premium at that time. Also, all summer long, Memorial Day through Labor Day, there are Indian dances nightly here at this park. These indoor performances, in the Marland Aitson Amphitheater, are $3 per person; children under 5 years are free. This is a high-class state park, in demand often as a convention center.

———————— WHERE TO EAT ————————

El Sombrero—$

Take exit 20 from Interstate 40, then go west on 66th. Known for authentic Mexican foods. Beer and wine available. **863-4554**.

Kristy's Coffee Shop—$

1310 E. Hwy. 66. Open 24 hours, seven days per week. **863-4742**.

Golden Dragon—$$

1808 E. Hwy. 66. Features Chinese and American food. Closed Sundays. 722-5652.

Pal Joey's—$$

1648 S. Second St. Restaurant and lounge in the Cedar Hills Plaza. Mexican and American food. 722-6383.

Earl's Restaurant—$$

1312 E. Hwy. 66. Big menu to choose from. 863-2401.

Roadrunner Cafe—$$

3014 E. Route 66. Serves good homemade Mexican and American food. Open 6 A.M.–9 P.M. Mon.–Sat.; until noon on Sun. 722-7309.

Almost all of the fast-food franchises you've ever heard of are operating in Gallup also. No one will go hungry, especially not during the ceremonial. Have you ever had a blue-corn tortilla? A Navajo taco? Try one—they're good.

——————— SERVICES ———————

There are fine indoor and outdoor swimming pools, parks, a golf course and all the amenities in Gallup.

Taxi service is provided by **City Taxi Cab, 863-6864. Rental cars** are available from **Avis, 863-9309; National Car Rental, 863-6578;** and **Fuhs Auto Sales, 863-6823.**

Radio entertainment comes from five local stations. And if you enjoy listening to disc jockeys who speak the Navajo language, try the Navajo station KTNN from Window Rock, Arizona. It comes in loud and clear.

═══ Bluewater Lake ═══
State Park

This lovely 5,000-acre state park is almost half water, impounding mountain runoff behind a small dam and producing a deep lake that furnishes good fishing for rainbow trout and catfish year-round. You get there by turning off of Interstate 40 onto N.M. 412, a loop road that connects Bluewater to both Prewitt and Thoreau.

The park is higher than 7,400 feet, so it freezes hard in the wintertime, making it one of the state's few good ice fishing spots. But in the warmer months, rainbows are taken from shore by fishing with salmon eggs, marshmallows and other modern baits. Purists also do well with wet flies, fished down deep and very slowly.

Bluewater is also popular with water skiers and boating enthusiasts. A concessionaire-operated marina, cafe and store provide the necessities for a camping vacation in the piñon and juniper trees that ring the lake. There is a campground, without hookups, priced at New Mexico state parks' usual $7 for developed sites. A dump station and showers are available.

The nearest commercial campground to Bluewater State Park is the fine **Grants West Campground** at Prewitt, right on Interstate 40 at exit 63 (this is where you turn off for Bluewater Lake, on N.M. 412). It offers 20 sites with full hookups at $15.50 for two people (summer rate). Also 55 sites with electricity and water. Open all year. **876-2662**.

Hedgehog cactus growing in the lava flow at El Mapais National Monument. (Photo by Mark Nohl, New Mexico Economic and Tourism Department.)

═══════════ Grants ═══════════

Seventy miles west of Albuquerque on Interstate 40, Grants is the city that bet its fortunes on uranium, had a tremendous boom, then saw uranium mining come to a virtual stop. The town suffered through some hard times, but it is now recovering, and there's lots going on in Grants. It's a recommended stop on the itinerary of every traveler in New Mexico.

─────────── HISTORY ───────────

The first known European settlement was the homestead of Don Jesus Blea (1872) on the south side of San Jose Creek. But we know that a certain Don Diego Antonio Chavez lived there at the time of the Civil War. Chavez controlled access to the only spring in the area and charged 10 cents to water a horse at "his" spring.

The railroad was building west, and the Grant brothers, Angus, Lewis and John, had the contract to build track this far. The area was known as Grants Camp, then Grants Station, and finally just Grants. After the railroad boom, Grants threw its energies into the logging boom, and millions of board feet of lumber off the Zuni Mountains went to Albuquerque for milling.

Then Paddy Martinez, who called himself 75 cents Navajo and 25 cents Mexican, discovered uranium. The uranium boom was on, and Grants grew. In 1980 Grants had 11,800 people, an all-time high. But things like the Three Mile Island debacle and fears of atomic meltdown changed things. The uranium boom was over. In 1983 Grants looked like a ghost town, with many stores and homes standing empty. To this day, Grants has never reapproached the 11,000 population figure.

Grants knows how to build on misfortune. The Chamber of Commerce— one of the most active in the state—is located in the **New Mexico Museum of Mining,** and that lovely new building stands over a former mine! You can descend into a real working mine and see for yourself how it was done, where workers risked their lives to bring out the yellowcake that became uranium that became atomic bombs and atomic power plants.

This was no hole-in-the-wall mine; modern drilling machinery removed tons of ore to the surface. The museum displays the giant machinery, and your guide is probably one of the former miners who participated in the great uranium boom. The mining museum is open

Mon.–Fri. 10 A.M.–12 P.M. and 1 P.M.–4 P.M., Sat. 10 A.M.–4 P.M., and Sun. 1 P.M.–4 P.M. Admission is $2.

The nearby **Laguna Pueblo and Mission** is one of the most prosperous of all the Indian pueblos in New Mexico for two big reasons. One was that uranium was mined on the Laguna Pueblo lands, so the tribe had good employment and received royalty payments for every ton of ore removed. Today the uranium mining is over, and the mining company—which was required by law to return the terrain to as close to its former condition as possible—has contracted with the Laguna Indians to do the reclamation and revegetating job. Naturally, the Lagunas are doing a good job, for this is their home. Take the short drive through **Old Laguna**, visit the white church there, then drive north on N.M. 279 through the reservation and on to the tiny towns of **Paguate** and **Cebolleta**—a good road, pretty country and a chance to see the revegetation work in action. If you're looking for a peaceful place to retire, you might want to look in Cebolleta.

The second reason for the Laguna Pueblo prosperity is that the Indians have a modern electronics manufacturing plant on the pueblo lands that hires many Lagunas and provides a steady payroll.

—— FESTIVALS AND EVENTS ——

Three Kings Day
In Jan. at nearby Laguna Pueblo. Honors the incoming president and officers.

Governors Feast Day
In Feb. at nearby Acoma Pueblo.

Winter Quadrathlon and the Mount Taylor Junior Quadrathlon
In Feb. on the slopes of Mount Taylor. This event is growing every year, producing legitimate claimants to the Iron Man and Iron Woman titles.

San Jose Day
In Mar. at the nearby Laguna Pueblo.

4-H Auction and Barbecue
In May.

Festival of Santa Maria de Acoma at McCartys
First Sunday in May.

San Juan Day
In June at Acoma Sky City.

Festival of San Juan
In June at Laguna Pueblo.

St. Peter and Paul Day
Celebrated June 29 at Acoma Sky City and also at Laguna Pueblo.

Wild West Days and Fireworks; Parade and Grants Rodeo and Jamboree; and Arts and Crafts Show
All happening in Grants over the Fourth of July weekend.

Arts and Crafts Fair
Mid-July at the Acoma visitors center.

Festival of St. Anne
July 26 at Laguna Pueblo.

Laguna Pueblo Cross Country Relay Race
Late July at Laguna Pueblo.

San Lorenzo Festival
In Aug., when all persons named Lorenzo or Lawrence throw gifts to visitors from pueblo rooftops—happens at Acomita, Old Laguna, Encinal, Mesita, Paguate, Paraje and Seama. Colorful festival!

Laguna Pueblo Triathlon
Mid-Aug. at Laguna Pueblo, of course.

Harvest Festival on the Feast Day of San Esteban del Rey
In Sept. at Acoma Sky City on the Acoma Pueblo.

Festival of the Blessed Virgin Mary
Sept. 8 at the Laguna village of Encinal.

Festival of San Jose de Las Lagunas
In Sept., with an arts and crafts fair at Old Laguna.

Festival of St. Elizabeth
Late Sept. in the village of Paguate.

Oktoberfest
First weekend in Oct. in Grants, believe it or not!
Call the Chamber of Commerce at **287-4802** for information.

─────── **SEEING AND DOING** ───────

The list of things to go see out of Grants is a long one. In addition to visiting Bluewater Lake State Park and the Laguna Pueblo, you should plan on seeing **El Malpais Lava Flow National Monument** (the office is in downtown Grants), **El Morro National Monument, Bandera Volcano**, the **Ice Cave** and the **Zuni Acoma Pueblos**. See individual sections on these attractions.

You can't do it all in one day, nor should you do it in just two days. I recommend the following routes: First, take a ride south of Interstate 40 on N.M. 117 for the best look at the Malpais laval flows. After that, take the very long circle tour, leaving Grants on N.M. 53 past another part of the Malpais, to Bandera Volcano and the Ice Cave. Then go on to El Morro (Inscription Rock), through the beautiful Ramah Valley, which is Navajo, and onto the Zuni Pueblo lands. Take some time in the Zuni Pueblo: Visit the old pueblo area, with its cross-filled churchyard, then compare that with the modern hospital and the thriving gift shops in the newer parts of town.

After visiting Zuni, drive north on 602 to Gallup, and you're back on Interstate 40.

This lovely natural bridge is located on Bureau of Land Management lands on Highway 117 south of Grants.

———— WHERE TO STAY ————

ACCOMMODATIONS

Econo Lodge—$$-$$$
Offers 212 rooms. Swimming pool. Lower prices on upper floors. At Interstate 40 interchange, 287-4426.

Desert Sun Motel—$
Has 29 rooms. 1121 E. Santa Fe, 287-7925.

Motel 6—$
Has 103 rooms. Swimming pool. At E. Interstate interchange. 285-4607.

The Inn—$$
Has 126 rooms and an indoor pool. At E. Interstate 40 interchange, 287-7901.

Sands Motel—$$
Has 4 rooms. 112 McArthur, 287-2996.

Leisure Lodge—$$
Offers 32 rooms and an outdoor swimming pool. 287-2991.

Western Host Motel—$
Offers 50 rooms. Has outdoor pool. 1150 E. Santa Fe Ave., 287-4418.

CAMPGROUNDS

Grants West KOA
Eighteen miles west of Grants, at exit 63, on old Route 66. More than 50 pull-through sites with all hookups. Grocery, laundry, pancake breakfasts June through Aug., horseshoe pitching, playground and gas and propane available. $15.50 for two; no additional charge for air-conditioning. 876-2662.

Cibola Sands RV Park
On the Interstate 40 interchange going east. Turn south and cross the interstate left on the frontage road. Has 46 sites with full hookups, at a cost of $13 for two people. Four tent sites at $10 per night. Small grocery store.

Well-designed, well-kept trailer park. Friendly people to deal with. They honor Good Sam, AAA, AARP, FMCA and senior discounts. **287-4376.**

Lavaland RV Park

On E. Interstate 40 interchange. Has 34 sites with full hookups. Electricity and water; $13.28 per night for two people. No hookups with shower privileges is $9.56 per night. There is a dump station. Senior discount available. **287-8665.**

—————— WHERE TO EAT ——————

La Ventana—$$

In Hillcrest Shopping Center. Good for steaks and seafood. Has full bar. Reservations are suggested, **287-9393.**

Monte Carlo—$$

721 W. Santa Fe, **287-9250.**

Tres Maria Bakery—$

831 E. Roosevelt. Open Mon.–Fri. 5 A.M.–5:30 PM. Sat. 5 A.M..–5 P.M. Closed Sun. This is the place for fresh-baked goods and the deli fixings to produce some great sandwiches. **287-7602.**

All the fast food restaurants are doing business in Grants.

—————— SERVICES ——————

Hospital telephone is **287-4446. Ambulance** service telephone is **287-7446. Fire department** telephone is **287-4401. Sheriff's office** telephone is **287-9476.**

═══ El Malpais Monument ═══

El Malpais means "badlands." It comes from the Spanish *mal* (bad) and *pais* (country). El Malpais is a 115,000-acre valley filled with black lava spewed out from volcanoes over the past three million years.

To learn all about it, go to the **El Malpais information center** at **620 E. Santa Fe St. in Grants**. The phone number is **285-5406.** The National Park Service and the Bureau of Land Management have teamed up here to avoid duplication of services, because both agencies control land in the monument. They'll answer all of your questions about this eerily beautiful land, and they have descriptive literature about most of it. But here are my suggestions for seeing much of the El Malpais, without long hikes.

If you are only a little interested, read about it and then take N.M. 117 off of Interstate 40. Drive a couple hundred yards on this slightly uphill road, and get out and look back at the laval flows. That's the minimal way and is only for the very lazy or those terminally in a hurry. I recommend continuing south on N.M. 117. This will take you to the Sandstone Bluffs lookout, which is truly spectacular, then on to the La Ventana, a lovely red-sandstone natural bridge that is reached by a Bureau of Land Management trail of about 700 yards. Take it slow and easy, and climb for a good look at La Ventana, which is Spanish for "the window." You are now 17 miles south of Interstate 40.

After you catch your breath from climbing back down from the "the window," keep going south on N.M. 117 to the narrows. Here the highway is squeezed between the black lava flow that looks to be about 12 feet high and the pastel sandstone bluffs. This is a good place for close-up looks at the convoluted black lava. You are now 19 miles south of Interstate 40.

If you are a real student and you have the time, you might want to continue on across County Road 42, which is all gravel and rock and not for motor coaches. It will take you past the West Malpais Wilderness and the Chain of Craters area. Slow going, but a very lovely trip. Last time over it I saw three big mule deer bucks in the velvet and two wild turkey gobblers—one of them sporting a foot-long beard.

Want still more? Talk to the people in charge, and go on foot, across the Zumi-Acoma footway. While you are at it, visit the Big Lava Tubes, formed by laval cooling on the outside while hot lava flows inside. This lava tube is 17 miles long! If your vehicle has enough clearance, you can drive into the area, about 10 miles off of N.M. 53.

There's a cruel, wild beauty about El Malpais, a wonderful example of what happens when the earth blows its top. This section of New Mexico has a violent past—as witness El Malpais and the Bandera Volcano and the Ice Cave.

═ Bandera Volcano and ═
the Ice Cave

Two of the most interesting things about the El Malpais Monument are not yet in the monument boundaries. The National Park Service has conducted an appraisal survey, and the wheels are grinding slowly to buy the Bandera Volcano and the Ice Caves from private ownership.

To find these attractions, take N.M. 53 southwest out of Grants for roughly 25 miles, and you'll find the well-marked entrance. It costs $5 to tour both the volcano crater and the Ice Cave. No, sorry, you can't take one or the other for half price. Let's do the volcano first before the day gets too hot. I'm guessing that the walk over a considerable climb is about three quarters of a mile long. You reach the caldera itself (the open cone from which the volcanic lava once blew out) and get a wonderful look into the mechanics of a volcano. Millions of tons of molten rock spewed out of this crater, probably many times in the past million years. Some of the lava was hurled out, flying miles before smashing to the ground. Most of the lava flowed out, just like water only slower. Try to imagine the tremendous heat of that eruption!

After you walk up to the volcano crater, the 300 yards on an easy path to the Ice Cave will be most welcome. Here's where you feel the cooling effect of nature's icebox. This is a small volcanic sink, formed when laval tubes collapsed as they cooled. Water flowing down into the tubes froze in the wintertime—remember, you are nearly 8,500 feet above sea level—and the perfect insulation of the lava walls kept it frozen. Many hundreds, and perhaps thousands, of tons of ice are still locked in blue-green brilliance down at the bottom of the solid stairway. The ice has remained frozen over hundreds of summers, even millions of summers. Its temperature is 31° F, and you'll find the Ice Cave a pleasant surprise and a comfortable spot to rest and cool off.

Bandera Ice Cave. (Photo by Mark Nohl, New Mexico Economic and Tourism Department.)

El Morro
National Monument

El Morro National Monument, operated by the National Park Service, ranks high on my list of the 10 things you *must* see when you visit New Mexico. This is the famous Inscription Rock upon which travelers carved their names and the dates of their travels. Some of them even told us why they were traveling this hostile land, others wrote poetry, and still others reported that they had to pay for their own travels, even though they were in the service of the king of Spain.

Names of western explorers date as far back as 1605, but prehistoric Indians carved their own inscriptions on the sandstones. They lived atop the huge sandstone mesa upon whose cliffs the writing is found. The most famous of the inscriptions is in *español*, and it starts out, *"Pasamos por aqui . . "* ("There passed this way.") De Onate left this message on his second visit to El Morro, in 1605. He first came here in 1598—almost 200 years before the signing of America's Declaration of Independence. This visit was about 15 years before the first pilgrim landed at Plymouth Rock.

A permanent pool of water at the foot of the sheer sandstone cliff was the lure for travelers—and even residents. Small handholds carved into the rock prove that Pueblo Indians climbed down from their mesa-top homes to the pool of clear, cold water (one can visit the ruins of Atsinna by taking a path that climbs the far side of the huge sandstone cliff). This is not a spring but is replenished by rainwater cascading down natural funnels in the rock. When full, it holds 200,000 gallons of water.

Pasamos por aqui. We passed this way, and we stopped to record our passing: Spanish explorers and missionaries, some of whom were martyred by the nearby Zuni Indians who preferred their own gods to those brought by the Franciscan friars; the earliest U.S. Army reconnaissance riders; Mormon colonists on their way west; and many people whose names are known but whose stories are yet unknown.

You should first check out the visitors center, looking at everything in the museum. Then pick up a trail guide—it's free to borrow—and set out on a walk into the past. The blacktopped path is easy walking, and you can go all the way around to the last of the inscriptions in 45 minutes or so.

Take time to read about each inscription, and try to envision the circumstances. For instance, one Spanish officer ordered his aide-de-camp to carve into the rock, "On July 14, 1736, passed by here the General Juan Paez Hurtado, Inspector." The man did what he was ordered to do, and then after the boss left, he carved an addition: "and in his company,

Corporal Joseph Trujillo." In so doing, he recorded his name for history and gave us a look into human nature.

This is a federal-fee area, so it costs you $3 to enter, but it's free for holders of the Golden Eagle Pass.

———— WHERE TO STAY ————

CAMPGROUNDS

El Morro National Monument

A nice but small campground is right at the monument. Only nine spaces, on a first come, first served basis, less than a mile from the visitors center. Water is available at the campground, but there are no hookups. Free at present, but undoubtedly there will be a charge later on when the campground is enlarged and improved. **783-4226**.

El Morro RV and Cafe

On N.M. 53, just half a mile east of El Morro. RV spaces are $15.00 for water, electricity and sewer. Tent spaces are $8. There's a 10 percent discount for senior citizens or Good Sam members. Cabins are $25.00 for one person, $30.00 for three or more. Meals and fast food are available at the cafe on the grounds. **783-4612**.

Tinaja RV Park

Just three and a half miles east of El Morro on N.M. 53. Has 20 sites with all hookups at $9.50 per night. Gas station and bar and lounge in connection. Big surprise for tenters—tenting is free. Says the owner-operator, "Tenters don't use anything but space, and I've got lots of space." **783-4349**.

Zuni Pueblo

The earliest Spanish explorers found their way to the Zuni Pueblo, thinking it was one of the fabled (but nonexistent) seven cities of gold. If you've visited El Morro, you've already learned that two of the earliest missionary priests were killed by the Zunis. Later on you read that the bishop of Durango (in old Mexico, not in Colorado) had visited there on his way to an inspection of the Zuni Pueblo. After the Pueblo Revolt in 1680 and the subsequent reconquest by De Vargas in 1692, the church and the Zunis seem to have gotten along famously for a couple of centuries. This is probably the most isolated of any pueblo in New Mexico, and the sturdy Zunis like it that way. They have long been famed for their ability to fashion lovely jewelry from turquoise and silver. Their crafts are for sale to an ever-increasing flow of tourists to this remote corner of the Land of Enchantment.

The Zunis have a proud tradition of being able to handle their own affairs. A Zuni named Robert Lewis—a memorable man—led a long struggle for increased responsibility for their own affairs. This campaign ended with Lewis's becoming the paid superintendent of the Zuni Reservation as well as the president of the pueblo. This was a first for all the Indians in America. I had the privilege of knowing Zuni Robert Lewis and remember him as a man of great intelligence, great memory and infinite patience.

Today Zuni (and Black Rock) sprawl along N.M. 53 for several miles. It is hard to find the oldest part of the town, where the distinctive church faces a courtyard crowded with the crosses of Zunis who died in the church, a courtyard that is usually colorful with floral tributes.

It is easy to find the silversmiths and jewelry makers and the busy shops that sell their products. Be sure to go to the arts and crafts information center and ask to watch the silversmiths at work. I was told that the turquoise now comes from the vicinity of Kingman and Globe, both in Arizona. The famed turquoise mines of Cerillos, New Mexico, were exhausted long ago. It is thought that the Zuni have been making their distinctive crafts since the original settlement in this spot. Zuni has been continuously occupied since about A.D. 740.

Jewelry and pottery from many other Indian pueblos and weaving products from the huge Navajo Reservation are also on sale through the shops in Zuni, and they are authentic and more reasonably priced than in many other outlets in New Mexico.

Logging was big business on the Zuni forests for several decades. The U.S. Forest Service offers a self-guided motor tour of the Zuni Railroad historic sites. Get your tour from the forest service in Grants, at **1800 Lobo Canyon Rd., 287-8833.**

⸺ Acoma, the Sky City ⸺

One of the oldest continuously occupied locations in North America, the Acoma Pueblo, situated on top of a high mesa, has been home to Indians since the 1200s, maybe even earlier.

To get to the Sky City, you turn south off of Interstate 40 6 miles west of Laguna. Or leave the interstate at the exit 12 miles east of Grants, where there is a well-marked turnoff and a blacktopped road all the way to the museum and visitors center of Acoma.

Once at the visitors center, register for the guided tour to the fascinating primitive world atop the impregnable mesa. It costs $5, a great bargain. You'll pay another $5 per camera if you want to take pictures— well worth it, in my opinion. Your guided tour will be called over the loudspeaker, so take time to look at everything in the museum. It is a good one.

You'll ride to the top of the mesa in a small modern bus. If you're lucky, your guide will be a young Acoma woman named Brenda. She adds a lot to the information you'll receive with her intimate knowledge of the place and her good sense of humor. The walking tour takes 45 minutes to an hour. Your guide will tell you about the construction of the beautiful Spanish-style church devoted to San Esteban del Rey, the patron saint of the Acomas since the 1600s, when the first missionaries arrived. Note the huge vigas, the logs forming the roof of the church. The vigas, 40 feet in length and more than 14 inches in diameter, were carried 40 miles from the slopes of Mount Taylor, on the shoulders of the Acoma.

Natural cisterns in the soft sandstone trap the infrequent rains, providing drinking water for the people who once lived here. Today there are about 4,000 Acomas in all, but only 13 or 14 families still live on top of the mesa year-round. Life on top is fairly primitive, with no running water and only outdoor privies. Digging a pit toilet in the sandstone is obviously impossible, so the toilets are set 20 to 40 feet down, over the edge of the mesa.

Most of the people now live in the communities of Acomita and McCarty on the lower level of the reservation. You will learn that ownership of the homes atop the mesa is passed down along youngest daughters of the owners! But there are strings attached. The youngest daughter must take care of her parents until they die before she has untrammeled use of the property. This form of Acoma old-age security has functioned well for perhaps a thousand years. Ours is much younger.

The walls of the Sky City kept invaders out for centuries. It was overrun by the Navajo, the Apache, the Comanche and the Spanish conquistadores, but the Acoma persisted after these various waves of conquest. But the Sky City finally fell in 1947—to Hollywood! Because the Acomas agreed to let the film capital make a movie set on top of Acoma, they allowed a road to be built up to the top to transport camera equipment. It's a mighty short road, but it changed things forever for the Acomas.

The road didn't change the essential nature of the Acoma people, however, and they are still friendly, happy people who smile readily. Their pottery patterns are recognized as some of the very best in all of New Mexico. Some small displays of pottery are offered for sale on top of the mesa, and you'll visit them during your tour. Far more and better pottery is on sale down at the visitors center.

There are several festivals celebrated on Acoma's high mesa during the year. See the Festivals and Events section in Grants. If you are lucky enough to be able to participate in one of the cermonies, check the rules about photography, and remember that the Indians' beliefs are sacred to them. Respect their beliefs, for the Indians have been here much longer than we have.

San Esteban del Rey Church, more than 250 years old, overlooks the sheer cliffs of Acoma Sky City.

THE LOWER
RIO GRANDE

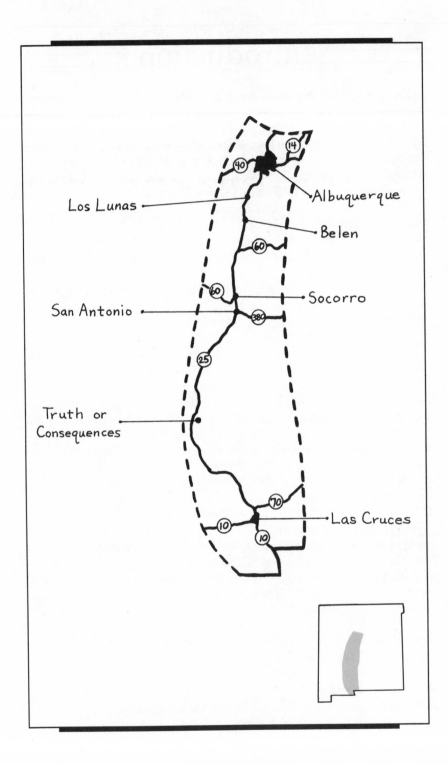

Introduction

The first Spanish explorers noted that when the Rio Grande dropped down through the gorge, it became a much more placid stream. Leaving the Rocky Mountains behind, the Rio entered a broad plain. The word *bajo* in Spanish is important here. The explorers called the upper river Rio Arriba and the lower river Rio Abajo. There's a big hill dropping down off the mesa top between Santa Fe and Albuquerque called La Bajada, the "coming down" or the "descent" in Spanish.

Where the river slowed, it became more useful for agriculture. It watered wide, flat areas that were home to the pre-Columbian pueblos, places like Isleta on the south edge of Albuquerque and the pueblos of Zia and San Felipe to the north of Albuquerque. Following the river was the easiest form of travel.

It still is. Interstate 25 closely parallels the Rio Grande from just south of Santa Fe, through Albuquerque and Socorro, on down to Las Cruces and into foreign land—El Paso, Texas. "El Paso" refers to "the passage," but it is the passage to the north . . . to Santa Fe!

The earliest conquistadores followed the Rio Grande from El Paso to Santa Fe, then they left the river and went to Taos and on into Colorado. The brown cloth of Franciscan missionaries was stained with sweat as the barefoot friars toiled north for the greater glory of God and the hoped-for wealth of the Spanish king. Armor was worn by the conquistadores on horseback, but it proved too much of a load for the foot soldiers. Despite the hardships, New Mexico was conquered for Cross and Crown by means of the path along the Rio Grande.

The Rio never flowed in a straight north-south line. Hoping to shorten the trip by at least a day, early travelers turned north, away from the river, at Rincon and made a straight line all the way up to San Marcial. It was a 91-mile stretch without any water at all! The San Andreas Mountains to the right were sufficient guideposts to keep from getting lost.

Indians attacked from Arroyos and out of the mountain ravines. Many laid their whitened bones alongside those of the cattle and horses that perished in the soft sands of the Jornada del Muerto ("Day's March of the Dead Man"), as this shortcut came to be called.

When the Atchison, Topeka and Santa Fe Railroad routed its lines southward, it also chose the Jornada del Muerto, but it was able to carry enough water for its steam engines and had no problems with thirst.

Today this central strip of the Land of Enchantment is far from a journey of death. This corridor boasts three great state universities: the University of New Mexico, in Albuquerque; the New Mexico Institute of Mining Technology, at Socorro; and the State University of New Mexico, at Las Cruces.

135

It has the biggest concentration of wintering waterfowl in the state, much of it on the Bosque del Apache National Wildlife Refuge, 12 miles south of Socorro. This strip of land holds some of the most successful irrigated agriculture in the state, using waters impounded behind Elephant Butte Dam. The town of Hatch is the center for the growing of New Mexico's famous chilis.

The Lower Rio Grande outdoes the rest of the state in the hunting of migratory waterfowl and also offers excellent hunting for mourning doves and two species of desert quail, the blue and the scaled. Elephant Butte Reservoir, year in and year out, is the most consistent producer of sport fishing—at times it has been acclaimed as one of America's 10 best bass lakes. This oldest of Bureau of Reclamation reservoirs, however, suffers from extreme fluctuations, and the fishing waxes and wanes with the water levels.

But enough of this introductory stuff. Let's get busy and retrace the steps of the conquistadores, backward. We'll travel the Rio Grande corridor from north to south.

First step is New Mexico's biggest city—Albuquerque!

Snow geese at the Bosque del Apache National Wildlife Refuge south of Socorro.

Albuquerque

More than one third of all New Mexicans live in the greater Albuquerque metropolitan area, one of the fastest-growing cities in the nation. With the privilege of choosing anywhere in the world to live, I chose Albuquerque and so did half a million others.

Sitting just west of the 10,628-foot-high Sandia Mountains (*sandia* means "watermelon" in Spanish; the late-afternoon sun on the mountains reminded the *españoles* of the flesh of the ripe watermelon), straddling the Rio Grande, Albuquerque has one of the best climates to be found anywhere. In the winter, we have snow on the mountains to look at but rarely any down here to walk around in. In the summer, daytime temperatures have been known to hit 105° F (rarely), but the humidity is way, way down, and we are not uncomfortable in the mid-90s. Because of the thin, dry air in this mile-high city, when the sun goes down, the thermometer goes with it. We always sleep under blankets.

The world's longest aerial tramway is in Albuquerque. It lifts you from the east edge of town to the top of Sandia Crest, 10,623 feet above sea level.

HISTORY

Albuquerque is a relative newcomer, compared to historic cities like Santa Fe or Taos. We weren't established until 1706, when Don Francisco de la Cueva Enriquez, Duke of Alburquerque, Viceroy of New Spain, authorized the settlement of a villa on the Rio Grande. Don Francisco Cueva y Valdez and a handful of colonists settled along the bend in the road. Today we call that area Old Town, and it centers on historic San Felipe de Neri Church.

Nothing much happened for almost 200 years, and then the railroad came to town in 1880, picking a location on higher ground, where the present business district of Albuquerque now stands. Notice that the first *r* in the name of our city was dropped.

The city was a hub of trade, with the Old Chihuahua Trail, an extension of the Santa Fe Trail connecting with the Spanish trails in old Mexico. Today it is still a crossroads of trade. Interstates 25 and 40 cross in Albuquerque. It is a major railroad hub, and the International Sunport is a major airport.

GETTING THERE

Just get your kicks on Route 66, sang the old song, and historic Route 66 ran right down Central Ave. Now Interstate 40 has replaced Route 66 as the main artery to the west coast.

Interstate 25 crosses Interstate 40 in Albuquerque. The crossing is often called the worst interchange in the world, but it really isn't that bad. Not quite. There is this one section where three lanes narrow to one lane, with a sharp curve—not exactly a speed-demon route.

All major bus lines service Albuquerque. It is also a stop on Amtrak, and many people ride from Chicago and other points to the distant east.

Albuquerque has a major international airport served by many airlines, including TWA, United, American, Southwestern and America West.

FESTIVALS AND EVENTS

Balloon Festival
Probably the biggest event of the year in Albuquerque, usually in the

first 10 days of Oct., starting at 6:30 A.M. Balloonists come from all states and a few foreign countries to take part in the festival, which features mass ascensions of as many as 650 balloons, the balloon night glow, hare and hounds competitions, and grab-the-brass-ring contests, in which the lucky person grabbing the brass ring wins a new car. It all happens at Balloon Fiesta Park, which is reached by taking Interstate 25 north to Alameda. Then just follow the crowds. There is special overnight parking for RVs, but put your name in early. Truly, there is no more room at the inn when it's Balloon Fiesta time in Albuquerque. To get exact schedules, call **821-1000**.

New Mexico State Fair
Takes place right in the middle of town and is one of the biggest such fairs in our nation. Runs for ten days in the first half of Sept. There's lots of horse racing and pari-mutuel betting, along with all the other attractions of a truly big fair. **265-1791**.

Ice Capades at Tingley Coliseum
In Apr. For prices and times, call Ticketmaster at **884-0999**.

Albuquerque's Founders Day
In Apr. A big wingding, mostly in Old Town. For dates, times and prices, call **243-3696**.

Gathering of Nations Powwow
Takes place in Apr. at University Arena—better known as the Pit—at Stadium and University. Indian dancing, arts and crafts, Miss Indian America beauty pageant. For prices and times, call **836-2810**.

Cinco de Mayo
Celebration in May. It is big with everyone who loves fun and good entertainment by big-name acts from south of the border. At Civic Plaza at Third and Marquette N.W. Free. For further details, call **768-3490**.

Great Rio Grande Raft Race
In May. A 14-mile race down the Rio Grande. For location and entry-fee information, call **768-3490**.

Summerfest
Starts in June and runs through Aug. Every Sat. night features a different ethnic group, with dances, singing, music and wonderful authentic ethnic foods. At Civic Plaza at Third and Marquette N.W. Free. For information, call **768-3490**.

San Felipe Fiesta
Takes place the first weekend in June. Three days of fun and fiesta in honor of Albuquerque's patron saint. Old Town is the place; admission is free. 243-4628.

Hispanic Celebration of the Fourth of July
Enjoy three fireworks displays and lots of fun for everyone on the glorious Fourth.

Albuquerque Bestfest
In July, featuring arts and crafts, food and entertainment. At the State Fairgrounds. For information, call 842-9918.

Cowboy Classic Western Art Show
In early July. Takes place at the State Fairgrounds. Admission free; parking $2. 265-1791, ext. 228.

La Luz Trail Run
In Aug., runners are challenged by the 12 percent grade up to the top of 10,678-foot Sandia Crest. Starts at the Juan Tabo Picnic grounds on the east edge of Albuquerque, at the foot of the mountain. For entry-fee information, call 268-6300.

Fiesta de Colores
In late Aug. Hispanic food, music, art and entertainment in Civic Plaza. Free. 768-3490.

State Fair
In Sept. At San Pedro and Central. Pari-mutuel horse betting, Professional Rodeo Cowboy Association rodeo, midway carnival, famous celebrity entertainers daily, livestock shows and Indian and Spanish villages. Wonderful food of all kinds. For information and admission fees, call 265-1791.

Duke City Marathon
In late Sept. Featuring full and half marathons, along with 10K races. For information, call 291-8250.

Oktoberfest
In late Sept. At our big northern suburb of Rio Rancho. Lots of beer, lots of food, lots of music and fun. For information about prices and times, call 892-1700.

Tour of Albuquerque Marathon
A full marathon in mid-Oct. For information, call **268-6300**.

Southwest Arts and Crafts Show
In Nov. Featuring the works of more than 200 artists from across the Southwest. This is a juried show, and the quality is high. Takes place at Exhibit Hall on the State Fairgrounds. **262-2448**.

Luminaria Display
During the Christmas season. Luminaries date from the days when *españoles* and Indians lighted signal fires to guide the coming of the Christ Child. We now have pathways, buildings, walls and sidewalks lined in luminarias, which are brown paper bags partially filled with sand to stabilize them, with a vigil light burning inside. The resulting lighting display is world-famous and very beautiful. Special bus tours are conducted through the most spectacularly lit neighborhoods. For information, call **1-800-284-2282** or **243-3696**.

——— OUTDOOR ACTIVITIES ———

Baseball
Baseball is king in the summertime with the Albuquerque Dukes, perennial front-runners in the Pacific Coast League. This is a farm team for the Los Angeles Dodgers—sometimes players wear the Albuquerque Dukes uniform one week and play in the big leagues the next! The ballpark is at Stadium and University, and the season runs from Apr. to Sept. Admission varies from $1 to $4. Call **243-1791** for schedule and game times.

Golf
There are four excellent municipal courses. **Arroyo del Oso** has been named one of the 50 best municipal courses in America. It's located at Osuna and Pennsylvania, **888-8115**. **Los Altos** is at **9717 Copper N.E.**, near the east end of town, **298-1897**. **Puerto del Sol**, a par 3 course, is at **1800 Girard S.E., 265-5636**. **Ladera** is west of the Rio Grande, at **3401 Ladera Dr. N.W., 836-4449**.

The University of New Mexico has two excellent courses: the **North Course** on Standard Dr. N.E., **277-4146**, and the **University South Course**, the longest and most challenging in the city, at University Blvd., S.E., **277-4546**.

Tee times are almost always necessary at all six of these courses, as Albuquerque is a good golf town.

Horseback Riding

Los Amigos Round Up offers riding on 300 acres of shady trails near the Rio Grande. Located at the intersection of Fourth and Second N.W., which is really in Alameda, a northern suburb. **898-8500**.

Swimming

The city operates 13 municipal swimming pools, open in summer only. For information, call **768-3520**. Los Altos, Sandia and Highland pools are also open in the wintertime.

Tennis Anyone?

There are 29 city-operated and city-maintained tennis courts, situated in all corners of the city, with never an admission fee. For further information, call **768-3520**.

Shooting Range State Park

Provides trapshooting ranges, as well as all rifle and pistol ranges. Open for practice five days a week; closed Mon. and Tues. This is an excellent facility, much used by hunters, especially for sighting in before big-game seasons. Drive west on Interstate 40, and watch for the signs leading off to the north. **768-7824**.

—— SEEING AND DOING ——

Indian Pueblo Cultural Center, at **2401 Twelfth St., N.W.**, just a block off of Interstate 40. A fine museum showcasing the history of the 19 Indian pueblos. Permanent museum exhibits on one floor. Changing exhibits on the upper floor feature murals and other art of contemporary Indian artists. Shops on the main floor. Open every day except Christmas, New Year's Day and Thanksgiving, 9 A.M.–5:30 P.M. Receives more than 300,000 visitors each and every year. Admission is $2.50 for adults, $1.50 for senior citizens and $1 for students. For more information, call **843-7270**.

Albuquerque Museum, just across the road from the Museum of Natural History, **2000 Mountain Rd. N.W.** Features exhibits of the area's history and changing exhibits of artwork from the past and the present. Open 9 A.M.–5 P.M.; closed Mon.; Admission is free, and they'll validate your parking. **242-4600**.

Maxwell Museum of Anthropology is on the University of New Mexico campus, one block north of Grand on University Ave. One of the best collections of Navajo rugs and Indian pottery, with other exhibits telling the history of man in the 10,000 years that we know he was in this area. First class in every way. Admission is free. Open Mon.–Fri. 9 A.M.–4 P.M., Sat. 10 A.M.–4 P.M., Sun. noon–4 P.M. **277-4404.**

National Atomic Museum on **Kirtland Air Force Base**, reached by driving east on Gibson or south on Wyoming. You need to get a visitor's pass at the gate. Besides showing you a full-size B-52 and F-105D fighter bomber up close, this museum traces the history of the atomic bomb. Free admission. Open 9 A.M.–5 P.M. except major holidays. **845-4636.**

New Mexico Museum of Natural History; on **1801 Mountain Rd. N.W.** near Old Town. I like to brag about this museum, for it does such a wonderful job of bringing the prehistoric past to life in the minds of young and old alike. Walk into the middle of the volcano? Sure. Why not? You can ride an Evolator, which will take you back 70 million years to the land of dinosaurs. Be sure to visit the Dynamax Theater. Admission is $4 for adults, $3 for seniors and students and $1 for children ages 3 to 11. Open 9 A.M.–5 P.M. every day of the year. **841-8837.**

Spanish History Museum, at **2221 Lead S.E.** Features a history of Spanish exploration, colonization and loss of the Southwest. Also memorabilia of New Mexico when it was a territory, before statehood in 1912. Donation of $1 requested. Open 1 P.M.–5 P.M. except major holidays. **268-9981.**

University Art Museum, in the Fine Arts Center on the university campus, on Cornell St. Holds the largest collection of fine art in New Mexico, both permanent and changing exhibits. Open Wed.–Fri. 9 A.M.–4 P.M., Tues. until 9 P.M., and Sun. 1 P.M.–4 P.M. Closed Mon and Sat. Free admission. **277-4001.**

Aerial Tram ride to Sandia Peak. At **10 Tramway Loop**, on the east edge of Albuquerque. The world's longest single-span tramway. It's 2.7 miles long and lifts you from the mile-high city to the two-mile-high Sandia Crest. Breathtaking views and the nicest way to reach a fine restaurant on top of the mountain. Costs $10.50 for adults, $8.50 for seniors and children ages 5 to 12, children under five go free. Open during the summer 9 A.M.–10 P.M. During other seasons, call for hours at **298-8518.**

Drive to Sandia Crest. Go east on Interstate 40 to N.M. 14, turn left on N.M. 536, Sandia Crest National Scenic Rd. and follow signs to the crest. Actual elevation is 10,678, and from the top you can see forever, including a beautiful view of the city spread out below you. Paved road can be slippery or snow-packed in winter. Call **243-0605** for information.

Petroglyphs National Monument is reached off of the north end of Unser Blvd. Take Interstate 40 west, and watch for signs. This is a marvelous display of prehistoric Indian writings, chiseled onto the black rocks. The area has just been made a national monument to be administered by the National Park Service. You'll do a lot of walking here as the volcano cliffs are 17 miles long. Open in the summer 9 A.M.–5 P.M. Admission is $1 per car. For more information, call **897-8814, 823-4016** or look up National Park Service in the phone book.

Rio Grande Nature Center is on the east bank of the Rio Grande on Candelaria. Excellent place for birders and others interested in migratory fowl. Open daily 10 A.M.–5 P.M. except major holidays. Admission is $1 for adults and 50 cents for children. **344-7240.**

Isleta Bingo Palace is located at **1100 Broadway S.E.** (exit 215 off Interstate 25). Bingo on an Indian reservation; big-money prizes. For other information, call **869-2614.**

Horse racing at the Downs of Albuquerque, in the state fairgrounds at San Pedro and Central. Racing Jan. through May. For post times and prices, call **262-1188.**

Lobo Basketball. Albuquerque goes absolutely ape over its UNM basketball teams. The 18,000 seat arena, commonly called the Pit, sells out for almost every game, even the exhibitions, which don't count in conference standings. The Pit is at Stadium and University, with lots of parking. The Lobos play in the Western Athletic Conference. Just on the chance that there might be tickets available, the box office phone number is **277-2116.**

New Mexico Symphony plays pops concerts along with classical music. Schedule varies through the year. **842-8565** or **1-800-251-NMSO.**

Albuquerque Civic Light Opera Association presents Broadway musicals at Popejoy Hall on the university campus during Mar., June, July, Sept. and Dec. Performances at 2:15 P.M. and 8:15 P.M. **345-6577.**

Opera Southwest is presented at the KIMO Theater in downtown Albuquerque. Presenting such standards as *Tosca*, *The Marriage of Figaro* and *Carmen*. Single-performance tickets as low as $22. For dates and other information, call **266-8043.**

Fine Spanish-language entertainment is provided by **La Compania de Teatro de Albuquerque.** (See? You're reading Spanish already.) For information, call **242-7929.**

Popejoy Hall Performances on the university campus. Home to many cultural events during the year. The box office phone is **277-3121.**

Rio Grande Zoo at **903 Tenth St. S.W.** has ample parking and displays more than a thousand wild animals in natural-appearing habitats. Sixty acres of fun for young and old. Open 9 A.M.–5 P.M. except major holidays. Admission is $4.25 for adults, $2.25 for children and senior citizens. **843-7413.**

Old Town, located where Albuquerque began in 1706. Historical buildings, arts and crafts and some excellent dining at La Placita and Hacienda restaurants. This is a district of more than one hundred shops and lots to see and do. My wife calls it one of New Mexico's top attractions. Guided tours available. Open 10 A.M.–6 P.M. Call the Chamber of Commerce for more information at **842-9918** or **1-800-284-2282.**

Coronado State Monument, 1 mile west of Bernalillo. Go north on

Interstate 25 to junction with N.M. 44, then west to the Coronado signs. Ruins of a small pueblo where Coronado spent the winter of 1540–1541. Open in summer 9 A.M.–6 P.M., in winter 10 A.M.–6 P.M. Admission is $2 for adults, children under age 15 are free. **867-5351.**

Sandia Shadows Vineyard and Winery, at **11704 Coronado N.E.** offers complimentary wine tasting right in the middle of a vineyard. To get there, take Tramway Blvd. north to San Rafael. Gift shop. Free admission. Open Wed.–Fri. 12 P.M.–5 P.M., Sat. 10 A.M.–5 P.M **298-8826.**

NEARBY ATTRACTIONS

Cochiti Dam and Reservoir

Fifty minutes from Albuquerque, and you can be at a popular swimming, fishing and boating place on the Rio Grande. It's a no-wake lake, so you won't be bothered by speedboats. There's a good camping area and lots of picnic tables. Take Interstate 25 north, and watch for the signs to turn off; the road goes to Pena Blanca, to the dam and reservoir, and to the Cochita Pueblo. Cochita Pueblo has a fine golf course, with a challenging layout, and it's open to the public.

Isleta Pueblo

On the southern edge of the city, this pueblo has one of the oldest churches in America. Go south on Interstate 25 to the Isleta turnoff, or go south on Broadway and keep going on its extension, N.M. 47, to the right turn into Isleta. This is a self-governing Indian reservation, so obey the laws while on the land.

Coronado State Monument

Thirteen miles out of town. It marks the place where Coronado spent the winter and avoided starvation. The remains of the Indian pueblo that served as Coronado's unwilling host are interesting. Go north on Interstate 25 to the junction with N.M. 44. Go through Bernalillo, and watch for the signs a couple of miles past the river bridge.

NIGHTLIFE

The Wool Warehouse

218 First N.W. Provides fine dinner theater. Dinner at 6 P.M, entertainment at 8 P.M. **764-9665.**

Caravans East
   7605 **Central Ave. N.E.** Features top-quality country music entertainers, with continuous music seven days a week 5 P.M.–1:30 A.M. **265-7877.**

Sundance Saloon
   12000 **Candelaria N.E.** (between Juan Tabo and Tramway). Features top country bands nightly. **296-6761.**

Chapter II Lounge
   2294 **Wyoming Blvd. N.E.** Offers continuous live adult entertainment on three stages. Features a five-hour happy hour, 3 P.M.–8 P.M. I'm told this is the oldest one-owner establishment of its kind in New Mexico. **298-1868.**

Our Place
   1517 **Coors Rd. N.W.** Calls itself the Westside's New Hot Spot. Restaurant, night club and lounge. **831-4323.**

Foxes Lounge
   8521 **Central Ave. N.E.** A gay bar, with disco dancing nightly starting at 9 P.M. **255-3060.**

La Posada de Albuquerque
   125 **Second St. N.W.** Live jazz Fri. and Sat. evenings. **242-9090.**

There are dozens of others, some better, some worse. You pay your money and you take your chances, but you won't lack for nightclubs and nightlife in the Duke City.

SCENIC DRIVES

The drive up to Sandia Crest is beautiful, taking you from the 5,000-foot level up to 10,623 feet on top of the mountain ridge, which affords a panoramic view of the city. Several good picnic spots dot the road up through the ponderosa-pine forest. Especially nice are sunsets and the lights coming on in the city below. To reach the crest, leave town to the east on Interstate 40, exit on N.M. 14, then follow signs to the crest. Caution! Road may be snow-packed in the wintertime.
   By the way, if you turn to the south on N.M. 337, instead of heading to the crest, you'll be on a slow, windy road to tiny villages of Hispanic origin—Chilili, Tajique, and slightly larger Mountainair. This is a different world from bustling Albuquerque.

———— WHERE TO STAY ————

ACCOMMODATIONS

How do you choose from nearly 1,000 hotels and motels? Let me suggest a few places in each price range. That doesn't mean the lodging is poor if I don't list it—there's enough room to mention only a few.

Sheraton Old Town—$$$
Close to Old Town, the Pueblo Cultural Center, the Albuquerque Museum and all of the specialty shops of this oldest part of the city. Offers 170 rooms and 20 suites. **800 Rio Grande Blvd. N.W., 843-6300 or 1-800-237-2133.**

Holiday Inn Journal Center—$$$
This big pyramid-shaped hotel has 311 rooms, two restaurants, pool, sauna, health club and whirlpool. West Interstate 25 on the north side of the city, **821-3333.**

La Posada—$$$
Close to the convention center. A good restaurant and bar and 114 rooms and suites and Limo to the airport. This hotel is listed on the National Register of Historic Places. **125 Second St. N.W., 242-9090 or 1-800-777-5732.**

Le Baron Inn—$$
Convenient to downtown and the Northeast Heights shopping centers. One hundred and sixty-one rooms, 28 suites. Has package plans that include entries to many attractions with transportation. Offers 25 percent senior discount. **2120 Menaul N.E., 884-0250 or 1-800-444-7378.**

El Vado Motel—$$
Close to Old Town on old Route 66. Senior-citizen discounts and good restaurants nearby. **2500 Central Ave. S.W., 243-4594.**

Pan American Lodge—$$
Near Interstate 25, University of New Mexico, Convention Center and Presbyterian Hospital. **817 Central Ave. N.E., 243-1321.**

Amfac Hotel—$$
Near the airport. Offers 266 rooms and 13 suites, two restaurants and a lounge. **2910 Yale, 843-7000 or 1-800-227-1117.**

Best Western Airport—$$$
Near the airport. Offers 120 rooms, complimentary breakfast. **2400 Yale S.E., 242-7022 or 1-800-528-1234**.

Radisson Inn at Airport—$$$
Has 148 rooms. **1901 University S.E., 247-0512 or 1-800-333-3333**.

Hyatt Regency Albuquerque—$$$
The city's newest hotel, offering 391 rooms and 13 suites, one restaurant and three lounges. **330 Tijeras N.W., 842-1234 or 1-800-228-1234**.

Albuquerque Hilton Hotel—$$$
Has 253 rooms and 6 suites. At the intersection of Interstate 25 and Interstate 40. **884-2500 or 1-800-821-1901**.

Fairfield Marriot
Has 190 rooms, **1760 Menaul Rd. N.E., 889-4000**.

La Quinta—$$$
Can be seen from Interstate 25. Offers 130 rooms and a restaurant. **5241 San Antonio Dr., N.E., 821-9000 or 1-800-228-5151**.

Howard Johnson Plaza—$$$
Close to Interstate 25 and Balloon Fiesta Park. Has 150 rooms and 12 suites, restaurant and lounge. **6000 Pan American Freeway, 821-9451 or 1-800-654-2000**.

Amberly Suite Hotel—$$$
Near Balloon Fiesta Park. Offers 170 suites, restaurant and lounge. **7620 Pan American Freeway, 823-1300 or 1-800-333-9806**.

Best Western Rio Grande Inn—$$
Near Old Town. Has 173 rooms, restaurant and lounge. **1015 Rio Grande Blvd., 843-9500 or 1-800-528-1234**.

Monterey Motel—$$
Close to Old Town. Offers 15 rooms. **2402 Central S.W., 243-3554**.

Royal Hotel—$$
Close to state fairgrounds, university and airport. Offers 70 rooms, swimming pool, restaurant and piano bar. Kids under 12 are free. **4119 Central Ave. N.E., 265-3585 or 1-800-843-8572**.

Econo Lodge of Albuquerque—$$
Eight blocks from Convention Center, easy access to both interstates. Exit 224B off Interstate 25, at Central Ave. **243-1321** or **1-800-446-6900.**

CAMPGROUNDS

COMMERCIAL

Albuquerque Central KOA
Just off Interstate 40, on exit 166, then you can see it. The usual KOA quality, including a heated swimming pool. Rates start at $17.95. **296-2729.**

Albuquerque North KOA
In Bernalillo, just 10 miles north of town. Its position alongside Interstate 25 makes it as close to downtown Albuquerque as you could wish. Also has tent sites. Rates start at $18.95. **867-5227.**

Palisades RV Park
9201 Central Ave. N.W., near Old Town. On bus routes to all parts of town. Costs $13 for two people with all hookups. All discounts honored. **831-5000.**

American RV Park
13500 Coronado Freeway S.W. Offers 184 spaces with all hookups, swimming pool, laundry, propane sales, video room and game room. Priced from $21.02 for full hookup. Good Sam discount honored. **831-3545** or **1-800-282-8885**.

HOSTELS

Albuquerque International Hostel—$
Has 12 rooms. Kitchen privileges. **1012 Central S.W., 243-6101.**

AYH/New Mexico Council
Has full information on hostels for all of New Mexico. **PO Box 9100, Bernalillo, N.M. 87004,** or call **867-6596.**

——————— WHERE TO EAT ———————

Albuquerque has a well-deserved reputation as a town full of good eating places. Obviously it is impossible to list *all* of the good ones, but I can give you some of my favorites. Bon appetit!

New Chinatown Restaurant—$
5001 Central Ave. N.E. I've been eating Chinese food at Kitty's for 20 years and have never had a poor meal. Complete Chinese menu in the evening. Call 24 hours ahead for Beijing duck. All-you-can-eat buffet at noon. Good deal. **265-8859.**

The Cooperage—$$
7220 Lomas Blvd. N.E. Specializing in steaks and prime rib. **255-1657.**

Beijing Restaurant—$
6900 Montgomery Ave. Full Chinese menu. I recommend the Manchurian lamb (Watch out for those dried red peppers—they're fiery!) and the Mongolian beef. **883-8770.**

Papa Felipes—$$
9800 Menaul Blvd. N.E. Serving excellent Mexican foods and the meanest margarita in town. My favorite dishes are the *chile rellenos* and the *chimichangas.* **883-5305** and **292-8877.**

The Holiday Inn Midtown—$$$
2020 Menaul Ave. N.E. Has an excellent restaurant with a wide range of cuisines. Especially good on seafood dishes. **884-2511.**

Le Marmiton—$$$
5415 Academy N.E. Traditional French cuisine. Dinner Mon.–Sat.; lunch Tues.–Fri. Open by special request on Sun. **821-6279.**

Bella Vista—$
Eight and one half miles from Albuquerque, high up on the east side of the Sandias. Perhaps the city's most patronized eating place. Featuring all-you-can-eat fried chicken and fish. Seats more than 1,100 in 12 dining rooms. Go east on Interstate 40, turn to the left on N.M. 14 and follow the signs. Call for reservations. **281-3370.**

La Placita—$$
208 San Felipe N.W. In Old Town. Features one of the oldest dining

rooms in America and offers old-world charm and authentic Mexican dishes, along with a good selection of American food and potent potables. **247-2204.**

The Luna Mansion—$$$

In Los Lunas, 20 minutes south of the city. Offers outstanding food and service in a historical old building that is a prime example of Spanish territorial architecture. Open evenings only at 5 P.M. **865-7333.**

La Hacienda—$$$

Close to La Placita in Old Town. Another historical jewel of early Mexican-American architecture, offering Mexican and American cuisine. See Los Lunas section. **243-3131.**

Mama Mia—$$

1430 Carlisle near Constitution. Offers fine Italian cuisine, featuring homemade pasta and lots of salads to go along with the usual Italian meat and seafood dishes. **265-4557.**

Oasis—$$

5412 San Mateo N.E. Restaurant and lounge. Offers Greek, Israeli, French and Lebanese cooking. If you like souvlaki or stuffed grape leaves, this is the place for you. **884-2324.**

Capos—$$

Lomas at Eighth St. N.W. Italian restaurant specializing in veal parmigiana, delectable lasagna and lots of other stuff that sings of Italy. **292-2007.**

High Finance Restaurant—$$$

Atop Sandia Peak. Has more than a breathtaking view to offer. Steaks, seafood and good pasta dishes. **243-9742.**

Maria Teresa Restaurant and 1840 Bar—$$

In Old Town. Offers authentic Mexican cuisine. Dinner seven days a week; lunch Mon.–Sat. Maria Teresa is in a building that has been here since 1840. Good food, along with history and tradition. **242-3900.**

Cafe Oceana—$$

Two blocks east of interstate 25 on **1414 Central Ave. S.E.** Lunch Mon.–Fri.; dinner Mon.–Sat. Oyster bar and fresh seafood. Full service bar, casual atmosphere. **247-2233.**

Ciao! Ristorante e Bar—$$

Tramway at Indian School. Northern Italian cuisine. Dinner seven days; lunch Mon.–Fri. Offers panoramic view of the city. **293-2426**.

Kachina Kitchen—$

Looking for something completely different? Go to Old Town, intersection of Central and Rio Grande, and look for the Kachina Kitchen. Don't get a hamburger; get a Kachina Ka-burger with chili and guacamole! Different! Try the green chile stew . . . or a Navajo taco—not like any taco you've had before. These are truly authentic Southwestern dishes. Go ahead! Be a sport! You'll come back for more. **243-6140**.

—————— SERVICES ——————

AIRLINES

American West, 247-0737 or 1-800-247-5692.
American Airlines, 842-4287 or 1-800-433-7300.
Continental Airlines, 1-800-525-0280.
Delta Airlines, 1-800-221-1212.
Mesa Airlines, 1-800-MESA-AIR.
Ross Aviation, 842-4161.
Southwest Airlines, 831-1221 or 1-800-531-5600.
Trans World Airlines, 842-4010 or 1-800-221-2000.
United Airlines, 1-800-631-1500.
USAir, 1-800-428-4322.

CAR RENTAL

There are several car rental agencies in Albuquerque. Many of them have counters at the Albuquerque airport. If you're not at the airport, here are the phone numbers: **Southwest Car Rental, 243-1899; Avis, 842-4080; Budget, 884-2666; Enterprise, 764-9100; Farr Better, 843-6693; General Rent a Car, 843-9386; Hertz, 842-4235; Rich Ford Rentals, 247-9255; Thrifty Car Rentals, 842-6201;** and **U Save, 242-8666.**

TAXI

Yellow Checker Cab, 247-8888. Twenty-four hour service every day of the year.

Albuquerque Cab Company, 883-4888. Twenty-four hours a day.

Classic Limousine Service, 247-4000. If you want to arrive in style.

HOSPITAL AND MEDICAL

Albuquerque is home to the world-famed **Lovelace Clinic,** the facility chosen to work with our astronauts ("Before they go into space, they come to us").

Archaeologists still have not deciphered the meaning of the symbols used in Albuquerque's Petroglyph Park.

═══════ Isleta Pueblo ═══════

On the south edge of Albuquerque lies the Indian pueblo of Isleta ("little island"), which has been there much longer than the Duke City. Once Isleta was the largest of the Rio Grande pueblos.

Take exit 215 off Interstate 25 south and follow N.M. 47 to the pueblo. On the way in, you'll pass a small pay-to-fish operation run by the pueblo. The biggest attraction of the pueblo is St. Augustine Church, which was built in 1613. That's about a century before Albuquerque came into being.

St. Augustine was destroyed by the rampaging pueblos in the Pueblo Revolt of 1680. When Isleta was reconquered by De Vargas in 1692, the church was rebuilt—using the same walls and foundations. It stands today much as it was 300 years ago. In late 1990 a disastrous fire did considerable damage to the interior of the church. I hope the redecorating is complete when you get there.

There's an interesting story about the church. A couple of decades ago, a Catholic priest named Stadtmueller had part of the courtyard paved over. The pueblo governor, Andy Abeyta, remonstrated because the old-way religion required the bare earth to dance upon. He accused the priest of trying to destroy the old way. The priest agreed that he was trying to get rid of such "idolatrous" practices. Incensed, the devout Catholic governor Abeyta arrested the priest and expelled him from the reservation. The archbishop promptly announced that the church of St. Augustine was closed and would remain closed until the pueblo governor apologized to the priest.

Years went by, with the Isleteños walking to other nearby churches each Sunday morning. Then the present archbishop, Robert Sanchez, was named to the Santa Fe see. He quietly assigned a young priest to Isleta Pueblo, and the problem was solved.

A lovely grandmother of the pueblo explained to me that the young people now all have jobs with the Anglo community, and they all prefer to build new frame homes on the hill above the ancient pueblo. "Nowadays, only we old people live in the old pueblo," she said. "We baby-sit for the young people and teach them about the old ways."

Some of the inhabitants of the old Isleta still bake in the adobe *hornos*. If you're lucky, you might be able to buy some of the blue-corn bread that they make so well.

Los Lunas

Next stop south of Isleta is the sleepy little village of Los Lunas. It was named for a family named Luna, which explains why it is Los Lunas, instead of Las Lunas. If it were "Las," we'd be talking about moons, which are *lunas* in *español*.

Although Los Lunas is the home of two prison facilities (don't pick up hitchhikers), the main reason we call your attention to it is the **Luna Mansion** ($). This is one of the most famous and best eating places in the center of the state. Built in a very old mansion, it offers classic elegance, good food and fine service. Open only for dinner, it starts service at 5 P.M. Reservations are definitely suggested. **865-7333.**

Elegance and style mark the Luna Mansion Restaurant in Los Lunas, New Mexico.

Belen

Belen means "Bethlehem" in Spanish. The name first appeared in 1740, but there is considerable evidence that both the Pueblo Indians and the Spanish settlers had been here long before that date. In fact, the Spaniards and the Indians fought over the place before then. Belen calls itself the Hub City of New Mexico. It's a big switchyard for the railroad, which has provided a steady payroll for many years. In addition, Belen is the trade center for a large agricultural area, much of it irrigated from the Rio Grande. Belen looks prosperous, but it has many vacant buildings.

But even the Chamber of Commerce in Belen told me that there "wasn't much to see or do in Belen for the tourist." I guess I'd have to agree.

But if you're traveling by RV or you are a tent camper, you might want to investigate **Senator Willie Chaves State Park.** Take River St. straight east from downtown, and watch for the sign on your right, just before crossing the new bridge. This is a small park, used mostly for picnicking by local folks. There are more than 100 acres of well-watered brush here on the state park, and nature walks are laid out to show you some of the wildlife of the *bosque*, which is Spanish for "woods." The park is kept clean and well maintained by laborers from the Los Lunas prison facilities. It offers 10 RV camping spaces. There are rest rooms but no showers. Cost is $7 for camping site; $11 with electricity. Good deal if you aren't ready for more driving to Albuquerque in the north or Socorro to the south.

Mariachi music is popular in New Mexico. (Photo by Mark Nohl, New Mexico Economic and Tourism Department.)

Socorro

Seventy-five miles south of Albuquerque on Interstate 25 is Socorro, a city of 9,500 people. It has a lot to offer to the traveler in the Land of Enchantment. Where else can you tee off at 7,000 feet in a golf tournament when the hole is 3,000 feet below the tee box? Where else can you witness the Big Bang, which detonates unused explosives from missile and military bases all over the country? It happens every other year at White Sands Missile Range. If you're not interested in *that* Big Bang, try driving 39 miles west on U.S. 60 to see the Very Large Array, the world's mightiest radio astronomy telescope, which listens in on the big bang, the possible beginning of the creation of our galaxy.

HISTORY

The people of Socorro are helpful. "Socorro" means help in Spanish. The name was coined by Juan de Onate in 1598 when the people of the nearby pueblo—Pilabo—provided help to his band, which was headed for Santa Fe to establish a colony. The Indians of the pueblo provided corn to the near-starving expedition, and the name was coined—and it lasted. But the name described only a locality until after the Pueblo Revolt in 1680. The Indians of the Pueblo del Pilabo did not join in the Pueblo Revolt but instead retreated southward with the Spanish. They never returned to their Pilabo and still live in Socorro Del Sur ("Socorro of the South") near El Paso. After the reconquest, Socorro was formally established as an outpost on the Camino Real—the "Royal Road"—which led all the way from Mexico City to Santa Fe, now the capital of New Mexico as it once was capital of New Spain. Even after the reconquest, Socorro remained a tiny, unimportant village until the coming of the railroad in 1880.

Socorro boomed with the advent of the rails. A silver smelter was going great guns, and when the rails were extended westward to Magdalena, things really exploded. Ore from mines all over that country were hauled to Magdalena by horses and mules, then railroaded into Socorro. Lumbering operations in the Magdalena Mountains brought logs to the railhead—known as Trails End—to load them on the rails. Livestock was driven as much as 60 miles from western New Mexico pastures to reach the railhead in Magdalena.

The mining, past and present, is still evident in Socorro, the home of the New Mexico Institute of Mining Technology—better known as

Tech—with more than 1,200 students and a faculty of nearly 700, many of them in vital research projects. The world's future came home to Socorro in the days before World War II, when the first atomic bomb was exploded at the Trinity Site on White Sands Missile Range, off to the east. A chunk of the metal container that held that first atomic bomb is on display on the east end of the old plaza in Socorro.

Days of Trinity are long gone, and silver mining is pretty much a thing of the past. Now Socorro is the center of a thriving agricultural area and the shopping town for a large area of New Mexico. You can still get a sense of the frontier days by visiting the old Valverde Hotel, just two blocks off of the main street, or the Garcia Opera House.

—— FESTIVALS AND EVENTS ——

Rare Whooping Cranes
Jan. is a good time to look for the birds on the Bosque del Apache National Wildlife Refuge.

International Students Exhibits
In Mar. On New Mexico Tech campus. Call Student Services at **835-0424.**

Open House at the Trinity Site
In Apr. and Oct. **678-1134.**

Conrad Hilton Pro-Am Golf Tournament
In June. **835-5335.**

San Antonio Fiesta
In June. Call the Chamber of Commerce for information. **835-0424.**

Old Timers Reunion
In July. Call the Chamber of Commerce for information. **835-0424.**

Ranchers Camp Meeting
In July. **835-0942.** Ask for Rev. Myron White.

San Miguel Fiesta
In Aug. Call Marian Porter, **835-1620.**

Fire Fighters School at the Fire Fighters Training Academy
In Aug. **835-7500.**

Women's Amateur Golf Tournament
In Aug. **835-5335.**

Annual Chile Chase Golf Tournament
In Sept. **835-5335.**

County Fair
Labor Day. Call the Chamber of Commerce for information. **835-0424.**

Hispanic Heritage Golf Tournament
In Oct. **835-5335.**

Fiesta de Octubre
In Oct. Call New Mexico Tech's Department of Humanities. **835-5445.**

Annual New Mexico Mineral Symposium
In Nov. Call the New Mexico Bureau of Mines, **835-5246.**

—— SEEING AND DOING ——

Walking Tour. See the historical buildings of Socorro, guided by a leaflet obtained from the Chamber of Commerce at **103 Francisco de Avando**—which is on the west side of the main street—set back half a block and marked with a big sign. It's near the north end of town. **835-0424.**

New Mexico Tech Golf Course is a challenging 18-hole layout. This is the permanent home of the Conrad Hilton Pro-Am. Located at the university. **835-5335.**

Be sure to get the informational leaflet about the **San Miguel Church** and read its fascinating history. It was built in 1615, and its 5-foot-thick adobe walls weathered the centuries and the Pueblo Revolt. Extensively restored in the last two decades, it remains an outstanding example of Spanish colonial architecture.

Socorro is a good place to headquarter while moving out to see the sights that include **Bosque del Apache National Wildlife Refuge, 835-1828,** 16 miles south; the **National Radio Astronomy Observatory, 835-7000,** 39 miles west; and the **Gran Quivira Ruins** in **Salinas Pueblo Missions National Monument, 847-2770,** 100 miles to the northeast.

—————— WHERE TO STAY ——————

ACCOMMODATIONS

El Camino—$$
Offers 43 rooms, restaurant, lounge and swimming pool. **713 California** (the main drag), **835-1500.**

Economy Inn—$
Offers 45 rooms, restaurant, heated pool. **400 California, 835-4666.**

Best Western Golden Manor—$$
Offers 40 rooms with full amenities, restaurant and heated pool. **507 California, 835-0320.**

Motel 6—$
Has 123 rooms, a pool. On U.S. 85, **835-4300.**

Sands—$
Has 25 rooms. **205 California, 835-1130.**

San Miguel—$$
Offers 40 rooms. Has a heated pool. **916 California, 835-0211.**

Super 8—$$
Has 63 rooms, a heated pool. **1121 Frontage Road N.W., 835-4626.**

Town House—$$
Offers 10 rooms. **803 Spring St., 835-4622.**

Vagabond—$$
Offers 70 rooms, a restaurant, lounge and bar, along with a heated pool. **1009 California, 835-0276.**

CAMPGROUNDS

Socorro RV Park
On the frontage road leading south out of town; used to be a KOA. Has electric and water hookups and a dump station, recreation room with pool tables, laundry, grocery and propane. Basic rate is $11.98. Good Sam members receive 10 percent discount. **835-2234.**

—————— WHERE TO EAT ——————

Socorro offers almost all of the fast-food restaurants and, in addition, some local eating places that are worth your patronage.

Armijos—$$
602 U.S. 85 S.E. Serves Mexican food. **835-1686.**

Don Juan's Cocina—$$
118 Manzanares. Mexican food. **835-9967.**

El Sombrero—$$
210 Mesquite. Mexican and American menu. **835-3945.**

Golden Manor—$$
507 California. American dishes. **835-0230.**

Jerry's—$$
1006 California. American cuisine. **835-2255.**

Vagabond—$$
1011 California. American and Chinese menu and a full liquor list. **835-1371.**

Val Verde Steak House—$$
203 E. Manzanares. American menu. **835-3380.**

The beautiful Spanish colonial church of San Miguel in Socorro.

══ Bosque del Apache ══ National Wildlife Refuge

Twelve miles south of Socorro on Interstate 25, you'll find the turnoff onto U.S. 380. The sign reads "San Antonio" and "Carrizozo." Now, Carrizozo is a long ways east, but San Antonio is right there, just off the freeway. Most tourists would go past or through San Antonio and not even know it existed. But there are three notable things about San Antonio. First of all, that small brown building on the corner, where you turn south to go to the Bosque del Apache Refuge, is the **Owl Bar & Cafe.** It claims to serve the world's best hamburger. Having judiciously sampled the green-chile cheeseburger about a hundred times, I agree that it is the finest. The place doesn't look like much on the outside, and the interior seems almost dark when you come in from the blazing New Mexico sunshine. Some of the floors are sloping just a bit. But the food is the best. If you're a beginner, you might ask to have the green chile served on the side so you can decide for yourself how much you want on your burger. Warning: the Owl Bar & Cafe is closed Sun. This famous little restaurant is owned by Adolph and Rowena Baca, and their phone is **835-9946.**

Second, this tiny town is the birthplace and childhood home of Conrad Hilton, who rented out a couple of rooms in his parents' house to railroad travelers, way back when. That gave him an idea, and he opened his first hotel in Cisco, Texas, and went on to build one of the greatest hotel chains the world has ever seen. Ask one of the locals to point out the Hilton home to you.

Third, right there at the Owl Bar & Cafe is where you turn south on good blacktopped road to the **Bosque del Apache National Wildlife Refuge**. This is a birders paradise from late Oct. until mid-Feb. because it is winter home to whooping cranes, about 60,000 snow geese, 20,000 greater sandhill cranes and countless other migratory waterfowl. Although the migrants start arriving in Oct., the peak time for seeing most of the species is in late Dec. and early Jan.

Although the refuge totals more than 57,000 acres, only about 7,000 of it is the prime river bottomland, which the waterfowl love. There's a 12-mile loop tour on good roads, open to the public from one hour before sunrise to one hour after sunset. Drive slowly, stay in your car and use good binoculars, and you'll see more waterfowl, up close, than you ever dreamed possible. New Mexico's bright sunshine makes this one of the best places in the world to photograph ducks and geese. There is also a good population of mule deer on the refuge and many coyotes.

There is a charge of $2 per car to travel on the refuge tour road, but a Golden Age Passport will get you all in free. Now, something new, the refuge will waive the entry fee to those who possess an up-to-date duck stamp. It's a good idea to stop at the visitors center before you tour the refuge because the exhibits will help you see and understand more.

In Nov., the refuge teams up with the city of Socorro and the Socorro County Chamber of Commerce to present the **Bosque Fall Festival**. The three-day event features tours of the refuge by the fish and wildlife personnel, celebrating the return of its famous winter residents, the endangered whooping cranes. A wildlife photography workshop is also offered on the refuge, with a tour of the habitat of the endangered species known as the Socorro isopod. Never heard of it? Time to learn.

The Bureau of Land Management offers a **tour of ancient Indian petroglyphs**, while the forest service weighs in with a full-day tour of the nearby **Cibola National Forest.** Call the Bureau at **835-0412** for tour information, or the Magdalena District Ranger office at **854-2281** for information on Cibola forest tours.

While all this is going on, there'll be retriever dog field trials, seminars about birds of prey, exhibits of wildlife art and workshops on landscaping with native plants. Obviously, some of the events are on the refuge, others are in the town of Socorro. For further information, call Bosque del Apache at **835-1828**.

The nearest hotels are in Socorro, 12 miles north. If you're traveling by recreational vehicle, note that **Bosque Birdwatchers RV Park** is on the road (N.M. 1) between San Antonio and the refuge. Open all year, it offers 20 spaces with hookups, at prices starting at $12.80 per night. **835-1366.**

A few miles southeast of the refuge is the place where the town of San Marcial used to be. At one time, it was perhaps the busiest town on the Camino Real, the most important outpost between El Paso to the south and Santa Fe to the north. It was also the northern end of the dreaded Jornada del Muerto, the "Day's March of the Dead Man." Travelers avoided a couple of days of the trip north by leaving the river at Rincon, about 96 miles to the south, and traveling straight up to San Marcial. There was little water available on the Jornada, so you can be sure that travelers were mighty happy to reach San Marcial and the Rio Grande, the only dependable source of water.

But you can't drive over to San Marcial now. The Rio Grande rose in flood and wiped it out in 1866. Then the residents moved to the higher west bank of the Rio and started the town up again. But in 1929, the Rio again flooded and removed San Marcial. Only a few of the foundations can still be found, and there's nothing there for the tourist.

⹀ The New Mexican Chile ⹀

New Mexico grows some of the finest chile peppers in the world. New Mexican cuisine features the savory chiles in many forms and many dishes. Here the chile pepper is used to flavor the food, not to sear the inside of your mouth. You won't find the Tex-Mex foods from our neighboring states, just the real flavor without the fire that is good New Mexico chile cooking.

There are many chiles, and they differ greatly. *Chile Verdes*, which means simply "green chiles," are big carrot-shaped peppers as long as 6 inches. They have great flavor and almost no burn. They are the basis of delicious *chile rellenos*, one of New Mexico's most representative dishes. *Rellenos* means "refilled." The *chile verde*, emptied of its seeds, is refilled with many tasty things, including ground beef, chicken, cheese, rice, tomatoes, and onions. Try them without worry. No *chile relleno* will burn your mouth. The only caution is that they often become addictive.

Chile Jalapeños, pronounced "hal-a-pain-yo," are two to four inches long and fatter and shorter than *chile verdes* by far. They vary considerably in the amount of heat they give, depending upon the soil they are grown in and the amount of water provided to the plant while it is growing its fruit. Some people eat *jalapeños* like peanuts; others claim that the spicy fruit causes blisters inside the mouth. Try the first one carefully. Nip off a dime-sized piece from the bottom and chew it slowly and carefully. Then wait for a couple of minutes before making up your mind whether or not you like *jalapeños*, because they do have a slow burn. Personally, I love them. They are great in stews and meat dishes. Sliced in tiny pieces, they are a welcome addition to a tossed salad. You most often find *jalapeños* served on the side in restaurants or canned in vinegar. In Spanish, pickled *jalapeños* are *jalapeño en escabeche*.

Chile Serranos are about the same length as *jalapeños* or smaller, and slimmer. When they are fresh, the skin is shiny green as compared with the duller skin of the fresh *jalapeño*. *Serranos*, my friend, are hot. Don't bite into a fresh one; you will regret it immediately. When you order a typical Mexican meal, you'll be offered a small bowl of *salsa picante*. This is composed of chopped *serranos*, onions, tomatoes and cilantro. The chemical temperature varies with the cook who prepared it. Dip a corner of a tostada into the *salsa picante*, and try it for taste. It is delicious when properly made. I spoon it over a tossed salad sometimes, sometimes over meat, even sometimes over *frijoles refritos*, which are refried beans—and very tasty.

The *serrano* is often called the "*quaresima*" in Spanish. The reference is to the 40 days of Lent in 90 percent Catholic Hispanic America. I was never sure whether the *serranos* were given as penance or whether they spiced up meatless meals for the penitent people. If you have fresh *serranos*, slice up a small one, and drop the slices into a big stew. Let it simmer for hours. It sure adds flavor.

Ristras are long strings of dried peppers turned purplish red—some say dried-blood color. They are hung on the sunlit adobe walls of the traditional New Mexican house, adding a welcome splash of color. When dry as powder, they are often crushed and put into shakers for use in spicy stews and meat dishes.

Chile Piquins, sometimes called "*chile pequeños*," are diminutive copies of the big *chiles verdes*. From two to three inches long and slender, they are picked when red and used in many authentic *mexicano* dishes. They can be hot or mild, again depending upon the variety, the amount of water they receive and the nature of the soil they grow in.

In some parts of southeast Texas, a tiny ball of fire is grown that is called *chile pitins*. These are badly misnamed, for their heat is no small pittance. These little balls of fire are only about the size of a pea, but they contain enough fire to blister the inside of your mouth. If you see them growing, you might think that they are fruit—like cherries or gooseberries or currants—but believe me, there is nothing sweet about them. One of them in a big pot of stew adds a delightful flavor. But even after it has stewed for a couple of hours, the *pitin* itself is still too hot to chew. I had a good friend who was raised on them. He often put two or three between

Chiles of all sizes and all varieties are featured in the Chile Festival, held every Labor Day weekend in Hatch, New Mexico.

slices of bologna in a sandwich. I tried that once—just once. I drank burning-hot coffee to get the *pitin* fire out of mouth and ended up with big blisters.

If you overdo a bite of a fiery member of the chile family, here's a tip. Chewing fresh bread will absorb the fire, putting it out faster than drinking a glass of water, which will spread it.

The active ingredient of chiles has been identified and named capsicum. It definitely does have healthful effects upon those who use it with caution. Work your way into New Mexico's tasty chile dishes slowly. When not overdone, chile adds much flavor to your cuisine.

The best peppers in the world are grown in the Mesilla Valley of southern New Mexico, where they are perhaps the number one cash crop. Chiles from Hatch draw raves from chile lovers all over the world.

In Hatch, chiles are the main crop, and their cultivation is a science. There you can buy bell peppers, maxibell peppers (which look the same but have more fire), Big Jim variety *chiles verdes*, Tam *jalapeños*, Sandias (which are hot), and the very hot *serranos* and *piquins*, along with the extra-hot varieties such as Barkers, Sante Fe Grande Española Improved, *jalapeños* (yes, they vary from mild to extra hot), and the yellowhots, sometimes called *torridos*. More than a dozen varieties are raised commercially near Hatch, the chile capital of the world.

Chiles are tasty and versatile additions to New Mexican cuisine. Enjoy them, but don't rush into anything. Taste slowly and in tiny bites until you find out how much is fire and how much is flavor. I love 'em.

A contestant of the Whole Enchilada
Fiesta, in Las Cruces, tastes his entry.
(Photo by Mark Nohl, New Mexico
Economic and Tourism Department.)

Truth or Consequences

Once it was called Hot Springs. Some 40-odd years ago, the town voted to change its name to Truth or Consequences. Now, why on earth would a relatively sane town do that? I'm going to tell you.

Ralph Edwards, a famous game-show master of ceremonies, hosted a popular program called *Truth or Consequences*. On this show, the contestants were given a question that was nearly impossible to answer. When they failed to "tell the truth," they were forced to face the consequences, which were usually undignified but safe enough. Ralph Edwards advertised to find a town that would change its name to Truth or Consequences to commemorate the tenth anniversary of that program. Hot Springs thought it over and decided that it had nothing to lose. Several other towns vied for the honor to become T or C, but Ralph Edwards' staff chose Hot Springs because of the mineral hot springs found here and because of the Carrie Tingley Orthopedic Hospital, which helped so many children.

The decision started a unique relationship that has provided publicity for the town and the program. Hot Springs, er, excuse me, T or C, changed the name of a street to Ralph Edwards. It built Ralph Edwards Park. Every year for more than four decades, it has had an annual fiesta and celebration. And for more than 40 years, Ralph Edwards has appeared to take part in the celebration. He brings a host of celebrities to help celebrate. He is revered in Truth or Consequences.

Twenty years after the name change, the residents were asked to vote on changing the name back to Hot Springs. The loyal residents stuck to their new name, and Ralph Edwards continues to highlight their annual celebration.

HISTORY

True, the town got on the national map in 1950 when it changed its name. But it had actually been there for many years before that. Spanish conquistador Juan de Onate came through here on his famed 1598 trip to establish Santa Fe. The discovery of copper, silver and gold in the surrounding mountains helped Hot Springs grow. The discovery was an added attraction to the mineral springs and lured new settlers. Hot Springs soon became the biggest and most influential city in Sierra County. To the east, across the Rio Grande, the railroad built the tiny town of Engle, the jumping-off place for prospectors who explored and settled southwestern New Mexico. Today Engle is almost gone. Only three buildings remain, and there is really nothing to see. But Engle once was an important spot in the region.

To most travelers, T or C is just the place where you turn off to go to Elephant Butte Lake, New Mexico's largest water area. The Bureau of Reclamation dam was built in 1916, making it one of the oldest in the Southwest. It piles up the waters of the Rio Grande and forms a lake that varies in length from 20 to 45 miles, depending upon the snowpack in Colorado and northern New Mexico and upon the needs of irrigation farming downstream.

The lake, often called one of the 10 best black-bass lakes in America, is host to at least a dozen bass fishing tournaments every year. But the fishing isn't limited to the bigmouths. I much prefer fishing for white bass, which are available by the untold thousands in May and early June. The whites taste much better than the largemouth black bass, and they are easily taken by trolling small white plugs 4 or 5 feet down. Best spots for both black and white bass are in and north of the Narrows when the lake is high. When it is low, move down near Rattlesnake Island. Black bass are often found among the dead trees that are still standing. I like spinner baits fished slow and careful down near the bottom among the snags and dead trees.

—— FESTIVALS AND EVENTS ——

Geronimo Days
In Oct., T or C remembers that Hot Springs was once the location of the sacred hot springs of the Apache people. There is an Indian village in Ralph Edwards Park, with Apache dancers, mariachi bands, bluegrass music and Spanish folk music. Lots of music culminates in the Street Dance on Sat. evening. The excellent **Geronimo Museum** shows the movie about Geronimo and the Apache resistance. Also speakers and a display by noted local artists. The museum is at **325 Main St., 894-6600.** It is one of the better museums in the state. Don't miss it. For other information call the Chamber of Commerce at **894-3536.**

—— OUTDOOR ACTIVITIES ——

There are three good marinas and launching ramps on the big lake. Best is the **Elephant Butte Lake State Park,** which also offers a bait store, some groceries and a lighted night-fishing area. The state park has lots of camping, with 56 sites sporting electricity and water at **Lyons Point** and another 47 sites with electricity and water at **Ridge Road.** Comfort stations with showers at these areas. There are hundreds more spaces of undeveloped camping. Portable toilets near all sites and a good comfort station at **Paseo del Rio Campground** but without showers. Rates are $6 for primitive camping, $7 for developed sites and $11 with electricity.

The three permanent launching ramps are at the main entrance to the park, the Dam Site Recreation Area and Rock Canyon. **Rock Canyon Marina** offers a fishing dock, gas station, store and complete bait and tackle selections, **744-5462.** In addition, the state park maintains temporary launching ramps to adapt to the rise and fall of the water levels.

A professional **bass-guiding service** is available to those who want help in locating the fish. For reservations, call Dale Wagy at **744-5314.** The price is $175 per day for one or two people. Guide service provides boat and motor and all fishing equipment.

A word of warning abut Elephant Butte Lake. Summer heat is high enough so that you need to take protective measures—suntan lotion, light but complete clothing cover, lip balm, etc. Also remember that this lake has a reputation for kicking up sudden strong winds. Be advised, and don't take the Butte for granted.

Unbelievable crowds jam into the state park area on Memorial Day, the Fourth of July and Labor Day. Outside of those three weekends, you'll not find it crowded, even though it definitely is the recreational center for southern New Mexico.

The municipal **golf course** in T or C is located at **700 Marie Ave.** Weekdays green fees are $5.25 for 18 holes. On the weekend the price goes up to $7.75. You can rent a cart for $11 for 18 holes, **894-2603.** The **Oasis Country Club** offers a challenging 18 holes on N.M. 52. Green fees are $10 for 18 holes, and a cart rents for $12 for 18 holes. **744-5224.**

—— WHERE TO STAY ——

ACCOMMODATIONS

Dam Site Recreational Area—$$

Offers cabins near the launching ramp, with a good restaurant, marina store and lounge. An RV park at the same location is advertised, but I've found it filled up with permanents, and there are seldom any spaces for overnight guests. Near the dam, **894-2073.**

Best Western Hot Springs Inn—$$
Just off Interstate 25. Heated pool. **2070 N. Date, 894-6665.**

Motor Manor—$$
Offers 14 units, close to downtown. **595 Main. 894-3648.**

Super 8 Motel—$$
At exit 79 off Interstate 25. Has 41 units. **2701 N. Date, 894-7888 or 1-800-843-1991.**

Elephant Butte Resort Inn—$$$
Out near the lake itself, this is perhaps the most luxurious accommodation in the area. Has 49 rooms and suites, restaurant and lounge, tennis courts, a heated pool. Follow the signs to Elephant Butte Dam. **744-5431.**

CAMPGROUNDS

Palomas Trailer Park
622 Van Patten. Has 19 sites all with full hookups. Close to downtown and mineral baths. Priced from $8. **894-6900.**

RJ RV Park
2601 South Broadway. Offers 36 sites with full hookups, laundry, showers. Nice view. Priced from $10. **894-9777.**

Some people thought that this butte looked like an elephant rising out of the waters of Elephant Butte Lake, hence the name.

Shady Corner RV Park
    100 Rio Grande in Williamsburg. Offers 22 sites, showers, recreation hall, full hookups. Priced from $10. Good Sam members receive a 10 percent discount. **894-7698.**

Cottonwood RV Park
    In town. Easily found on the road leading to the state park. Charges only $8.75 for two people with all hookups. **894-2181.**

KOA
    Just off Interstate 25, at town of Caballo. Has 56 sites, all facilities, laundry, store, overlooking fish-filled Caballo Lake. Priced at $14.50 and up. **743-2811.**

——————— WHERE TO EAT ———————

La Cocina—$$$
    220 N. Date. My personal choice for excellent Mexican and American cuisine. **894-6499.**

Los Arcos—$$
    1400 N. Date. My personal choice for steaks and other traditional American foods. **894-6200.**

Elephant Butte Resort Inn—$$$
    On N.M. 195. Overlooking the lake. Fine dining, lounge and (often) live entertainment. **744-5431.**

Hilltop Cafe—$$
    1301 N. Date. Good salad bar. Fri. special is catfish. **894-3407.**

Cuchillo Cafe—$$
    Fourteen miles west of T or C on N.M. 52 in Cuchillo (pronounced "coo-chee-oh"). If you've got the time and wish to try something different, try a blue-corn enchilada. Dinners only on Wed., Thurs. and Sat. Other days 11:30 A.M.-7 P.M.

══════ Caballo Lake ══════

Just a few miles out of Truth or Consequences on Interstate 25 is another lake to the east, a mile or 2 off the road. This is Caballo. I thought of it as merely the stilling basin for irrigation waters out of the Butte. But its fans, and they are legion, call it New Mexico's best-kept secret. Caballo's level fluctuates as much as 38 feet up and down. This is bad for the aesthetics of the place, and no one calls Caballo beautiful. But when I say, "The lake is way down," its supporters retort, "You mean our beaches are much bigger." They've got a point.

Despite the extreme fluctuations in depth, Caballo holds a fine population of game fish. Several times in the past three years, walleyes that flirted with the state record have been taken from this lake. It is also good for both white and black bass. Blacks have been taken up to 9 pounds, which is a fine black bass in any water.

Caballo is a family-fun lake, good for swimming, picnicking and laying in the sun, in addition to fishing.

There's a marina in Caballo Lake State Park, with everything you need for **boating** and **fishing.** For a fine KOA campground see the Campgrounds section on Truth or Consequences. In addition, Caballo and Percha state parks, so close together that they really are operated as one park, provide lots of **camping.** Caballo offers 15 sites with electricity and another six primitive sites. Percha has six sites with electricity and lots of open territory that invites primitive camping. Both state parks offer showers in nice, clean rest rooms.

Near the entrance gate of **Caballo State Park (743-3942)** is an educational exhibit of all the cactus species, each one identified. If you can't tell a fishhook cactus from a prickly pear, this is your chance to learn.

Both state parks are near the southern end of Caballo Lake. Camping fees are $6 for a primitive site, $7 for a site with water and picnic table and $11 for a site with electricity. Like all of southern New Mexico's state parks, these are most heavily patronized by snowbirds, who spend their winter in the land of sunshine.

Hatch

Less than 20 miles south of Caballo, Interstate 25 brings you to the turnoff for the small town of Hatch. If you agree that T or C was the town that fell in love with a broadcast show, then you'll easily see that Hatch has fallen in love with chiles.

Shortly after De Onate began to settle in New Mexico in 1598, small Spanish towns sprang up in the fertile valley of the Rio Grande. The people brought chile peppers with them. What they started nearly 400 years ago has grown to the point where Hatch is the undisputed chile capital of the world. See the section The New Mexican Chile.

Today, the New Mexico chile farmer tends more than 22,000 acres of chiles, most of it in the irrigated flatlands along the Rio Grande, New Mexico's lifeline. By comparison, the nearest competitor—California—plants only 2,300 acres of chiles.

Caballo Lake State Park lies alongside the lake, facing the rugged Sierra Caballo Mountains off to the east.

Hatch produces many varieties of chiles, and Hatch residents love them all. Best time to visit this chile town is over the Labor Day weekend, when the residents celebrate the **Hatch Chile Festival.** Stop in at the **Cotton Patch Restaurant** on the main north-south street, and talk to Peggy Meyers. She runs the restaurant, but she is "hep to the step" with regard to chiles. Then go back out on the access road from Interstate 25 to the **Chile Express,** a small building on the north side of the road. There you can talk to either Jo or Johnny (both women). See all the various kinds of fresh chiles; watch chiles being roasted; buy bottles of *salsa picante*, made from chiles; and sample some excellent bottled *pico de gallo*, also made from chiles, and even chile honey. Peggy, Jo and Johnny can answer questions about chiles that you haven't even thought of. But you must attend the chile festival to get the real flavor of this small town and its love affair with its main crop, the delicious, savory, spicy chile.

During the festival, Hatch crowns two queens; one is the red-chile queen and the other is the green-chile queen. There's a chile meal and a chile *ristra* and wreath contest. A *ristra* is a bunch of red chiles strung on cords and used as a wall decoration. In many parts of New Mexico, *ristras* are the preferred Christmas ornament. There's a chile-recipe contest, a fiddler contest, a drawing for the chile capital artist painting, horseshoe-pitching contests, stick races, lots of western music and lots of western and Mexican dancing. Most important of all, there's lots of fun!

If you're traveling by RV, Hatch people allow you to park (without facilities) at the Y where the road north separates from N.M. 44, which leads west to Deming and Lordsburg.

There's really only one motel to recommend, on the main east-west street in town. It's the **Village Plaza Motel** ($$), with only six rooms and six suites. **267-3091.**

You'll find good eating in Hatch all year long, at the **Cotton Patch**, at the **Country Kitchen** and at the **B & E Burrito**. During the festival, you'll be allowed to taste many exotic dishes featuring Hatch chiles, of course. Try them all, but don't over do it.

For more information about Hatch and the chile festival, contact the Chamber of Commerce at **PO Box 38, Hatch, N.M. 87937, 267-4381.** Ask for Chuck Watkins.

Fort Selden
State Monument
and Leasburg State Park

May I make a small suggestion? When you leave Hatch going south, don't take the fast but uninteresting Interstate 25. Take the back road, N.M. 185, which is an extension of the north-south main street of Hatch. This road will take you through a greenbelt of irrigated farmlands with lots of trees, a peaceful land. Follow it down the west side of the Rio Grande until you find the signs pointing to Fort Selden State Monument across the river. Sure, this road is slower than Interstate 25, but it's lots more fun, and who's in a hurry, anyway?

Fort Selden is now just a collection of ruined adobe walls built around a military quadrangle. This historical fort was built in 1865 to protect settlers from Apache raids. In the early 1880s a young captain was detailed to command this frontier outpost. His name was Captain Arthur MacArthur. His son, Douglas MacArthur, who played in the fort as a child, grew up to be the Supreme Commander of Allied Forces in the 1941–1945 war against Japan.

By 1890, the Apache were no longer a threat, and Fort Selden was abandoned in 1891, declared obsolete by the army. It became a state monument in 1973, after nearly a hundred years of neglect. Today it features an interpretive trail through its ruins, with explanatory sign-posts to give you a good idea of what life must have been here 110 years ago. Excellent **visitors center** and **museum** in connection with the monument. For further information, call **526-8911**.

There is no camping at the Fort Selden State Monument, but good **camping** is available in **Leasburg State Park**, which is only a mile and a half away. Leasburg doesn't have a visitors center. Seems logical that the two should be combined into one state park (and monument) because they complement each other so well.

The day fee is $3 per car, and the state park offers 18 sites with electricity and many more undeveloped camp sites. Prices are $7 for developed sites and $11 for sites with electricity, as with all New Mexico state parks. This park gets little use in the hot months. But from Sept. to Apr., Leasburg State Park is usually filled up. Many people escaping the cold northern months come to these parks every winter. I was impressed with the hard work by park manager Armando Martinez and his crew that has resulted in a pleasant place to spend some time.

The **Leasburg Dam** on the Rio Grande diverts water to irrigate the upper Mesilla Valley, one of the most productive areas in the state. The reservoir also provides fishing for catfish and other species and is much used by kayakers and canoeists. If you plan to camp here in the winter, call ahead to make sure that there is space available. **524-4068.**

You'll find no motels near this interesting park and monument, but it is not far to Las Cruces, with hundreds of accommodations of all kinds.

As the interpretive marker says, General Douglas MacArthur lived in these mud-walled ruins as a child. He said he learned to ride and to shoot while living in Fort Selden.

====== **Las Cruces** ======

With more than 60,000 people, Las Cruces is New Mexico's second city—no matter how much Roswell, Farmington or Santa Fe might protest. It's located at the crossroads—las cruces—of Interstate 25, Interstate 10, the Atchison, Topeka and the Santa Fe railway and U.S. 70. But it wasn't that kind of crossing that gave this lovely city its name.

Legend says that the *cruces* were crosses erected over Spanish settlers who had been buried after an Indian massacre in 1848. Another story says that the *cruces* were crosses erected over the graves of Spanish settlers who were ambushed and massacred on their way back from Taos in 1830. In any event, Las Cruces, like Albuquerque, is a relative newcomer among New Mexican cities. But the Las Cruces area possesses archaeological sites that prove that the Mesilla Valley was occupied by Pueblo Indians as far back as 200 B.C.

HISTORY

This area figured in the story of Alvar Nuñez Cabeza de Vaca, who survived a shipwreck somewhere in the Gulf of Mexico and got ashore in the 1530s. With three companions he traveled on foot across the entire length of Louisiana and present-day Texas in search of Spanish settlements. He finally found his way to the Mesilla Valley in 1535 and thus has the distinction of being the first European to see this land. Five years after Cabeza de Vaca's arrival, the Coronado expedition passed through the Mesilla Valley on its way to search for the fabled (and nonexistent) Seven Cities of Cibola.

Sixty-three years after the arrival of Cabeza de Vaca, Don Juan de Onate led colonists all the way from Chihuahua, Mexico, to Santa Fe. Some colonists stopped in the area and thus avoided traveling the 90 miles of hell that came to be known as the Jornada del Muerto.

In Mesilla, the Gadsden Treaty was signed in 1854, establishing the border between the United States and Mexico. Here too was the Butterfield Stage route stopover. It was said that the only place you could rent a bed on the Butterfield Stage route between San Antonio and San Francisco was here in Las Cruces. The historic church of San Albino was built in Mesilla in 1850.

Lots of things happened here. The notorious William Bonney, otherwise known as Billy the Kid, was tried for murder in a building that still stands on the Mesilla Plaza. The "Kid" was sentenced to hang, but he escaped and was the subject of quite a manhunt. Pat Garrett finally tracked him down and shot him. Pat Garrett was himself shot and killed just outside of Las Cruces under mysterious circumstances. He is buried in a local cemetery.

Las Cruces has shed its wild-west frontier image and is now a cosmopolitan city, boasting the New Mexico State University, a symphony orchestra, two theater repertory companies and the Branigan Cultural Center in the rebuilt center of town.

—— FESTIVALS AND EVENTS ——

Antique and Collectible Show
First full weekend in Jan. Takes places at Dickerson's Auction Barn. **526-8624.**

Cinco de Mayo
The Fifth of May celebrates Mexico's independence day, with lots of bands, parades and interesting activities. Takes place in Old Mesilla Plaza, naturally. **646-4543** or **524-8521.**

Mesilla Wine Festival
In late May, Memorial Day weekend, in Old Mesilla Plaza. **646-4543.**

Antique and Collectible Show
First weekend in June.

Juneteenth Celebration
Third Saturday in June.

Southern New Mexico State Fair
In Sept. The fair features the Sheriff's Posse rodeo. **526-8179.**

Whole Enchilada Fiesta
In Oct. Three days of celebrating the local chile harvest. Food booths, street dancing, beer halls and the world's largest enchilada! **524-1968.**

Renaissance Craftfaire
First full weekend in Nov. Exhibition and sale of works by southwestern artists and crafts people. Lots of extra entertainment. Takes place at Young Park. **523-6403.**

Gem and Mineral Show

In Nov., the weekend before Thanksgiving, at Dickerson's Auction Barn. This part of New Mexico is famed for its gems and minerals and is a favorite of rock hounds. For information, call **523-9244.**

Fiesta of Our Lady of Guadalupe

In Dec. Features a torchlight procession on Tortuga Mountain and Matachine dancing by Indians. This takes place at Tortugas, on U.S. 80/ 85. **526-8171.** Incidentally, Tortugas was founded by the Isleta Pueblo Indians fleeing southward to escape the rampages of the 1680 Pueblo Revolt. They were headed for El Paso, but when they got here, the slower ones, the aged and the infirm could go no farther. So they stayed here, and the town was called Tortugas, or "turtles" in Spanish, because of the slow pace of its founders.

Las Cruces Symphony Guild Walking Tours

In Dec. Tours of the historical homes, churches and other buildings of the city.

When you first get to Las Cruces, go to the convention and visitor's bureau at **311 North Downtown Mall**, and ask for a more detailed calendar of events for the particular time of year that you are visiting Las Cruces.

——— SEEING AND DOING ———

Concerts by famed artists from all over the world are held in the Pan American Center on the NMSU campus, which is also home to the "Aggie" basketball team, which has won national acclaim. For information and tickets, call the Special Events office at **646-4413**.

Bicentennial Log Cabin, which dates back to 1879, is located at the north end of the Downtown Mall. Closed in winter, strangely enough. Las Cruces temperatures average a low 26° F and a high of 57° F in Jan., which is lovely, in my opinion. In July the average low is 59° F and the average high is 94° F.

Branigan Cultural Center, a highlight of the Downtown Mall, displays the work of local artists and craftsmen and exhibits artifacts from Fort Selden days, **526-0205.**

Amador Hotel, at the corner of Amador and Water streets, once housed both Billy the Kid and Sheriff Pat Garrett. Now it houses the county offices, **525-6602.**

Our Lady at the Foot of the Cross Shrine, near the Main and Lohman street intersection, is a reproduction of Michelangelo's *Pieta*.

Aguirre Spring Recreation Area, east of town on U.S. 70, offers picnicking, hiking and horseback trails. Administered by the Bureau of Land Management, **525-8228**.

Burn Lake, at the intersection of Amador Ave. and Interstate 10, offers fishing, swimming and picnicking.

Farmer's Market in the Downtown Mall is open Wed. and Sat. mornings and features baked goods, produce of the fertile Mesilla Valley and arts and crafts.

New Mexico State University, on University Ave., was established in 1888. State is home to the Solar Energy Institute, the Water Resources Institute of New Mexico and the Clyde Tombaugh Observatory. Williams Hall and the Corbett Center house art exhibits. Kent Hall offers archaeological exhibits. The university switchboard is **646-0111**.

Las Cruces is home to three **vineyards** and **wineries.** Tours can be arranged, sometimes with wine tastings! **Binns Winery, 526-6738; Estrada Winery, 526-4017;** and **La Vina Winery, 882-2092.**

Stahlmann Farms is probably the world's largest single producer of pecans. It's 12 miles south of town on N.M. 28. For a free tour call **525-3470** or **1-800-654-6887.**

There are two public **golf courses** in Las Cruces. Las Cruces Country Club offers a good 18-hole course. Green fees run from $8.45 on weekdays to $10.55 on weekends. NMSU has another 18-hole course, with green fees ranging from $9 on weekdays to $11 on weekends. **526-8731.**

Gadsden Museum, on N.M. 28 and Barker Rd. in Old Mesilla, holds an interesting collection of memorabilia of the Albert Jennings Fountain family. He was a prime mover in the historic Mesilla Valley. **526-6293.**

Sunland Park, 40 miles south of Las Cruces, is a favorite horse-racing spot from Oct. to May. Its location, just outside of El Paso, attracts Texans, who have only recently voted for legalized pari-mutuel betting for their state.

Old Mesilla Plaza, in a southern suburb of Las Cruces, is a must for anyone visiting Las Cruces. Its historical buildings include the famed San Albino Church, built in 1850; the place where they tried Billy the Kid; and the stagecoach station served by the Butterfield Stage. Now most of its historical buildings are occupied by interesting gift shops that offer the usual southwestern arts and crafts. This is where the Confederate army took possession of the so-called Arizona Territory in 1861. The Union forces arrived one year and two weeks later, defeated the rebels and again claimed this area for the United States.

—— WHERE TO STAY ——

ACCOMMODATIONS

Las Cruces Hilton—$$$
Has 202 rooms, heated pool and an excellent restaurant. **705 S. Telshor, 522-4300.**

Days Inn—$$
Has 132 rooms, indoor pool. **2600 S.Valley Dr., 526-4441.**

Best Western Mesilla Valley Inn—$$
Has 167 rooms. **901 Avenida de Mesilla, 524-8603.**

La Quinta Inn—$$
Offers 100 rooms, prices start at $44. **790 Avenida de Mesilla, 524-0331.**

CAMPGROUNDS

Coachlight RV Park
301 S. Motel Blvd., 526-3301.

KOA of Las Cruces
Located about 5 miles west of the city on U.S. 70. It is a well-planned, well-managed park, but what makes it exceptional is its location. High on the mesa, it overlooks all of the city and the Mesilla Valley. You can even see east to the Organ Mountains. It's a beautiful sight every evening when the lights come on. Swimming pool and all the usual attributes of a KOA. Priced from $15 for two people with all hookups. **526-9030.**

Belmont's RV Park
2224 South Valley Dr. Offers sites with all hookups for two people at $11.50 plus tax. **523-2992.**

El Patio RV Park
1557 Calle de Vista. Priced at $10.50 for two people with all hookups. **524-7504.**

Siesta RV Camp
1551 Avenida de Mesilla. Well located for visiting historic Mesilla. Charges $14.75 for two people with all hookups. Ask for Good Sam discount. **523-6816.**

Lunts RV Park
2851 W. Picacho Blvd. Conveniently located for seeing Las Cruces. Economically priced. 526-6781.

St. John's RV Park
3115 El Camino Real, 526-6290.

There are many others, but most of them seem to be primarily mobile home communities that sometimes take in overnight campers and RVers.

———————— **WHERE TO EAT** ————————

There are several hundred good restaurants in Las Cruces. Naturally, many of them feature Mexican cuisine. But you can find all kinds of food, and here are some of my favorites.

China Temple—$$
1510 S. Solano. Recommended for Chinese food. 522-9951.

Chinese Phoenix—$$
1202 E. Madrid. Also highly recommended. 524-4241.

Eddie's Bar and Grill—$$
901 Avenida de Mesilla (in the Best Western Mesilla Valley Inn). A favorite for family dining. 524-8603.

Henry J's Gourmet Hamburgers—$$
 A slightly off-beat recommendation. Serving only hamburgers, but what hamburgers! 525-2211.

Hieberts—$$
2401 N. Main. Good family dining. 524-0451.

Mama Marie's—$$
2190 Avenida de Mesilla. Italian food is well represented. 524-0701.

Pullaro's—$$
901 W. Picacho. Italian food. 523-6801.

La Posta—$$
In the Old Mesilla Plaza. Mexican food. 524-3524.

My Brother's Place—$$
336 S. Main. Mexican food. 523-7681.

Pancho Villa Cantina—$$
In the Holiday Inn, 201 E. University. Mexican food. 526-4411.

BK Steakhouse—$$$
In the Holiday Inn, 201 E. University. Steaks. 526-4411.

Double Eagle—$$$
In Old Mesilla Plaza. Steaks. 523-6700.

Peppers on the Plaza—$$$
Yes, it's in old Mesilla Plaza. And if you feel like trying something different, I recommend this. 523-4999.

SERVICES

Air service to Las Cruces is good, with several flights per day to Albuquerque, Dallas and Houston. It is only 45 miles to the El Paso International Airport, which has connections to the whole world.

Las Cruces is served by both the Southern Pacific and the AT & SF railroad, as well as Greyhound and Trailways bus services. There are four car rental services, all available at the airport. There's also a good taxi service.

Las Cruces has 57 parks, 18 tennis courts and four swimming pools open to the public.

A recent survey listed Las Cruces as one of the best places in which to retire. I can't argue with that, and it's a good town to visit also. It's a good place to headquarter for trips to Sunland Park to bet on the horses, to the White Sands Missile Range and National Monument, to Elephant Butte for bass fishing, to Fort Selden and Fort Craig for historic places, and to the Gila Wilderness and Black Range Mountains.

THE SOUTHEAST REGION

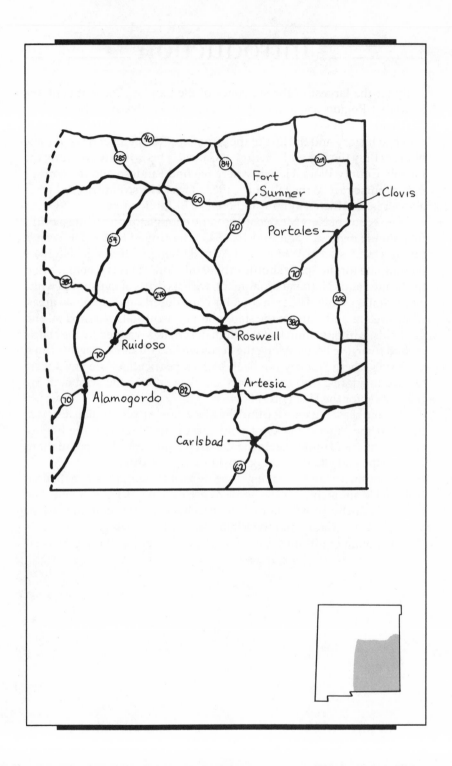

Introduction

By far the largest of the six zones of the Land of Enchantment, the Southeast Region has much of interest. The Southeast is the home of Carlsbad Caverns, the greatest single attraction in the state. The region is rich in history and the lore of the gunmen of the pioneer days; it is the home of Billy the Kid and Sheriff Pat Garrett. This is where we study the Lincoln County Wars. Here is where we find Ruidoso and the world's richest horse race in the tall pines, the Quarter Horse Futurity, which is all over in less than a minute and offers a $1 million purse.

This section of New Mexico was roomy enough to contain the world's first atomic explosion, on July 16, 1945. The United States' long-range missiles are tested at White Sands Missile Range. This is the alternate landing site for the space shuttle orbital missions. This is where we find the White Sands National Monument, with its drifts of gypsum as white as new-fallen snow. The area contains cruel deserts and alpine ski areas, trout streams and some of the state's best agricultural areas and oil and gas fields. Although much of it is high desert, it is watered by the state's second river, the Pecos. Along the Pecos we find this area's largest cities.

This is where Smokey the Bear, a black-bear cub whose paws were burned in a forest fire, got his start. Smokey became the symbol of fire prevention for the U.S. Forest Service.

The southeast is where we find the Mescalero Apache Indian Reservation and the biggest flocks of wild turkey and probably the biggest concentrations of mule deer in the state. It is home to healthy populations of antelope and elk. It's a big-game hunter's paradise.

The Southeast holds amazing stone ruins of ancient cities in the Salinas National Monument. It is the home of petroglyphs at Three Rivers, and the visitor can find out the latest in high tech science as exemplified by the Sun Spot Observatory and the White Sands Missile Range.

But enough of this introduction. Let's take a look at the southeast.

Salinas
National Monument

Until 10 years ago, we had Abo State Monument and Quarai State Monument, 30 miles away from one of the least visited of all national monuments—Gran Quivira. All three of these fascinating reminders of the three centuries past are located in the northwest corner of our Southeast Region and now make up the Salinas National Monument. They are only an hour's drive south of Albuquerque, but few Duke City residents have ever heard of them.

Charles F. Lummis, one of the most charismatic writers about this state, wrote of Quarai, "An edifice in ruins, but so tall, so solemn, so dominant of that strange lonely landscape. . . . On the Rhine it would be a superlative, in the wilderness of the Manzano it is a miracle."

The Spanish conquistadores first saw this part of New Spain in 1583. They found two different Indians—the Piro and the Tiguex ("tiwa")—who spoke different languages. There were cool fresh water springs at Abo and Quarai (pronounced "kwah-rye," as in rye bread and peaceful people numbering more than 700 at Abo and 900 at Quarai. There were perhaps as many as 3,000 at another larger pueblo farther to the east, which they called Las Humanas, or Las Xumanas, or any of a dozen other spellings. The name had nothing to do with our English word for humans. Las Humanas had no visible surface water, but early records tell us that the Indians at the big pueblo had dug at least 34 wells, about three quarters of a mile away from the pueblo, from which they carried their water every day.

Las Humanas (which we now call Gran Quivira) was built on a low hill, giving it a commanding view in all directions. It is not known whether or not it was planned for defense, but a century after the Spanish arrived, it was under constant attack from roving banks of Apache and Comanche. Most of the Indians sat astride the horse, which came to the New World with the Spaniards and made the hit-and-run tactics of the Comanche much more dangerous.

At first the Spanish Franciscans stationed priests at Abo and Quarai, then conducted a mission to the much bigger Gran Quivira. Fray Alonzo de Benavides first preached in the plaza of Gran Quivira in 1627. Fray Francisco Fonte arrived in Abo in 1621. In 1629, Fray Esteban de Perea, who was in charge of the entire area, assigned Father Francisco Acevedo to Abo as a second missionary. Father Acevedo later became "guardian" or headman of the Abo mission. He had big plans, and he was vigorous in carrying them out. He built the huge stone church of San Gregorio de Abo on the ruins of an earlier church.

Today, San Gregorio rises above the sparsely vegetated plain, reminding me of the hymn "Rock of Ages." It has stood empty for 300 years, but it is living still in spite of fire and sword, in spite of drought, in spite of Comanche attacks and in spite of the Pueblo Revolt, in which it was nearly burned in 1680.

Eight miles north of Mountainair, at the tiny town of Punta de Agua, is a turnoff to an even more beautiful ancient pueblo mission. This is Quarai, established by De Perea in 1630. De Perea built a small church, but when the indefatigable Fray Francisco de Acevedo took over its operation, a huge and very beautiful stone church was built. This is the Church of the Immaculate Conception, whose internal measurements are 104 feet by 46 feet. Its remarkably clean lines, sharp edges and excellent planning remain a tribute to those Spanish priests who labored here more than 300 years ago. It has a stone floor instead of the hard-packed adobe of most mission churches. Early travelers wrote that the congregation had a very good choir that sang the praises of God from the choir loft.

In Gran Quivira, which is now reached on paved N. M. 55, 25 miles south of the town of Mountainair, the biggest church of all was built. An earlier mission church, San Isidro, had served the population well until the parish priest left. Then devout Indians from Abo, with their priest, walked for eight hours each way to celebrate mass on Sunday in Gran Quivira. But things changed when Father Diego de Santander arrived in Gran Quivira in 1659.

Picking a site just outside of the pueblo itself, Father Santander sketched out his huge church, the Mission of San Buenaventura. Certainly he planned it to last and to be a comfortable home for those who labored in God's vineyard, saving souls for Christ. The outside length of the church is 140 feet! The walls are 6 feet thick. It was built of the blue-gray limestone rock common to the area and laid up with adobe cement.

Even today, it is easy to see that this was a beautiful building, a well-planned edifice with shaded benches in rooms for the people to wait upon the priest with their problems or petitions. An inner courtyard offered a lovely place for the mission priest to read his Holy Office, to tend his small garden or just to have a few minutes to himself, away from his many duties.

By 1650, all three great missions were in the height of their glory. But storm clouds were gathering. These pueblos had always prospered by trading salt from the salt lakes (Salinas) to the east. Now Comanche raids shut off that source of wealth. Repeated droughts had ruined the agricultural basis of their economy. The steady conflict between the priests, who wanted most of all to make converts, and the civil administrators, who wanted most of all to make a profit, continued to divide the peaceful pueblos. Enforced labor on the *encomiendas* was resisted by the Indians. The Apache, who saw some of their members captured by the Spaniards and sold into slavery, raided more often, and their raids were more deadly. Now the Comanche and Apache wanted more than a few measures of corn; now they wanted the death of the Spaniards and of all Indians who supported the Spanish.

Buffalo meat from the wide plains no longer came to the plaza of Abo and Quarai in trade for corn and chiles. The vineyards and fields became scorched under the merciless sun, without rain for several years at a time.

In the early 1670s all three of these grand missions, with their peaceful peoples, were almost deserted. Many of the people, tired of fighting the Comanche and Apache raids, moved west to the Rio Grande pueblos, especially to the one near modern-day Socorro.

When the Pueblo Revolt of 1680 flared up, the last of the Salinas Pueblo Indians followed their Spanish friends and masters to Socorro and then south to the vicinity of El Paso del Norte. They never returned.

The story of the Salinas pueblos is one of the most interesting in all of New Mexico. Today, all three are protected by the National Park Service. Mountainair has a good visitors center. Interpretive movies tell the stories of the salt pueblos, their rise and fall.

Although picnicking is allowed at all three sites, there is no camping allowed in any of them. The nearest **camping** is at **Manzano State Park**, at the town of Manzano, 13 miles northwest of Mountainair on N.M. 14. There are spaces for RVs, and a dump station is provided. Rates are the same as at all other state parks ($7 and $11). It's at 7,200 feet above sea level, which makes it quite cool. State park phone number is **847-2820**.

Although Mountainair is in the center of the three attractions, it does not seem to be much interested in tourism. I've eaten at **El Coyote** ($) a few times and learned to beware of the green chili, which is not for beginners. There is also the **Pueblo Cafe** ($), in the historic Shaffer Hotel. The visitors center for the national monument was once in this hotel, but that's no longer true. It is on U. S. 60, one block west of the junction with N.M. 55, which goes south to Gran Quivira.

I certainly hope that you see all of the Salinas Monument, but if you can see only one of the three, please pick Quarai. Its beautiful setting, classic lines and peaceful atmosphere make the trip more than worth it.

Valley of Fires

It was once the hottest place in North America. A short 1,500 years ago, about when Romulus, the last emperor of Rome, was deposed by a barbarian army, a gigantic volcanic eruption spewed forth from Little Black Peak, sending molten lava streaming down the gentle valley slope for 42 miles. This is perhaps the newest of all lava flows in North America, still sharp-edged and fascinating. This lava flow is just 4 miles west of the town of Carrizozo, on N.M. 60, which runs from Carrizozo to San Antonio and is a junction with Interstate 25.

Valley of Fires used to be a state park but is now operated by the Bureau of Land Management. The lava and the vegetation that grows everywhere in this desolate lunar landscape have a different, stark form of beauty. A quarter-mile nature trail gives you easy walking to see some of its twisted black world.

Twenty **camping** sites are available; five of them have electricity, ten have water. There is a comfort station. Camping fee is $7, discounted by half if you have a Golden Eagle Passport. Electricity is $4 more, with no discount. If you are self-contained and enjoy using a primitive site, you get by for $5 a day, or only $2.50 with the passport. For more information about Valley of Fires, phone **624-1790.** That's the Roswell office of the Bureau of Land Management. Ask for Paul T. Happel; he's most knowledgeable. If he isn't in the Roswell office, he is probably out at the Valley of Fires site.

Valley of Fires State Park. (Photo by Mark Nohl, New Mexico Economic and Tourism Department.)

Carrizozo

Just 4 miles east of the Valley of Fires recreation area and at the important junction of U.S. 380 (east and west) with U.S. 54 (north and south), we come to the pleasant little town of Carrizozo. It was originally called Carrizo ("reeds" in Spanish), which is the name of the nearby springs. The El Paso and Northeastern Railroad arrived here in 1899 to haul cattle from the large ranches of the area. James Allcock, the foreman for a local cattle ranch, added the second zo, which indicates abundance.

WHERE TO STAY

ACCOMMODATIONS

Four Winds Motel—$$
Has 22 rooms. At the junction of the two highways. **648-2356.**

Cross Roads Motel—$$
Has 22 rooms. **648-2373.**

Dos Amigos—$
Offers 10 rooms. **648-2511.**

Sands Motel—$
Has 8 motel rooms. On U.S. 54 going south out of town, **648-2989.**

CAMPGROUNDS

Sands Motel and RV Park
Located with the Sands Motel on U.S. 54 going south out of town. Offers 25 nice looking spaces with all hookups, shower room and laundry facilities. Priced at $13 per night. Gives Good Sam discount. **648-2989.**

Tularosa

Just 12 miles northwest of Alamogordo, on U.S. 54, you'll pass through the lovely little town of Tularosa ("red reeds" in Spanish). Be sure to stop for a few minutes and walk around the shaded grounds of the Franciscan Mission church on the west side of the highway. It is beautifully designed and was built in 1865 as a mission to the Apache. I think people had more time to "live" in those days, when a shaded portico was considered a good use of space. The churchyard also has an interesting monument, in Spanish, to the fallen soldiers of the battle of Cerro Redondo in 1868.

Fifteen miles north of Tularosa is the turnoff leading to the **Three Rivers Petroglyph Site.** The turnoff is well marked, and the 5-mile road to the site is paved. There's a 1,400-yard long walk leading to more than 5,000 individual carvings, where prehistoric Indians who once lived here carved their drawings on the sides of black rocks. Some drawings have religious meaning of some kind; others depict the game animals of the area. There's a lot to see, and there is also a nice primitive campground, which makes a quiet and peaceful spot to spend the night. From the ridge where most of the petroglyphs are carved, you can see the gleaming White Sands National Monument far to the southwest, and 12,003-foot Sierra Blanca marks the eastern rampart of what geologists call the Tularosa Basin.

Did this symbol have a religious meaning? Or did it stake out a claim of ownership? Or did it record the passing of a roving band of Indians? Three Rivers Petroglyphs Site.

Fort Sumner

Fort Sumner, located at the junction of U.S. 84 and U.S. 60, out on the high, dry eastern plains of New Mexico, stakes its chief claim to fame on the story of Billy the Kid, a.k.a. William Bonney; his real name was Henry McCarty. Even the top athletic event of the area is a tombstone race. Believe it or not, contestants go over an obstacle course while carrying 80-pound tombstones! The event is based on the history of Billy the Kid's tombstone, which was twice stolen and taken off to states that wanted yet another attraction: California and Texas. The first governor of the New Mexico Territory had to send the county sheriff all the way to California to bring it back. Now the tombstone is where it belongs, on the grave of Billy the Kid, just a couple of miles south of the town of Fort Sumner.

One of the biggest and best privately owned museums in the Southwest, the **Billy the Kid Museum**, is right on the main street of Fort Sumner. Operated by Don and Lula Sweet, it contains memorabilia of this teenage outlaw, mementos of the original fort and lots of Indian artifacts. Well worth the $2 entrance fee. Open every day 8:30 A.M.–5:00 P.M. May 15 through Sept. 15. Closed Sun. Sept. 15 through May 15.

Fort Sumner was built to house soldiers who fought the Apache, who once called all of southeastern New Mexico theirs. During the Civil War and shortly thereafter, the soldiers won the battle with the Apache and the Navajo, who had threatened white settlers for so long. It was decided to move all of the hostile Indians to Fort Sumner and keep them on a long stretch of woods, watered by the Pecos River. The journey of the defeated Indians to this area, known as the Bosque Redondo, went down in history as the Long Walk. The hapless Indians were kept here for five years, and hundreds died of disease, malnutrition and exposure. John Chisum brought cattle to Fort Sumner to feed the Indians. Remember that name. You'll run into it again as we follow the trail of Billy the Kid. Cattlemen Goodnight and Loving also trailed Texas longhorns to Fort Sumner and thus started the New Mexico cattle industry.

In 1868 General William Sherman inspected the Bosque Redondo situation and decided to send the Indians home. The relocation reservation was an admitted failure. In 1870 the buildings of Fort Sumner were sold to Lucien Bonaparte Maxwell, who probably was the biggest landowner in the history of the United States, as he already owned the huge Maxwell Grant near Las Vegas. His total land holdings amounted to more than 2 million acres!

When Lucien B. Maxwell retired, he came to Fort Sumner and remodeled the old officers' quarters as his own home. In that home, Sheriff Pat Garrett gunned down Billy the Kid in 1881.

Be sure to see the **Old Fort Sumner Museum**, located just to the east of the Fort Sumner State Monument, where both Billy the Kid and Lucien Maxwell are buried.

Sumner Lake, formed by a dam on the Pecos River, is just 10 miles north and 6 miles west of the town of Fort Sumner on N.M. 203. Fishing is good here for walleyes, catfish, both white and black bass, bluegills and crappies. The waters from Sumner Lake are used for irrigation all the way down the valley of the Pecos, so its level fluctuates drastically. Nevertheless, fishing has remained good even though, the park manager tells me, the lake has not been stocked since 1984. Biggest crowds are in May, when the walleye fishing is phenomenal. The state park offers 20 camping sites, 18 of which have electricity. There's a dump station, two boat ramps and two comfort stations with showers. **355-2541.**

Speaking of fishing, the historic **Bosque Redondo**, on the southern approaches to Fort Sumner, offers good black-bass fishing. This land was bought with Land and Water Conservation Fund monies. It offers camping and a fishing dock that is excellent for children's use. There are no hookups, but portable toilets are provided.

In Fort Sumner, there are two motels, the **Oasis** ($$) **1700 E. Sumner Ave.**, which has 28 units, **355-7414**, and the **Coronado** ($$) **305 W. Sumner Ave., 355-2466**.

De Baca General Hospital, a 25-bed facility with good equipment and staffing, is located at **500 N. Tenth St., 355-2414.**

The legend of Billy the Kid runs all through the history of this part of New Mexico. We won't give you all the story. Besides Fort Sumner, the towns of Mesilla, Lincoln, Capitan and even Stinking Springs all play a part in the story. You'll be able to put the pieces together when you tour the museum at Lincoln. Was Billy the Kid a hired killer or a young man fighting for what he thought was right? You make the choice.

The Elusive Tombstone

BILLY THE KID'S TOMBSTONE WAS STOLEN IN 1950, FOR 26 YEARS IT REMAINED A MYSTERY UNTIL 1976, WHEN JOE BOWLIN RECOVERED IT IN GRANBURY, TEXAS

STOLEN AGAIN IN FEB. 1981 - RECOVERED FEB. 12, 1981 IN HUNTINGTON BEACH, CALIF.

GOV. BRUCE KING ARRANGED FOR SHERIFF "BIG JOHN McBRIDE TO PERSONALLY RETURN THE MARKER VIA TEXAS INTERNATIONAL AIRLINES.

CHAMBER OFFICIALS, WITH JARVIS P. GARRETT, SON OF PAT GARRETT OFFICIALLY RESET THE MARKER IN "IRON SHACKLES" MAY 30, 1981

OLD FORT MUSEUM
CONTAINS HISTORICAL DOCUMENTS ON "BILLY THE KID"

Self explanatory, the Tombstone of Billy the Kid was well traveled.

Clovis

In contrast to some of the truly old places in New Mexico, Clovis didn't even exist until 1907. At that time it was known as Riley's Switch, and the Santa Fe Railroad decided to build a branch line out to this area, connecting with the main line at Belen. The railroad looked back to about A.D. 486 to pick a name and chose Clovis, in honor of the Frankish king who defeated the Germans and converted to Christianity, thus changing the history of the continent of Europe for all time to come.

HISTORY

Long before the coming of Europeans, this area had been home to prehistoric Indian tribes who tracked mastodons and saber-toothed tigers over these plains, as evidenced by the discovery of finely made arrow and spear points, known as Clovis points. When the warriors of these Plains tribes discovered the horse—and stole them from the Spanish newcomers—life was greatly changed. Horseback Indian raiders were the scourge of the area for centuries.

Despite only scrub vegetation and absolutely flat land for hundreds of miles to the north, south and east, Clovis promptly started growing when the railroad came and is now a city of about 35,000 people. Today Clovis is the location of the Cannon Air Force Base, a stabilizing force in the economy of this high-plains agricultural and ranching area. Another stabilizing influence and the source of steady paychecks is the Clovis campus of Eastern New Mexico University.

FESTIVALS AND EVENTS

Pioneer Days
First week or so of June. Recalls when homesteaders and ranchers first fought the elements in Curry County. Features a parade, a Professional Rodeo Cowboys Association rodeo and pageant. For information, call the Chamber of Commerce at **763-3435, 215 N. Main.**

Gem and Mineral Show
Takes place in the last few days of July. Call Don Hogg at **762-5901.**

Clovis Music Festival

In mid-Aug. Features music of all kinds, from teeny-bopper rock to gospel and sock hops, with exhibits of antique cars. **763-3435**.

Curry County Fair

Last week of Aug., first week of Sept. All of the usual competitions for crop and livestock growers, plus exhibits and entertainment, square dancing, tractor pulls and who-knows-what-else. Everyone has fun. **763-6505**.

Cannon Air Force Base Open House

Usually in Sept. Features aerobatics of the famed Air Force Thunderbirds and an air show. For information, phone **784-3311**.

Allsups Races

In late Oct. Features everything from a half marathon to a 1-mile fun run. Phone J.R. Jacobs at **769-2311**.

Arts and Crafts Show

Scheduled for Nov. in the North Plains Mall. Call Kathy Adair for information at **762-5021**.

——— SEEING AND DOING ———

Hillcrest Park and Zoo, at Tenth and Sycamore, offers a petting zoo for children, a good variety of birds and animals for all ages, a swimming pool, a sunken garden, a public golf course and soccer and softball fields. Admission is 50 cents for adults, 25 cents for kids. Call **762-1101** for information.

Ned Houk Park is just 6 miles north of Clovis. It provides a stocked fishing lake, volleyball courts, archery range, hiking trails, motorcycle dirt track and a model airplane 'drome. In addition, there's the Pappy Thornton Farm Museum, with its fine collection of vintage farm equipment.

Caprock Amphitheater, which we described in the **Tucumcari** section, is about 45 miles north. Melodrama featuring—who else?—Billy the Kid.

R & S Gun Shop and Indoor Range. If you are interested in guns and pistol shooting, a surprise is waiting for you at this gun shop and complete indoor pistol range. As good a stock of merchandise as you'll find anywhere, along with people who can really talk guns with authority. It's just a block from the old railroad depot, a block south of the old Hotel Clovis. **762-1853**.

Eula Mae Edwards Memorial Museum, on the Clovis campus of ENMU, features good displays of prehistoric artifacts, such as mastodon bones and the weapons of Stone Age Clovis residents who hunted those pre-Columbian beasts. **769-2811.**

Oasis State Park is just a few miles southwest of Clovis. Head west on 84, and just as you clear Clovis, you'll see the sign pointing south on N.M. 467. It is just about 14 miles away. This state park made a good impression on me both times I stayed overnight. It offers 13 camping sites with electricity and 23 developed sites. Surprisingly, it has many big trees. Shade is often at a premium here in southeastern New Mexico, which is blessed with about 350 days of sunshine every year. Those trees were planted in 1902 by a homesteader named Will Taylor, and we all owe him a vote of thanks. Another reason I liked the park is that I was awakened in the early morning by the singing of coyotes, lots of coyotes. There's a small fishing lake that is always productive of catfish, and in the winter it comes up with a lot of good trout, thanks to the state's hatchery trucks. The little lake was once fed by an artesian spring, but now it is filled from wells that tap the famous Oglalla Aquifer. Lots of bird life, a nice place. **356-5331.**

Blackwater Draw Museum is halfway between Clovis and Portales on U.S. 70. The museum is located at one of the most important archaeological finds on the continent. The Carnegie Institute, the Smithsonian Institution and the Academy of Natural Sciences have all supported archaeological work here. It is now under the direction of ENMU at Portales. For more information, call **562-2254.**

———— WHERE TO STAY ————

ACCOMMODATIONS

Holiday Inn—$$$
Luxury class. Offers an indoor pool, restaurant, racket ball court and Jacuzzi. **2700 Mabry Dr., 762-4491 or 1-800-HOLIDAY.**

Sands Motel—$$
Has an outdoor heated pool and an outdoor play area for kids. **1400 Mabry Dr., 763-3439.**

Best Western La Vista Inn—$$
Offers a pool and free HBO. **1516 Mabry Dr., 762-3808.**

Motel 6—$$
Offers cable TV in every room. **2620 Mabry Dr., 762-3186.**

Super 8—$$
Cable TV, free Continental breakfast. **2920 Mabry Dr., 769-1953.**

Kings Inn Motor Hotel—$$
Offers pool, free coffee and cable television. **1320 Mabry Dr., 762-4486.**

Days Inn—$$
Offers free HBO and free tennis courts. **1720 Mabry Dr., 762-2971.**

Comfort Inn—$$
Offers free HBO, game room with free pool table. **1616 Mabry Dr., 762-4591.**

CAMPGROUNDS

KOA Campground
4707 W. Seventh. The usual KOA quality. Rates start at $12 with all hookups. **763-4650.**

West Park Inn and RV Park
1500 W. Seventh. Offers all hookups starting at a flat rate of $12.50 per night. 10 percent senior discount. **763-7218.**

———— WHERE TO EAT ————

El Charro—$$
805 E. First. A *charro* is a fancily dressed good-roping, good-riding *mexicano*. Now you know what to expect here. **769-1345.**

El Monterey—$$
118 Mitchell. Good Mexican food. **763-4031.**

La Villa Steak House—$$
600 Pile. Gets you back to the American cuisine, featuring steaks. **762-3838.**

Ranchers and Farmers Steakhouse—$$
816 Lexington. Another good spot for steaks. **763-6335.**

Guadalajara—$$
916 W. First. Tasty Mexican food. **769-9965.**

Kelley's—$$
2208 N. Prince. Just plain good family eating. **762-0044.**

SERVICES

I think Clovis ought to take a bow for yet another reason. It has no fewer than 67 churches. You ought to be able to find your church here.

This is the Torreon (tower in English) built by earliest Spanish colonists to protect themselves against Apache raiding parties.

Portales

Just 18 miles southwest of Clovis on U.S. 70 lies Portales, a different sort of town. Portales is the home of Eastern New Mexico University, and it has the look of a peaceful college town. Lots of trees, clean, quiet streets and friendly people make Portales a standout on the eastern Plains. Many towns lay claim to being friendly, but Portales calls itself the "Warm Heart of the Sunbelt," and the welcome sign to Portales says, "Home of 12,000 friendly folks, and three old grouches"—or words to that effect. With that sign, Portales tries to stake its claim.

Slightly fewer than 4,000 students are enrolled at ENMU. The major crops grown in the Portales area are wheat, milo, corn, cotton, potatoes and peanuts. Peanut processing is a big business here.

Nearby Portales Springs, where water trickled out of a series of caves, was a stop on the cattle-drive trails that led northwest to Denver. The area's first settler, Doak Good, ran about 400 head of cattle in this area in the 1880s, and Josh Morrison built the first store here about a year before the railroad arrived. The present town of Portales grew up around that store.

FESTIVALS AND EVENTS

Heritage Days
In May. For information, call the Chamber of Commerce, 7th and Abilene, **356-8541**.

Annual Homecoming at ENMU
In Oct. Everyone turns out for this. **356-8541**.

Peanut Festival—ENMU
In Oct. Arts and crafts. Peanut Olympics. **356-8541**.

SEEING AND DOING

Blackwater Site and Museum. This famous archaeological dig is administered by ENMU; it is the property of the state of New Mexico. Scientists found proof of human occupation here. Man has used this area since the late Pleistocene era. Scientists also found the bones of the hairy mammoth and the saber-toothed tiger, which lived here at the same time as man. Then the Blackwater area was a large freshwater pond. But the pond dried up about 7,000 years ago. The museum is 7 miles northeast of Portales on U.S. 70. Open Tues.–Sat. 10 A.M.–5 P.M., Sun. 12 P.M.–5 P.M. Admission is $2 for adults, $1 for children and senior citizens. **562-2202.**

ENMU's Natural History Museum, on the campus, features live and stuffed specimens of much of the wildlife of eastern New Mexico. **356-8541.**

Jack Williamson Science Fiction Library contains manuscripts and letters from Jack Williamson, one of the most successful pioneers in the sci-fi genre. Here are housed letters to and from most of the science fiction greats, including Ray Bradbury. **356-8541.**

——— WHERE TO STAY ———

ACCOMMODATIONS

Dunes Motel—$$
Heated pool. Close to Eastern New Mexico University. Gives AARP discount. On the Roswell Highway, **356-6668.**

Portales Inn—$$
Offers complete hotel and restaurant accommodations. **2318 W. Third St., 359-1208.**

Hillcrest Motel—$
On the Roswell Highway, **359-1215.**

Sands Motel—$
1130 W. First, 356-4424.

Super 8 Motel—$$
Continental breakfast, spa, 24-hour desk, suites available. On the Roswell Highway. **356-8518, 1-800-800-8000.**

CAMPGROUNDS

Your best bet is the pleasant, peaceful surroundings of **Oasis State Park,** a few miles north of town. See Seeing and Doing section in Clovis. The **KOA** at Clovis is just 18 miles away. See Campground section in Clovis.

———— WHERE TO EAT ————

There are many good eating spots in Portales, but I want to recommend two above all others.

Wagon Wheel Cafe —$$
521 W. Seventeenth. Don't miss this tiny cafe. It doesn't look like much on the outside, or the inside for that matter, but the Mexican cuisine is absolutely tops! 356-5036.

Cattle Baron—$
1600 S. Avenue D. Has locations in Ruidoso, Hobbs, Roswell and Las Cruces. A good seafood and steak restaurant, along with complete lounge. Varied menu lists a cup of chowder all the way up to a lobster tail and prime rib dinner. 356-5587.

Riccardi's Italian Restaurant—$
813 South Avenue C Place. Authentic Italian food in an atmosphere not generally found on the high plains of eastern New Mexico. 356-4431.

La Hacienda—$
909 North Avenue K. Favorite with locals. Outstanding Mexican food. 359-0280.

Capitan, New Mexico, honors the real "Smokey the Bear," Forest Service symbol of fire prevention.

═══ Carlsbad Caverns ═══

First of all, to avoid problems, I must warn you that the world's greatest cave—Carlsbad Caverns—is not located at the town of Carlsbad. It is 27 miles southwest of Carlsbad, 7 miles on excellent park service road west of Whites City.

Carlsbad Caverns is by far the most majestic cave ever discovered on this earth. It has stalactites and stalagmites, flow rock, every color of the rainbow painted in stone, and lakes of still waters more than 1,700 feet below the dry New Mexico landscape. Weird and lovely sculptures in limestone are still being created by the slow but certain activity of tiny drops of water. The force of dripping water caused a 100,000-ton rock of limestone to slip and come crashing down into the cavern below it.

How big are the caverns? Well, one room has a floor space that covers 14 acres! The largest underground room in America, it is so big that a 30-story building could be erected in it without touching the top.

You can experience the beauty of Carlsbad Caverns in an easy two-hour walk on blacktopped paths, protected by guardrails and illuminated enough to make it safe. That walking tour starts at the entrance, where the bats come in and out. I forgot to mention the bats? Hundreds of thousands of them live and bear their young in the cool darkness inside the cave. When they go out to feed on insects—which happens at sunset—they exit at the rate of about 5,000 bats a minute, making a dark spiraling cloud. These Mexican free-tailed bats are harmless to humans and one of the most efficient insect eaters the world has ever known. They are only seen at exit time, when they leave to go foraging on the wing. They return before dawn and swing into their upside-down roosting sites. Sadly, we must report that there once were 12 million of the bats, consuming 100 tons of insects each and every night. Today only about 375,000 bats are left.

The walking tour doesn't include the bat sighting or the room where they spend their daylight hours. The tour continues by slow stages down to the big room, where there is even a snack bar. More important, an elevator takes you back to the surface. If you can't handle the easy walking tour, you can use the elevator both ways. On the big-room level, you can walk amid monster statues, colossal formations, stalactites and stalagmites, then have a cup of coffee and return to the sunlit world above.

No one really knows how extensive the underground caverns are. In 1984 park rangers crawled through a narrow entrance and found themselves in New Cave, a tremendous unadorned series of rooms and channels that go on for miles. Special ranger-led tours of New Cave are arranged upon request. There may be other, still undiscovered caves, but their discovery would only put Carlsbad Caverns farther out front as the foremost cave attraction in the world.

In 1985 Readers Digest Books put out a lovely book entitled *Our National Parks*. It contains a thorough description of the process that formed Carlsbad over the last hundred million years and that is still at work, adding to its formations at a rate measured in centimeters per century. The main reason I recommend that chapter of reading is that I wrote it. I've been a Carlsbad enthusiast for 30 years. For your own sake, don't miss seeing Carlsbad Caverns, the most beautiful cave in the world.

Admission to the caverns is $4 for adults, half price for holders of the Golden Age Passport, $2 for children ages 6 to 15 and free for children under 6 years of age. Tours of the entire cavern can be enjoyed from 8:30 A.M. until 2:00 P.M. Tours of the big room only can be enjoyed starting any time from 8:30 A.M. to 3:30 P.M. Every night at 7:00 P.M. the rangers give an interesting free talk about the bat flight, at the walking entrance to the

Temple of the Sun, Big Room, Carlsbad Caverns.
Courtesy of the National Park Service.

cave. Stay on after the talk, and watch the bats head out for a night of insect eating. It's a sight you won't soon forget.

In addition to its unsurpassed underground beauty, Carlsbad Caverns National Park offers an interesting 9.5-mile driving tour of the surface features. This is for automobiles only. Don't try it with a trailer or a motor home.

WHERE TO STAY

ACCOMMODATIONS

Best Western—$$
Offers 62 rooms, restaurant and swimming pool. **Whites City, 785-2291** or **1-800-CAVERNS.**

Guadalupe Inn—$$
Offers 44 rooms, restaurant and swimming pool. **Whites City, 1-800-CAVERNS.**

Walnut Canyon Inn—$$
Restaurant and swimming pool. **Whites City, 1-800-CAVERNS.**

CAMPGROUNDS

There is an RV park at Whites City, reached by calling **1-800-CAVERNS** or **785-2291**.

For many good accommodations of all kinds, see Carlsbad. The town is only 20 miles north on good highways.

═══ Lovington ═══

Twenty miles northwest of Hobbs on N.M. 18, the town of Lovington was founded in 1908 by Robert Florence Love, on his homestead farm. Lovington slept along through the years as a farming and ranching community, until the Denton Pool Discovery after World War II turned it into an oil-boom town. Today, it is prosperous, dedicated to the oil industry and not at all oriented toward tourism. Still, there's lots going on here.

── FESTIVALS AND EVENTS ──

Lovington Auto Show
In Apr. at the fairgrounds. If you're interested in any facet of old automobiles, there's something here for you. **396-5311.**

Country Music Festival
In July. Takes place right on the lawn of the county courthouse. Admission is free. For information, call **396-5311.**

Fourth of July
Lovington goes all out with fireworks. One of the best displays in the state. Admission is free.

Lizard Race
On the glorious Fourth of July, Lovington stages this annual race, with about 60 lizards competing for the title of fastest lizard. **396-5311.**

Lea County Fair and Rodeo
In mid-Aug. One of the biggest county fairs in the nation, as you might expect when you realize that Lea County is the biggest oil-producing county in the nation. **396-5311.**

Southeastern Arts and Crafts Festival
Early Nov. With more than 100 exhibitors from all over the Southwest. For more information, call the Chamber of Commerce at **396-5311, 1535 N. Main.**

—————— WHERE TO STAY ——————

ACCOMMODATIONS

Lovington Inn—$$
1600 W. Avenue D, 396-5346.

Mack's Motel—$$
805 W. Avenue D, 396-2588.

Power's Motel—$$
215 E. Avenue B, 396-3627.

Western Inn —$$
2212 S. Main, 396-3635.

—————— WHERE TO EAT ——————

Lovington Inn—$$
1600 W. Avenue D, 396-5346.

Ribeye Steak House—$$
1422 S. Main, 396-8553.

Artesia

Roughly halfway between Roswell and Carlsbad, the thriving community of Artesia owes much to liquid from under the earth. It was originally homesteaded by J.F. Truitt, a Union soldier, who was attracted by the flowing spring water. The old stage line stopped here because of the water. But in 1923 a different liquid was discovered underground—oil! The oil industry is today the leading economic impetus to Artesia's growth. The big Navajo Refinery in Artesia is the state's largest. Irrigated farming is also strong in the Artesia vicinity, using water from impoundments on the Pecos River as well as from aquifers. It's a good place to live but is not tourism oriented.

Laid up stone walls up to five feet thick typify the construction of the mission churches of Abo, Quarai and Gran Quivira.

———— WHERE TO STAY ————

ACCOMMODATIONS

Best Western Pecos Inn—$$
Offers indoor heated pool, good restaurant and lounge. **2209 W. Main, 748-3324** or **1-800-676-7481.**

West Winds Motel—$$
Has a swimming pool and HBO. **1820 S. First, 746-9801**.

Starlite Motel—$$
1018 S. First, 746-9834.

CAMPGROUNDS

The Odd Stop RV Park
On U.S. 285 on the south side of town. **748-3779.**

———— WHERE TO EAT ————

Artesia Country Club—$$$
Twenty-sixth and Richey, **746-2055.**

Kwan Den Restaurant—$$
2209 Pecospecos. Good Chinese and American menu. **746-9851.**

La Fonda—$$
210 W. Main, 746-9377.

Hobbs

This city of 35,000 people is just 3 miles outside of Texas, but like most of that state, it has suffered through the deep depression in the oil and gas industry. Hobbs was named for 1907 homesteaders J.B., James and Grandma Hobbs. It never amounted to much until the state's #1 oil well came in, in 1928. Since then Hobbs has bloomed and faded along with the oil industry.

But there has always been more than oil in Hobbs—rich red beef. Today it is processed and sold to the Japanese. At one time the Hat Ranch had 60 employees to round up no fewer than 31,000 calves for market per season.

Two colleges, New Mexico Junior College and College of the Southwest, add a $9 million payroll to the Hobbs economy.

——FESTIVALS AND EVENTS——

Cinco de Mayo
The celebration of Mexico's independence, takes place in City Park. Cinco de Mayo means "fifth of May," of course. Call Hermilo Ojeda at **393-8053**.

Miss New Mexico Pageant
The pageant, which you know all about, showcases feminine beauty of New Mexico. Takes place at the R.N. Tydings Auditorium. The dates vary so call Phil Millender at **393-3463** for information.

Juneteenth Celebration
Sponsored by the NAACP. Phone Mattie Johnson at **393-8878**.

National Soaring Glider Championship
In July. Call the Chamber of Commerce at **397-3202**.

Pro-Am Golf Tournament
In July, at both the Hobbs Country Club and the Ocotillo golf courses. **392-5561**.

Softball Tournament
In July. Sponsored by the USSA. For information call the Chamber of Commerce at **397-3202**.

Lea County Fair
August 11–15, **397-3202**.

Hoedown Days

In late Sept. Gives Hobbs residents the chance to have one of their own "arrested" and placed in the "jail" by payment of a $10 arrest fee. The culprit is then tried before a kangaroo court and usually fined. It's all part of the fun that includes performances by country music stars. Four top country bands are selected from dozens that apply, and the lucky four play to capacity audiences at Norte Vista Plaza. There's also a parade, hot air balloon rides, a chili cook-off, a beard-growing contest and a *jalapeño*-eating contest. (If you don't know about *jalapeños*, see The New Mexican Chile.) Lots of dancing and fun for all.

When you get to Hobbs, please ask for a more detailed calendar of events. Get it at the chamber office at **400 N. Marland**. If you're lost, call them at **397-3202**. Ask for events coordinator.

—— SEEING AND DOING ——

Lea County Cowboy Hall of Fame, at **5317 Lovington Hwy**. on the campus of the Junior College. Interesting exhibits that prove that the cowboy surely played a part—and still plays a part—in the development of this area. Open 8 A.M.–5 P.M. Mon.–Thurs., Fri. until 3 P.M., **392-4510**. **Confederate Air Force Museum,** located at the Hobbs-Lea County airport. Usually open from 8 A.M. until sunset, but if the door is locked, just telephone Bill Razo at **392-5342**.

Thelma A. Webber Southwest Heritage Room, in the library of the College of the Southwest on N.M. 18. Collection of prehistoric, Indian, pioneer and oil-discovery artifacts. **392-6561, ext. 315**.

Soaring Society of America. An association of 16,000 soaring glider enthusiasts, located at the airport. For information, call **392-1177**.

Hobbs offers one municipal **golf course**, a good 18-holer, with carts available. Located on the Lovington Hwy. Phone number is **397-9297**. The other course is the Country Club, for members only.

—— WHERE TO STAY ——

ACCOMMODATIONS

Motel 6—$$

Has 80 rooms. **509 N. Marland, 393-0221**.

Executive Inn—$$
Offers 62 rooms. **211 N. Marland, 397-6541.**

Hobbs Motor Inn—$$
Has 76 rooms. **501 N. Marland, 397-3251.**

Inn Keepers Motel—$$
Offers 63 rooms. **309 N. Marland, 397-7171.**

CAMPGROUNDS

Harry McAdams State Park
5000 State Park Rd. Camping sites, some with electricity at the usual state park rates of $7 for developed sites and $11 for electric sites. Comfort stations with showers, playgrounds and a lot of interesting exhibits describing the history of the area. **392-5845.**

——— WHERE TO EAT ———

Hobbs is not a small town. For proof, there are three locations for Ma Brown's Hamburgers, three Pizza Huts and almost every franchised food store you've ever heard of. In addition, I'd like to recommend:

Cattle Baron—$
1930 N. Grimes. Big menu, reasonable prices. **393-2800.**

Lamplighter Restaurant—$$
114 E. Marland, 393-8350.

Peking Restaurant—$
2404 N. Grimes. Good Chinese food. **392-2411.**

Saxony Room—$$
At the Hobbs Motor Inn. **501 N. Marland.** American Cuisine. **397-3251.**

══════ Carlsbad ══════

Since 1888 there's been a city here, but until 1899 it was named Eddy, honoring pioneer Charles Eddy. Then the local fathers decided that the minerals in their spring water reminded them of Karlsbad in Bohemia, so they renamed it Carlsbad. It's a good thing they changed the name because now there are more than 30,000 people living in this dynamic city and most of them are not named Eddy.

Carlsbad is in extreme southeastern New Mexico, at the junction of U.S. 62/180 and U.S. 285. Its chief claim to fame is that is just 25 miles from world-famous Carlsbad Caverns. Even without the caverns, Carlsbad has a lot going for it, including the Pecos River, which flows through it.

────── HISTORY ──────

A couple of hundred million years ago, Carlsbad was on the shore of the Permian Sea and the Gulf of Mexico. At that time, potash was being laid down in huge quantities and oil was being formed. Both are important to the Carlsbad economy.

The first Europeans to visit this area were Cabeza de Vaca, in 1536; Coronado, who came close in 1541; and Espejo, who followed the Pecos River through this area in 1583. The first railroad tracks came from Pecos, Texas, in 1891. Oil was discovered in 1913, and the entire Eddy County is a big producer today.

The WIPP, an isolation project for radioactive waste, is under construction near the city, and the arguments for and against storing radioactive wastes in the salt domes underlying this desert area are still raging. People on one side claim that WIPP produces lots of new jobs; people on the other side shout, "Don't Waste New Mexico," because they feel that it is not wise to accept the nuclear-waste problems of other states and just hide them away under the huge deposits of salt, hoping that they will stay harmlessly hidden for a quarter of a million years.

"Fertilizer" is an important word in Carlsbad. First of all, bat guano from the Carlsbad Caverns was used in 100,000 tons of fertilizer that went to California orange groves from 1903–1923. Mineral potash underlies the area and is mined in greater tonnage than anywhere else in the United States. It is one of the best fertilizers in the world.

The Pecos River, which runs through Carlsbad, is the primary irrigation source in the eastern half of the state. Its waters fill Brantley, Avalon and McMillan reservoirs, storing water for the irrigation of crops. The Pecos also keeps Lake Carlsbad at a constant level, providing the water-sports area for the city.

——— **SEEING AND DOING** ———

The foremost attraction is the **Carlsbad Caverns**, located 25 miles south of the city. Carlsbad Caverns is the number one attraction in all of New Mexico, and we want to make sure you don't miss it. See Carlsbad Caverns.

Potash Steam Locomotive, the first train to operate at the first mine in the potash basin when production began in the 1930s. It is located at Carlsbad Riverfront Park. Carlsbad is still the largest producer of potash in the United States.

Lake Carlsbad Beach is a 1,000-foot-long beach, offering good swimming in a spring-fed pool of cool water. Boasting slides, diving boards and a bathhouse, it is a favored area in summer's heat. It's in the municipal beach park.

George Washington Paddlewheel Boat. Originally built in 1858, this boat takes you for a cruise on the Pecos River. It runs daily from Memorial Day to Labor Day. On Park Dr. Adults cost $2.50, children go for $1.50. **887-0512.**

Centennial Princess cruises farther and longer than the George Washington. $2.50 per person. On Park Dr. **887-0512.**

Carlsbad Spring. Located at Calloway Dr. and Westridge. The same mineralized water that caused the town to change its name still flows.

Pecos Flume. This is the flume that carries the river on a path that makes it cross over itself. Part of an early irrigation project, it has been rebuilt a couple of times and is still in use. Right by the Carlsbad Spring.

Living Desert State Park, on U.S. 285 just north of Carlsbad. Turn to your left on a well-marked road to see an amazing collection of cacti and succulents from all over the world. It also houses a good collection of animals living in the desert Southwest, ranging from bear and mountain lion to elk and prairie dog. Summer hours are 8 A.M.–8 P.M. After Labor Day, it is open 9 A.M.–5 P.M. Admission is $3 for adults, free for children 6 and under. **887-5516.**

Carlsbad Museum and Art Center. Located at **418 W. Fox St.** Prehistoric bones of mastodons and camels, Apache Indian relics, pioneer artifacts and a featured art collection, the McAdoo Collection. Open Mon.–Sat. 10 A.M.–6 P.M. Free. **887-0276.**

WIPP Visitors Center tells all about the project to store nuclear wastes under the earth near Carlsbad. You might just as well learn all about it, for the storage of such wastes is a big problem confronting our country. Free. Call to set an appointment. **101 W. Greene St., 885-8883.**

Carlsbad Shooting Range Area. North of Happy Valley on the east side of the truck bypass to Artesia. Offers four trapshooting ranges, standard rifle ranges for small and large bore and silhouette range. Free. Closed Mon. **885-0138.**

The 18-hole municipal **golf course** is on the east side of Lake Carlsbad. Green fees $6. Closed Tues. **885-5444.** There is also the **Riverside Country Club**, which is open to visitors from reciprocal clubs. Pro shop phone is **885-4253.**

Lake Brantley is a lake just filling for the first time, formed by a dam on the Pecos River. Boat ramps, picnic areas, comfort stations, overnight camping facilities with the usual state park fee system. It is north of Carlsbad on U.S. 285; watch for sign on right side. **457-2384.**

Lake Avalon is much nearer, being only 4 miles north of Carlsbad. Follow Canal St. out of town, then turn left on County Road 602. Fishing for bass, walleyes, crappie and catfish.

———— WHERE TO STAY ————

ACCOMMODATIONS

Best Western Motel Stevens—$$
Offers 151 rooms. **1829 S. Canal St., 887-2851** or **1-800-528-1234.**

Park Inn International—$$
Offers 123 rooms. **3706 National Parks Hwy., 887-2861** or **1-800-437-PARK.**

Carlsbad Inn—$$
Offers 117 rooms. **601 S. Canal St., 887-3541.**

Motel Six—$
Offers 80 rooms. **3824 National Parks Hwy., 885-0011.**

Rodeway Inn—$$
Offers 107 rooms. **3804 National Parks Hwy., 887-5535.**

There are many more motels, and don't forget about accommodations at Whites City, close to Carlsbad Caverns. See Where to Stay section of Carlsbad Caverns.

CAMPGROUNDS

COMMERCIAL

Carlsbad Kampgrounds
4301 National Parks Hwy. Used to be a KOA and still has all KOA amenities, including indoor swimming pool. Gives Good Sam discount. Rates from $9.50. **885-6333.**

PUBLIC

Brantley Lake State Park
Twelve miles north on U.S. 285. Brand new, on a newly filling reservoir of the Pecos River. Developed sites at $7 and electric sites at $11. **457-2384.**

———— WHERE TO EAT ————

Park Inn International—$$
3706 National Parks Hwy. Has two restaurants. Both are good. **887-2861.**

Lucy's Restaurant—$
701 S. Canal. Serves a big list of authentic Mexican dishes, plus excellent margaritas. **887-7714.**

Southwest's Choice—$$
1511 S. Canal. Known for its good steak meals, plus a fine salad bar. **887-6278.**

Tina's Cafe—$
3122 San Jose Blvd. Offers lots of good homemade Mexican dishes (none of the thaw-and-serve stuff here) and features a big *chimichanga* for a little money. **885-4239.**

Roswell

Located at the junction of U.S. 70/380 and U.S. 285, Roswell is the largest city in the southeastern region, with more than 50,000 people. It is home to New Mexico Military Institute, which turns out military leaders for America. It is also the center of a great irrigated farming area and a shopping center for the oil industry and for ranchers.

HISTORY

It all began in 1869, when gambler Van C. Smith built two adobe buildings here and named the town Roswell in honor of his father, Roswell Smith. Eight years later Captain Joseph C. Lea bought him out and can claim to be the father of Roswell. When artesian water was discovered in 1890, the town really began to grow as a center of irrigated agriculture.

There's a good spirit in Roswell. Evidence of that was plain when the air force base closed. Instead of moaning its fate and the loss of a great part of its economy, Roswell went to work and developed the **Roswell Industrial Air Park**. Attracting businesses from all corners of the map, Roswell ended up stronger and more stable than it had been before the big loss. At the same time, tiny Roswell Community College became the ENMU Roswell campus and moved to the industrial air park location.

FESTIVALS AND EVENTS

Updated monthly, the calendar of events for this area can be obtained from the local Chamber of Commerce office at **131 W. Second St.** The phone is **623-5695**. The listing of activities would be the envy of a city 10 times the size of Roswell. In addition, there is a continuously updated calendar of events for the RIAC—the Roswell Industrial Air Park—and there is a lot more than industry going on out there. Best bet is to stop in at the Chamber of Commerce offices and visit with the friendly folks there to make sure you don't miss anything.

——— SEEING AND DOING ———

Golf. There's a municipal course of 18 holes, located at **1612 W. Eighth**. Green fees are $6 for 18 holes and $8 for all day long. Carts are available at only $14 for 18 holes. Pro shop phone is **622-9506**.

There's another 18-hole course at New Mexico Military Institute, open to the public. Located at **201 W. Nineteenth St.** Green fees are $10 ($6 before 10:30 A.M.) for 18 holes, but you can also buy a $50-per-month ticket. Electric carts are available. **622-6033**.

Roswell Country Club course is open for members only.

Bitter Lake Wildlife Refuge, located 9 miles to the northeast of Roswell, is an important wintering ground for migratory waterfowl and cranes. Springs feed a series of man-made lakes, which provide roosting areas for the birds. Crane populations as high as 70,000 have been recorded in recent years, along with 20,000 ducks and at least 20,000 geese. The refuge dates back to 1937, when the Dust Bowl years were winding down and the land was cheap. Its most important segment wasn't purchased until 1988. It is open to the public year-round. The refuge is a favorite of birders, photographers and picnickers. No camping is allowed on the refuge. **622-6755**.

Spring River Park and Zoo, the only free zoo in New Mexico, at College Blvd. and Atkinson Ave., features a children's zoo, a prairie dog town so natural that wild burrowing owls have taken up residence with the dogs, a fishing lake open to children only and longhorn cattle, which were a part of Roswell's heritage. Open every day 10 A.M. until sunset, weather permitting. **624-6760**.

Chaves County Historical Museum at **200 N. Lea,** right off of U.S. 70 going west. It is open only Fri., Sat. and Sun. 1 P.M.–4 P.M. The building was once the palatial home of James Phelps White. Built in 1910, it is filled with the furniture, clothing and memorabilia of that era. Small admission fee. **622-8333**.

Roswell Museum and Art Center, located on Eleventh St., just west of Main St., is a great place to visit. It features the works of Southwestern artists, such as Peter Hurd (born in Roswell) and Georgia O'Keeffe. It also houses the memorabilia of Dr. Robert Hutchings Goddard, the first person to test liquid rocket fuels and a progenitor of our space program. It also features the space suit worn by Dr. Harrison J. Schmidt, a New Mexican who was sent into space and later was elected to the United States Senate. Free. **624-6744**.

Roswell Community Little Theater, at **1101 N. Virginia,** presents a full season of modern plays. The theater has been in action for more than 33 years and has an excellent reputation for producing the works of Neil

Simon and Molnár, along with the other less-famous playwrights. For more information, call **622-1982**.

Roswell Symphony Orchestra presents an average of five orchestral performances per season, along with three chamber music evenings. **623-5882**.

Hunting in the Roswell corner of New Mexico is among its greatest attractions. Scaled quail and California quail are found all over the area, and New Mexico laws allow a daily bag limit of 15 birds. Open season lasts for months. The lesser prairie chicken is found only in this part of New Mexico, and a short open season occurs every fall. The hunter who works the areas near Bitter Lake National Wildlife Refuge can expect to shoot ducks, geese, sandhill cranes, ringneck pheasants and two species of quail. The nearby mountains offer goodly populations of mule deer and wild turkey. On the open plains, pronghorn antelope roam, and there's a permit season every year. Even the majestic elk is open game for those fortunate enough to own a permit to hunt on the Mescalero Apache Indian Reservation.

——— WHERE TO STAY ———

ACCOMMODATIONS

Sally Port Inn—$$
Has 124 rooms. **2000 N. Main, 622-6430.**

Roswell Inn—$$
Offers 12 rooms. **1815 N. Main, 623-4920.**

Budget Inn—$$
Offers 42 rooms. **2101 N. Main, 623-6050.**

Budget Inn West—$$
Offers 29 rooms. **2200 W. Second, 623-3811.**

Comfort Inn—$$
Has 58 rooms. **2803 W. Second, 623-9940.**

Crane—$$
Has 29 rooms. **1212 W. Second, 623-1293.**

Best Western El Palacio—$$
Offers 45 rooms. **2205 N. Main, 622-2721.**

Frontier Motel—$$
Offers 38 rooms. **3010 N. Main, 622-1400.**

Days Inn—$$
Offers 62 rooms. **1310 N. Main, 623-4021.**

Leisure Inn—$$
Offers 104 rooms. **2700 W. Second, 622-2575.**

Royal Motel—$$
Has 67 rooms. **2001 N. Main, 622-0110** or **1-800-247-6831.**

Zuni Motel—$$
Has 35 rooms. **1201 N. Main, 622-1930.**

Belmont Motel—$
Offers 60 rooms. **2100 W. Second, 622-8633.**

El Capitan Motel—$
Has 12 rooms. **1636 S.E. Main, 622-9375.**

Hacienda Motel—$
Has 34 rooms. **2331 N. Main, 623-9425.**

Mayo Lodge—$
Offers 26 rooms. **1716 W. Second, 622-0210.**

Navajo Motel—$
Has 30 rooms. **1013 W. Second, 622-9220.**

CAMPGROUNDS

COMMERCIAL

Daltons Trade Village
2200 S. Sunset. Offers full hookups, but no rest rooms or bath. $7.50 per night. **622-7410.**

Trailer Village Campground
1706 E. Second St. Full hookups for two people costs $14.00. Gives Good Sam discount. Laundry facilities. **623-6040.**

Town and Country RV Park
333 W. Brasher Rd. Full hookups, recreation room, cable tv, showers. Prices start at $10. **624-1833.**

PUBLIC

Bottomless Lake State Park
Ten miles east of Roswell on U.S. 380, then 6 miles south on N.M. 409. At usual state park rates of $7 for developed sites and $11 for electrical sites. Comfort stations with showers. Not really "bottomless," the lakes do have depths to 90 feet. Favorite of scuba divers. **623-4173.**

———— WHERE TO EAT ————

Cattle Baron—$$
Twelfth and Main. Good steaks and seafood. **622-2465.**

Beijing Chinese—$$
1509 W. Second, **623-9380.**

Los Ranchos—$$
911 E. Second. Offers good Mexican American dishes. **622-9545.**

Italian food seems to be quite popular in Roswell, which has no fewer than eight pizza parlors.

———— SERVICES ————

Roswell is served by **MESA Airlines,** with daily flights to El Paso, Texas and Albuquerque.

Claiming to be the cultural hub of southeastern New Mexico, Roswell boasts a symphony orchestra and museum and art center.

Lincoln and the Lincoln County Wars

In Lincoln County, halfway between Roswell and Carrizozo on U.S. 380, you come upon the tiny town of Lincoln in a lovely mountain valley watered by the Rio Hondo. This town was the scene of a wild west shoot 'em-up that was far more deadly than anything seen in the wild west movies.

Let's talk about the cast of characters. Start with a skinny teenager named Henry McCarty, who traveled with his oft-married mother around the southern half of the state and came to Lincoln County. He started using the name of William Bonney, not as an alias but just because he liked the sound of it. Enter two other main actors, a couple of retired army officers named L.G. Murphy and James J. Dolan, who built a merchandising empire in the tiny town. They made most of their money by supplying the needs of nearby Fort Stanton and by overcharging farmers and ranchers, who were forced to deal with them as the only source of most everything. These two controlled the law in Lincoln County. Sounds like the plot for a B western movie, but it's all true.

Now, a wealthy young Englishman named John Tunstall came on the scene with his pockets full of family money to invest. He started a mercantile business in competition with the retired army officers, and this didn't earn him their gratitude. Tunstall teamed up with Alexander McSween, an attorney, to promote his business. They worked with John Chisum, a pioneer cattleman, in trying to get the supply contract from Fort Stanton.

John Tunstall, realizing that he wasn't getting a fair shake from the law, built his own group called the Regulators to make sure that justice was served. One of the Regulators was young William H. Bonney, known as Billy the Kid. It seems that Billy worshipped the suave, urbane Tunstall. Tunstall liked Billy because he needed his ability with the gun.

Action started! Tunstall was ambushed and murdered. Billy swore to kill everyone guilty of this foul deed. The entire county found themselves forced to choose up sides; it was not permitted that anyone remain neutral. A three-day gunfight in Lincoln resulted in the death of McSween. (Some claim that his wife poisoned him during the excitement.) It wasn't safe to walk the one street of Lincoln.

Sheriff Pat Garrett got on the trail of Billy and his partners and caught them holed up in a small shack at Stinking Springs. (No, I'm not making this up.) In the cold and with no food, Billy surrendered. He was taken to Mesilla, a suburb of Las Cruces, for trial and was sentenced to hang.

Billy escaped, killing two deputies, and made it back to Lincoln County, with Sheriff Garrett hot on his trail. In the home of the greatest landowner New Mexico has ever seen, Lucien Bonaparte Maxwell, Sheriff Pat Garrett surprised Billy the Kid and killed him.

Eighteen years later, Sheriff Pat Garrett was killed by a hidden gunslinger in an arroyo near Las Cruces.

The fascinating story of Billy the Kid and the Lincoln County Wars comes alive in the pioneer setting of the town of Lincoln. Today you can walk where the Kid walked, visit the *torreón* in which earliest Spanish colonists took shelter from raiding Apache and enter the big store that was the first mercantile business in Lincoln County. You'll visit a museum of memorabilia from that day—and you can make up your own mind. Was Billy the Kid really a hired gun? Or was he an idealistic young man who fought for the right? You can decide in Lincoln.

The **Historical Center** on the highway exhibits the story of old Fort Stanton, Pat Garrett, Billy the Kid and the Apache wars that were won by the Buffalo Soldiers, the black cavalry of the U.S. Army. Well worth the $4 admission fee. Open daily in summer 9 A.M.–6 P.M.,until 5 P.M. after September. **653-4025.**

Last Escape of Billy the Kid, a historical drama, is reenacted usually the first full weekend in Aug. This is a pleasant time to vacation in the tall pines of Lincoln County. Admission is $2. **653-4025.**

The **Lincoln State Monument** on the same one street of Lincoln operates the Tunstall Store Museum and the Lincoln County Court-house—the place from which Billy made his escape in 1881. **653-4372.**

The **Wortley Hotel** is owned and operated by the state, but you can still spend a night in one of its historical rooms, if you are of a mind to. You'll need reservations, so call ahead to **653-4500.**

The **San Juan Mission**, built in Lincoln about 1888 and much restored, is open to the public 9 A.M.–6 P.M.

The people of Lincoln work hard at preserving the town of 110 years ago. Guides dressed in period clothing are most knowledgeable about your leisurely tour through history. I urge you not to miss Lincoln while seeing the Land of Enchantment.

Alamogordo

Alamogordo is roughly translated as "fat cottonwood" or "thick cottonwood." Either way, it's an odd name for a thriving city of 31,000 people—the home of Holloman Air Force Base, the White Sands Missile Range, the White Sands National Monument, the International Space Hall of Fame, the Alameda Zoo (one of the best in the Southwest), and Oliver Lee State Park. Alamogordo is the only big city near the Mescalero Apache Indian Reservation and the high ski areas of the Lincoln National Forest.

Lately, Alamogordo has become something of a retirement community. Military and park service personnel stationed here learn to love the area, and they come back to retire. One of its greatest assets is its location.

Alamogordo is nestled against the towering Sacramento Mountains on the west edge of the Tularosa Basin. The Sacramentos are real mountains with lots of territory reaching higher than 10,000 feet. As a result, they are covered with tall, cool pine forests and get lots of snow in the winter, providing some of the nation's most enjoyable skiing, at Ski Apache Basin. The mountains' clear, cold streams are home to rainbow trout and flow down to contribute to irrigated farming in the area.

FESTIVALS AND EVENTS

Hang-Gliding Contests
In June. From the cliffs of the Sacramento Mountains.

Western Roundup and Bluegrass Festival
In June. In nearby Cloudcroft.

Moonlit Tour of White Sands National Monument
In July and Aug. Something really different. Phone **479-6124** for details.

Old Fiddlers Contest
Fourth of July. At the Alameda Park Zoo. Phone **437-1292**.

White Sands Tour of Lake Lucero
Tells you all there is to know about the source of the alabaster-white gypsum dunes. **479-6124**.

Induction into the Space Hall of Fame
First Sat. in Oct. **437-2840.**

Gun Show
Late Oct. At the fairgrounds. **437-7116.**

High Rolls Apple Festival
Late Oct. Yessir, there's a small village named High Rolls, and the residents sure grow some delicious apples. **682-2403.**

There's always something special going on in Alamogordo. For detailed calendar of events and update, contact the Chamber of Commerce, located near the Alameda Park Zoo, just a few steps off of U.S. 54, **437-6120.**

——— SEEING AND DOING ———

White Sands National Monument is 15 miles southwest of the city. It is the largest area of pure-white gypsum sands in the world. Here's how it happened: Prehistoric seas laid down tremendous deposits of gypsum during the days when this was probably a shore of the Permian Basin or even a brackish part of the Gulf of Mexico. Thousands of tons of gypsum were dissolved in the waters of prehistoric Lake Otero.

Over eons, Lake Otero dried up completely, depositing a million tons of gypsum, whose crystal is brown on the outside but becomes gleaming white—alabaster white—when scratched. Constant winds blowing from southwest to northeast tumbled the gypsum crystals along, grinding them smaller and smaller until they became white powder. These are the dunes of White Sands, wind-moved and irresistible, as they slowly cover vegetation and pile up in dunes more than 50 feet high. It takes a hardy plant, indeed, to grow here in this land of pure gypsum. However, the water table is sometimes only five feet below the surface. We could not drink the gypsum-laden water, but it does nourish some plant life.

A 16-mile drive takes you through the best of the White Sands: picnicking sites and comfort stations dot the route. You are invited to stop and climb on the dunes, and if you are one of the hardy ones, back-country camping is allowed at the end of a long hike. One of the 10 greatest attractions of New Mexico. Don't miss it! National Parks Service visitors center telephone is **439-6124.**

Alameda Park Zoo, on U.S. 54 and U.S. 70 at their intersection with Tenth St. This is an old-timer of a zoo, built in the first place as a diversion for railroad passengers while the locomotives refueled and took on water. Its first animal collections were displayed in 1898! More than 300 species are on exhibit now, tastefully displayed in a well-shaded environment, which is nice on this land of bright—and hot—sunshine. Open every day 9 A.M.–5 P.M. except Christmas and New Year's Day.

International Space Museum and Hall of Fame, known locally as the Golden Cube, is easy to find. Just raise your eyes unto the Sacramento Mountains backdrop to the east of town. Look low along the horizon, and you'll see the gleaming gold building with the 90-foot-tall white rocket standing alongside it. Easy to get to. Interesting exhibits of man's journey into space. All of the pioneers of space travel are honored here, Russians as well as Americans, along with the rockets and satellites that have been lofted into the heavens by mankind. You ride the elevator to the fourth floor, then journey slowly downward on sloping ramps that lead you past the exhibits. Open daily 9 A.M.–6 P.M. except Christmas. Admission is $2.25 for adults, $1.75 for children. Senior citizens pay half price, and children under six go free.

Clyde W. Tombaugh Space Theater is located on the other side of the parking lots from the Space Hall of Fame. Its 180-degree movie screen presents the stories of space exploration. The top-notch movies are brilliantly conceived and well done. This is no Mickey Mouse affair but a highly professional presentation of our odyssey into space. Narrated by Walter Cronkite. You'll lean back in your seat to get farther away from the rocket blasts that launch our biggest satellites. You'll have the feeling that you are right in the middle of the action because of the authentic sound

Alabaster white, the gypsum white sands are blown by the winds to cover and kill off vegetation. The dunes are always on the move at White Sands National Monument.

track. Truly great. It costs $3.75 for adults, $2.50 for children. However, there are combination visit entrance fees that allow you to see the movies and tour the museum. For example, a senior citizen going to both attractions will pay only $2.75. Children as well as adults are fascinated by both the exhibits and the movies.

National Solar Observatory is atop the Sacramentos in a place chosen for the purity of its air, at 9,200 feet above sea level. It's reached by driving east on U.S. 82 through the tunnel to Cloudcroft, then 15 miles south on N.M. 24. The main purpose of this observatory is to monitor sunspots, which have a direct effect upon our weather. An informative self-guided tour is available every day. A guided tour of the entire facility runs Sat. at 2 P.M. May–Oct., led by a member of the observatory staff. There is no charge for either of the tours. No picnic or camping facilities, but rest rooms are available on the grounds. The drive to the solar observatory is an attraction in itself. For further information, you'll have to call the Tucson, Arizona, office, **(602) 325-9204**, or the Alamogordo Chamber of Commerce, **1-800-545-4021** from outside of New Mexico or **1-800-826-0294** inside of New Mexico.

Oliver Lee State Park, some 20 miles south of the city, is located at Dog Canyon, where the very earliest white settler lived. A man named Frenchy built a cabin where the stream comes out of Dog Canyon. Cattle baron Oliver Lee followed him and appropriated his land. Then Lee built a nice home half a mile to the south on more-level ground. Because a Hollywood film company didn't think it authentic enough, builders added a veranda. There is an excellent campground near the visitors center, with all hookups. Prices are $11 for each of 10 sites with electricity and $7 for each of the 34 other sites without electricity. And what a view. From your camp site, you can see all the way to El Paso across a tremendous flat. To the northwest you can see the shining ribbon of pure white that is the White Sands. Peaceful and quiet. **437-8284.**

Trinity Site was where the first atomic bomb was exploded. Don't get your hopes up. It can be visited only on the first Sat. in April and the first Sat. in Oct., when the military takes sightseers on a trip to the famous spot. I possess a bit of green glass, fused from sand by the heat of the first blast. You use your own vehicle for most of the trip (about 150 miles), and the army furnishes transportation to the McDonald House, where the plutonium core of the bomb was assembled.

Driving a few miles north on U.S. 54, you'll come to pistachio-nut farms. A little farther along is one of the world's largest pecan farms. Combine this sight-seeing with a visit to the lovely old Mission Church in Tularosa.

—————— WHERE TO STAY ——————

ACCOMMODATIONS

There are many motels in Alamogordo, ranging from very luxurious to very small and poorly furnished. It's a good idea to ask to look at the rooms first.

Ace Motel—$
Has 12 units. **2615 N. White Sands Blvd., 437-5671.**

Alamo Inn—$
Has 40 units and an outdoor swimming pool. **1400 N. White Sands Blvd., 437-1000.**

All American Inn—$$
Offers 28 rooms and an outdoor swimming pool. **508 S. White Sands Blvd., 437-1850.**

Budget Motel 7—$
Offers 23 rooms. **2404 N. White Sands Blvd., 437-9350.**

Desert Aire Motor Inn—$$
A Best Western Inn. Offers 102 rooms, swimming pool. **2110 S. White Sands Blvd., 437-2110.**

Econo Lodge—$$
Has 40 rooms. **907 S. White Sands Blvd., 437-5090.**

Holiday Inn—$$–$$$
Has 106 rooms, swimming pool, restaurant and lounge. **1401 S. White Sands Blvd., 437-7100.**

Motel 6—$
Has 122 rooms and a pool. **251 Panorama Blvd., 437-5970.**

Satellite Inn—$$
Offers 40 rooms, swimming pool. **2224 N. White Sands Blvd., 437-8454.**

Super 8—$$
Has 60 rooms. **3204 N. White Sands Blvd., 434-4205.**

Townsman Motel—$
Has 19 rooms. **710 N. White Sands Blvd., 437-0210.**

Western Motel—$
Has 25 rooms, **1101 S. White Sands Blvd., 437-2922.**

White Sands Inn—$$
Has 93 rooms and a swimming pool. **1020 S. White Sands Blvd., 434-4200.**

CAMPGROUNDS

COMMERCIAL

KOA Campground
One block east of U.S. 54 and U.S. 70 on Twenty-fourth St. Award-winning KOA, with lots of shade trees. Priced from $16 for two people, with all hookups. Handy location to all the sights. **437-3003.**

PUBLIC

Lincoln National Forest
Pick up a map at the Alamogordo office of the U.S. Forest Service. **1-800-283-CAMP.**

Oliver Lee State Park
Just half an hour south, 44 nice camp sites. See Seeing and Doing section.

———— WHERE TO EAT ————

Angelinas Italian Restaurant—$
415 S. White Sands Blvd. Like the name says, Italian food. **434-1166.**

Alfredo's Mexican Restaurant—$
Good Mexican menu as befits Alamogordo's location close to the border. **437-1745.**

Chinese Dragon Restaurant—$$
606 First St. Tops in Chinese. **434-2494.**

Classic Cafe—$$
607 S. White Sands Blvd. Well-rounded menu. **437-2851.**

Crystal Dining Room—$
1021 S. White Sands Blvd., **437-9213.**

Furgi's—$$
817 Scenic Dr., **437-9564.**

The Golden Cube, the Space Hall of Fame, towers above the eastern horizon in Alamogordo.

═ Mescalero Apache Land ═

Many times in these United States, the native Americans got the short end of the stick when the invading Europeans forced the Indians onto less-than-favored lands. Not so this time. When the Mescalero Apache finally left the paleface-planned experiment that tried to make farmers out of them, the Apache returned to their ancestral lands, the high mountains of what is now the Mescalero Apache Indian Reservation.

The reservation is a beautiful land of high mountains, sparkling trout streams, pine forests, blue skies and peace. It separates the two largest chunks of the Lincoln National Forest.

From its headquarters town of Mescalero, on U.S. 70, the tribe operates a good-sized tourism industry, based on hunting, fishing, skiing and just plain fun. The U.S. Fish and Wildlife Service built a trout hatchery at Mescalero, and much of its output goes into the streams and lakes of the reservation.

Fishing is popular in the summer months, with Snake River cutthroat trout in the lovely big lake at the **Inn of the Mountain Gods** ($$$) and rainbow trout in all other waters. This is quite possibly the loveliest resort in North America. Here at 7,200 feet above sea level, just a few miles out of the town of Ruidoso, the Mescalero provide a gorgeous 18-hole **golf course** on their 460,000-acre reservation. They offer fishing, hunting, skiing, trapshooting, tennis on both indoor and outdoor courts, horse-back riding, bicycling, boating, badminton and volleyball. Every bit of it is top-notch. Prices are top-notch also. Golf costs guests $30 per 18 holes, and the required cart another $20. A fishing permit is $8 per day. There are packages, of course, which reduce the prices considerably. But you'll find more Lincolns, Cadillacs and BMWs in the parking lot than Fords and Chevrolets. For information, call **257-7967** or **1-800-545-6040**.

Hunting on the Mescalero Reservation is also high-priced. For example, a regular public hunt for bear will cost $350 while an all-inclusive package for bull elk will run to $4,200. But let's go first class, shall we? The Mescalero offers a package elk hunt, which includes your personal guide and driver, six days at the Inn of the Mountain Gods, breakfasts and box lunches, horses, packing out of the meat and trophy, processing of the meat, and your Mescalero permit for a bull with five points on each side. The total cost of $7,863.53 does not include the 5 1/2 percent tax or the gratuities. Do these luxury hunts sell? Yes, they are booked well in advance, mainly because of the 98 percent hunter success ratio. For more information, talk to Jonathan Adams, director of the package hunts, at the **Inn of the Mountain Gods, Box 269, Mescalero, NM 88340**, or telephone him at **257-9770**. And even if, like me, you can't afford to hunt there or stay there, you might enjoy driving through the layout, just to see how beautiful it is at the Inn of the Mountain Gods.

═══════ Ruidoso ═══════

The town of Ruidoso is just off of the Mescalero Apache Indian Reservation, on U.S. 70. The name means "noisy" and comes from Ruidoso Creek, the lovely stream that babbles along through town.

Ruidoso is strictly a tourism town, and it's quite good at it, thank you. Just out of town is the famed Ruidoso Raceway, home of the richest horse race, the Quarter Horse Futurity. One half mile east of the entrance to the downs is the Sports Theater, where you can wager (pari-mutuel) on horse races all over the country. See the race on big-screen TV. Also other sporting events. For more information, call **378-4431**. A couple of miles in the other direction is the fabulous resort the Inn of the Mountain Gods. See Mescalero Apache Lands.

Northwest of Ruidoso is Ski Apache. Just to the north lie Lincoln and the places made famous by the Lincoln County Wars, and it's only a few miles to Capitan, where the story of Smokey the Bear began.

────── FESTIVALS AND EVENTS ──────

All American Festival
In Aug. through Labor Day. Horse racing, hot air balloon rides, fiddling contest, beauty contest, street dance, golf tournament. Call Chamber of Commerce for exact dates each year, **257-7395**.

All American Gold Cup
First week of Sept.

Ruidoso Thoroughbred Futurity
Late Aug.

Ruidoso Mile Handicap
In Sept.

Cloudcroft Days
Last week of Sept. In that neighboring town. With fiddlers contest.

Golden Aspen Motorcycle Rally
Last week in Sept.

Aspenfest

In Oct. Street festival, street dances, arts and crafts fair, chili cook-off, parade and marching-band contests.

Square Dance Festival

In Oct.

Oktoberfest

In mid-Oct. The biggest thing of the year in Ruidoso.

For a more detailed calendar and an update of things happening, call the Ruidoso Chamber of Commerce, **257-7395**.

———— WHERE TO STAY ————

ACCOMMODATIONS

Cree Manor Inn—$$$

Close to golf and skiing (not in the same month, of course) and five minutes from the racetrack. Motel-type rooms, with color cable TV, Jacuzzi and indoor pool. Boasts of fabulous views of Sierra Blanca. Also apartments. Mile and a half north of main street, **257-4058**.

Swiss Chalet—$$

Has 82 units, restaurant and lounge. Swimming pool and spas. **1451 Mecham, 258-3333** or **1-800-47-SWISS**.

Ruidoso Super 8—$$

Has 63 units. Highway to West 70 **100 Cliff Dr., 378-8180** or **1-800-843-1991**.

Villa Inn Motel—$$

Has 60 rooms and restaurant. Highway 70 at the Y, **378-4471**.

There are also many different kinds of cabins, condominium rentals and bed and breakfast lodgings in and near Ruidoso. For help in finding just what you want, please call the Chamber of Commerce at **257-7395**.

CAMPGROUNDS

COMMERCIAL

KOA Campground

Six miles east of Ruidoso Downs on U.S. 70. Open all year. Priced at $12.50 with all hookups **378-4655.**

Tall Pines RV Park

On the main drag in Ruidoso. Offers 80 sites with all hookups. Right on the river with lots of shade trees. Priced at $15.00 per night and also gives Good Sam discount. **257-5233.**

Blue Spruce RV Park

Right on the river at **302 Mechem**. Offers 22 sites with full hookups. **257-7993.**

PUBLIC

Don't forget the public camping available in the Lincoln National Forest.

———— WHERE TO EAT ————

The Bull Ring—$$$

1200 Mechem. Prime rib, steak, shrimp and Mexican cuisine. 5 P.M.–10 P.M. **257-5271.**

Cattle Baron Steak House—$$

627 Sudderth. Offers fresh steaks cut in-house, seafood, prime rib. Reduced hours in off-season. **257-9355.**

La Lorraine—$$$

2523 Sudderth. Offers French cuisine, specializing in veal, fowl and seafood. Open 11:30 A.M.–2 P.M., 6 P.M.–9:30 P.M. Fine wine list. **257-2954.**

THE SOUTHWEST
REGION

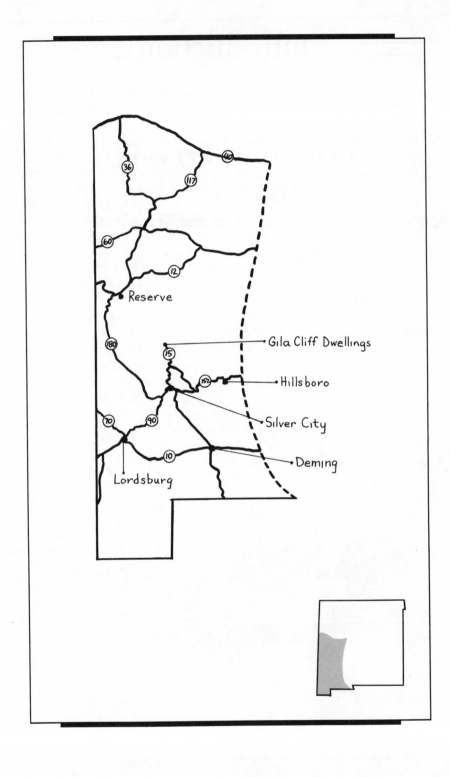

Introduction

There is lots of room in the Southwest Region of the Land of Enchantment. For example, when you turn off of U.S. 60 to go the 6 miles into the Very Large Array, west of Magdalena, you'll notice the sign that says, "No food, no lodging for the next 62 miles." That sign isn't kidding, folks!

This area includes some of the oldest Anasazi ruins, the Gila Cliff Dwellings and lands on which the New Mexico Game and Fish Department has established herds of exotic Persian ibex goats. Some of the largest wilderness areas in America are here, including the first-ever-established wilderness area. You'll find huge copper mines and the place where Pancho Villa and his Mexican army raided the town of Columbus. It is a happy hunting ground for those who pursue desert quail, wild turkey, mule deer and even the diminutive Coues whitetails. This area contains four of the best fishing lakes in the state—Bill Evans, Roberts, Wall and Quemado.

This is a land of extreme contrasts, of great expanses of cool pine-clad mountains and great expanses of bone-dry desert. See the Very Large Array radio telescope, which listens in on the secrets of creation. Then follow N.M. 52 a few miles away from the telescope, and you can go through about a hundred miles of land left exactly as the good Lord made it, full of turkey and mule deer as it was in the days of the Apache heyday.

The southwest corner sports many ghost towns, for it was the original mining country of New Mexico, and millions upon untold millions of dollars came out of these mountains and deserts.

It's a land of diversity. Come along. Let's take a look.

View of the strange rock formations at the City of Rocks State Park.

Deming

Deming bills itself as the city of pure water and fast ducks. It straddles Interstate 10 exactly halfway between Las Cruces and Lordsburg. Should we explain the "fast ducks" business now or wait till after we describe other things that should lure you to Deming? We'll hold off on the fast ducks.

Three interesting state parks can be visited from a headquarters in Deming. First is **Pancho Villa State Park**, located on the Mexican border at Columbus. Here is where United States soil was invaded on Mar. 9, 1916, by Pancho Villa and his ragtag army, which had no official status in Mexico. In fact, the Carranza armies were fighting against Villa at the same time that American forces under Black Jack Pershing pursued him. The American army penetrated 516 miles into Mexico.

The entire affair was a disaster for the Mexican irregulars. Although they caught the Americans asleep at Camp Furlong—attacking at 4:15 A.M.—and although the Americans had to draw ammunition before they could start to fight, the American soldiers pursued Pancho Villa and his men into the sleeping village of Columbus. Villa led between 900 and 1,000 soldiers in the raid. *Los mexicanos* looted many stores in Columbus and set several buildings on fire. The soldiers arrived about that time and shot the bandits silhouetted against the blazing fires. In all, the Villistas lost 142 men in Columbus and in the military camp. Another 75 were killed in close pursuit when the U.S. Army followed them as they retreated into Mexico. American casualties added up to 10 civilians killed, 2 wounded; 8 soldiers killed, 8 wounded.

Why did Villa raid Columbus? He was a rival of Mexican president Carranza, and our president, Woodrow Wilson, had recognized the Carranza government. Pancho thought his raid would embarrass the American president. This was the first time in American history that used airplanes in a war. The flimsy outmoded biplanes were not equal to the job and failed utterly.

Pershing did not capture Pancho Villa, and our army withdrew to Columbus on Feb. 5, 1917. Villa continued his bandit operations until July 1920, when the Mexican president De la Huerta bribed him to stop. On July 20, 1923, Pancho Villa was assassinated outside the town of Parral.

It is somewhat of a surprise to Americans from the north to find a state park dedicated to a man who raided American territory and killed Americans. However, you have to remember that this town is as close to Mexico as you can get without crossing the border; most of the people were (and are) of Mexican ancestry. Pancho is a hero, with a big statue in Chihuahua City. Many of the locals looked upon his raid with some pleasure—Pancho twisted Uncle Sam's tail and got away with it, or so it seemed to many.

There are few traces remaining of Camp Furlong. The railroad depot in Columbus has been converted into a Pioneer Museum, which houses much of the memorabilia of 1916–1917. The state park does a good job of telling the story of Pancho's raid in pictures.

——— SEEING AND DOING ———

Rockhound State Park, located just a dozen miles from Deming on a good—mostly paved—road, is unique among parks because the visitor is urged to take mineral rock samples home. There's an exhibit of common gemstones found in the area, so that you can become a rock hound without a long period of apprenticeship. Rock hounds find blue agates, common opals, thundereggs (geodes), quartz crystals, perlite and pitch stone. While you're out clambering around the rocky mountains in search of geodes, you can **camp** comfortably in the park. There are 29 sites, 22 of them with electricity, and a dump station. The campground is high on the slope of the mountain, affording an unlimited view of everything to the west. **546-6182.**

City of Rocks State Park is the third of the three parks visited from a headquarters in Deming. The entrance to the park is located 23 miles north of Deming on U.S. 180. This park is nothing at all like Rockhound State Park. City of Rocks is a large arrangement of weird and strangely beautiful rock formations. The geological explanation says that these rock shapes are welded tuff: It was spewed out of a prehistoric volcano as fine particles and became fused together. Erosion has softened and shaped the outlines, creating New Mexico's own Stonehenge. **Camping** is available at primitive sites—you can park in the shade of one of the monoliths if you wish—at usual state park fees ($7 and $11). There's no water at the sites, but good drinking water and showers are provided at a central rest room. I hope you camp there on a bright moonlit night. If you do, drive around the loop road to enjoy the weird landscape in the lunar light. I don't recommend that you hike after dark, because this is rattlesnake country. **536-2800.**

Deming itself is a busy small town, a major motel and refueling spot on Interstate 10 and perhaps the busiest east-west truck route in the Southwest.

The Chamber of Commerce is located at **800 E. Pine**, and the people there are experts at helping you plan what you want to see. After you've visited the **Deming Luna Mimbres Museum,** which features some excellent examples of Mimbres culture pottery, you'll probably opt for one of the three color-coded tours from Deming. Red, blue and green, the tours are mapped out for you in a free brochure.

Oh, yes! Deming is the home of **fast ducks**. On the last weekend in Aug. each year, duck racers congregate in Deming. These are real, honest live ducks, and they waddle in real, honest-to-goodness races to win the crown of the fastest duck! A man whose ducks won more than anyone else's is actually named Duck. Believe it. I wouldn't lie to you.

There are also many other attractions during the time of the **Great American Duck Race**. Such as choosing the Darling Duckling of the year, crowning the Duck Queen, a golf tournament, a Duck Queen Ball, a hot air balloon rally, softball tournaments, chili cook-offs and the annual outhouse race. But the climax of everything is the duck race itself, when the world's fastest ducks compete for a purse of $7,500. You have to be there, I guess, but very many people come to Deming for the race.

In March, Deming stages the **Annual Rockhound Round Up** at the fairgrounds. It is sponsored by the Deming Gem and Mineral Society. Gems and minerals are bought, sold and swapped, and there are guided field trips led by local experts. For more information, write the **Deming Gem and Mineral Society, PO Box 1459 Deming, NM 88031**.

——— WHERE TO STAY ———

ACCOMMODATIONS

Motel 6—$$
Offers 102 units, swimming pool. Air-conditioned, of course. East of town, at exit 85 of Interstate 10, **546-2623**.

Best Western Chilton Inn—$$
Offers 57 units and a restaurant. **1709 E. Spruce, 546-8813**.

Grand Motor Inn—$$
Offers 62 units, heated pool and restaurant. On east U.S. 70/80, **546-2632**.

Super 8 Motel—$$
Has 43 units. No pets allowed. **1217 W. Pine, 545-0481**.

CAMPGROUNDS

COMMERCIAL

KOA-Roadrunner RV Park

Take exit 85 from Interstate 10 east of Deming; follow signs. Offers 90 twelve-foot-wide sites; can handle rigs up to 73 feet. All usual KOA amenities. Rates from $9 to $12. **546-9035.**

Sunrise RV Park

2601 E. Motel Dr. Has 51 sites with full hookups. Rest rooms and hot showers. Rates start at $7.63 per night. **546-8565.**

Little Vineyard RV Park

2901 E. Motel Dr. Has 60 units with lots of long pull-throughs. Rest rooms, showers, cable TV. Rates start at $10.90. Gives Good Sam discount. **546-3560.**

There are other, smaller RV parks and many mobile-home parks, some of which sometimes rent spaces to overnighters.

PUBLIC

Pancho Villa State Park

Sixty-one camp sites are distributed through a botanical garden that includes almost all of the southwestern plants. I guarantee you'll see cacti you never knew existed. As in all New Mexico state parks, the cost is $7 for a camp site without electricity and $11 for a camp site with electricity. Good place to spend some sunshine time when it's cold up north. **531-2711.**

And remember, one of the nicest things about Deming is that it is only 53 miles from Silver City.

Lordsburg

One hour's drive west of Deming on Interstate 10, you come to Lordsburg, which was created when the Southern Pacific tracks reached here from the west. Before that, there was a small community known as Grants, which was renamed Shakespeare. When the rails came by, the residents of Shakespeare moved a mile north to the present site of Lordsburg. Today, Lordsburg is the last town of any size on the New Mexico portion of Interstate 10. It is a town of many motels, campgrounds and gasoline stations, for its main reason for being is as a support system for the interstate and the railroad. Lordsburg is also the eastern terminus for the scenic U.S. 70/60 corridor, a highway route that runs westward to Apache Junction, Arizona. Lordsburg offers a fine opportunity to look back into history, especially at the two nearby ghost towns.

——— SEEING AND DOING ———

Shakespeare ghost town is almost inside of Lordsburg. Go south on the main drag, under the Interstate, and keep on going for 2 miles until you find the signs leading you to Shakespeare. Definitely not a tourist trap, the ghost town is open only to tours, which can be arranged even on short notice and for very small groups. For information about tours and costs, call **542-9034**.

The town was born in 1870 with a silver strike and a diamond swindle. It grew to about 3,000 people under the name of Ralston City. In 1879 it changed its name to Shakespeare in an attempt to look like a cultured city. It was in operation as a mining center until the 1893 depression, when it was abandoned. During this period, desperadoes often holed up in Shakespeare. Two of them, Sandy King and Russian Bill, were surrounded by a vigilante posse of local citizens. The posse strung the two to the rafters and left them hanging. The next morning the stage stopped there for breakfast. The passengers found the corpses still hanging, cut them down and *then* had breakfast. From 1908 until 1932, Shakespeare was again booming as a mining town and earned its reputation for lawlessness and frequent hangings.

Since 1935 the Hill family has owned the place, and trespassers are definitely not welcome. But tours are conducted on two weekends each month in tourist season, and there is a series of reenactments, which would be called melodramas in other, more tourist-trapish communities.

For information about dates of these historical reenactments, contact the Lordsburg Chamber of Commerce, or write directly to **Shakespeare Ghost Town, PO Box 253, Lordsburg, NM 88045**. This has been designated as a national historic site. It's authentic.

If you're really into ghost towns, there is another one close by. **Steins** (pronounced "Steens") is yards off of Interstate 10, just before you get to the Arizona border. It's reached from exit 3 off the highway. There are junky-looking relics of the prosperous town of 1,000 residents that was first set up as a station on the Butterfield Stage line in 1858. It is named for Major Enoch Stein, a member of the U.S. Dragoons who camped there in 1856.

During the Civil War, congressional order closed the Butterfield Stage Line. In defiance of the closure order, one last stage left Mesilla for Tucson, Arizona. It was ambushed by Apache near Steins, and all the passengers were killed. In fact, lots of folks were killed near Steins, including the town's namesake, who was killed in Doubtful Canyon. Travelers called the canyon "Doubtful" because they were doubtful that they would get through it without being ambushed by Indians. Water, hauled from Doubtful Canyon, sold for $1 a barrel in Steins, which was drier 'n a mouthful of cotton. The rocky terrain and lack of water were the main reasons why Steins never made it. Today it is possible to take a good long look at life of a century and a half ago. There is a minimal fee charged for the tour. **542-9791.**

A promotional brochure from Lordsburg provides this quotation: "Hidalgo County has the best thing in the world to offer our visitors—Nothing." The brochure goes on to explain that Hidalgo County has lots of

Part of the ghost town of Steins, west of Lordsburg.

open space, great expanses of mountains and deserts, all of it land to enjoy in its original condition, just as God made it. With an average of 358 days of sunshine per year, a flat terrain and a healthy dry climate, Lordsburg seems to be a natural as a retirement community, but that hasn't happened yet.

If you are one of those who thinks America is getting crowded, I'd like to recommend a half-day auto trip out of Lordsburg. Drive west on the interstate to its junction with U.S. 80, and go south to Rodeo. I once asked a Rodeo resident, "Why would anyone come to Rodeo?" He retorted, "You tell me, and we'll both know." This landscape appears to be empty, although it is home to many forms of wildlife, from desert quail to javelina and the rare Coues deer (in the Peloncillo Mountains to the west). Then go back north a few miles to the junction of N.M. 9, and head east, through Animas and on over to Hachita. Then go north on N.M. 8 to the interstate. Now, do you still think that America is getting crowded?

I would like to add that Lordsburg is the happy hunting ground for desert-quail seekers, offering good supplies of Gambel's and California quail in most years. These desert quail are unpredictable in numbers from year to year, because their hatching success depends so greatly on when the rains come to this semidesert country. It also takes lots of walking to get them to fly, for they prefer to run away from the hunter.

───── WHERE TO STAY ─────

ACCOMMODATIONS

Best Western American Motor Inn—$$
Offers 88 rooms, with restaurant, lounge and pool. **944 E. Motel Dr., 542-3591 or 1-800-528-1234.**

Bel Shore Motel—$
Offers 30 rooms, with swimming pool. **508 W. Motel Dr., 546-2717.**

Holiday Motel—$
Has 48 rooms, restaurant, lounge and swimming pool. **600 E. Motel Dr., 542-3535.**

Aloha Motel–Friendship Inn—$
Offers 42 rooms and a swimming pool. **816 E. Motel Dr., 542-3567 or 542-3568.**

Oasis Inn—$
Offers 35 rooms and a swimming pool. **1032 E. Motel Dr., 542-9007.**

Western Skies Inn–Best Western—$$
Offers 40 rooms, swimming pool and a restaurant next door. **1303 S. Main, 542-8807.**

Super 8 Motel—$$
Offers 41 rooms. **110 E. Maple, 542-8882.**

CAMPGROUNDS

KOA
1501 Lead St. The usual KOA amenities for $13.50 per night for all hookups. **542-8003.**

Range RV Park
836 Motel Dr. Rates from $9.55 per night. All utilities available. **542-9918.**

Chapparal Trailer Park
100 E. Second St. Offers sites at $7 per night and $8 if you take cable TV. **542-9814.**

Tumbleweed Trailer Park
904 E. Second St. Offers all hookups including cable for as low $7 per night and $30 per week. **542-8284.**

———— WHERE TO EAT ————

American Inn—$$
Good American and some Mexican cuisine at reasonable prices. On Motel Dr., going east from Main St., about a mile, **542-3591.**

And another nice thing about Lordsburg is that it is only 44 miles from Silver City.

══════════ Silver City ══════════

Silver City is very much different from nearby Deming and Lordsburg. It is in the cooler and wetter high country. Silver City receives more than 16 inches of rain and more than 8 inches of snow in the average year. It is definitely tourism oriented, which sets it apart again.

Silver City is 143 miles from El Paso, Texas, and 190 miles from Tucson. It is a highway hub: U.S. 180 passes through and N.M. 15 leads north to the fabled Gila Cliff Dwellings and joins up with N.M. 152, leading east to Kingston and Hillsboro. That road is one of the most scenic in all of New Mexico; it also has the most curves of any road besides N.M. 15 to the cliff dwellings. Silver City is the jump-off place for four tours that take in a good part of the most beautiful parts of New Mexico.

This is silver country, and the ruins of old silver mines still exist side by side with modern operating and prosperous silver mines. Nearby Bayard is home to the huge Santa Rita open-pit copper mine, and nearby Hurley is the site of the huge Chino smelter. Copper and silver have played a major role in the history of this area, and they still do, now that Silver City's population has grown to more than 11,000.

Western New Mexico University is home to about 2,000 students, adding another wage-stabilizing element as well as a good education.

You definitely should start your enjoyment of Silver City and its surroundings by making a visit to the Chamber of Commerce visitors information center, which is along the highway coming into town from the south. It is well marked with signs. In addition to answering your questions about Silver City, the chamber people will provide you with maps and literature about the four wonderful driving tours available from a base of Silver City. These tours will take you to the best attractions, and I'll describe them separately after our rundown on Silver City. These major attractions, in my mind, are the **Gila Cliff Dwellings, Lake Roberts**, the **Tyrone Open Pit Mine, Piños Altos, N.M. 152 over Emory Pass to Hillsboro, City of Rocks State Park** (see Seeing and Doing in Deming), the self-guided **mining tour** at Hanover and the Mimbres Valley—and so, so much more!

────── SEEING AND DOING ──────

Right in Silver City, you'll want to visit the **MacComas House** site at **500 N. Hudson**. Once this was a fashionable area of town, but a flood wiped it out, and the area then became a famous red-light district.

Close to the MacComas House, you can visit the sites that figured in the early story of the infamous Billy the Kid. He lived here in Silver City with his mother when he was but a teenager. Jailed for stealing from a Chinese laundry, the 15-year-old Billy escaped by squirming up through the chimney. He also waited tables here for a living after his mother died.

Be sure to see **Big Ditch City Park**. When a series of floods eliminated Main St. and eventually dropped the ground level as much as 55 feet, the city fathers turned the area into a park—a very unusual park.

The **Silver City Museum** at **312 W. Broadway**, houses a fine collection of local Victoriana as well as Mimbres pottery, some of the most beautiful of all Indian pottery. This structure was once the home of a man named Ailman, who came here penniless and became the richest man in the county and the founder of the Meredith and Ailman Bank. Take your time roaming around the historic districts of Silver City—there's more than meets the eye at first glance.

Golf? The 18-hole **Scott Park Municipal Golf Course** is 5,816 yards long and has a rating of 66.4. Green fees start at $7.75, $1 less for seniors. Carts are available at $14 for 18 holes. Pro Jim Smith can be reached at **538-5041**. Tee times are seldom needed here.

——— WHERE TO STAY ———

ACCOMMODATIONS

Copper Manor—$$
Offers 68 rooms, pool and restaurant. Discounts for senior citizens and members of AARP. **710 Silver Heights Blvd., 538-5392.**

Drifter Motel—$$
Offers 69 rooms, pool and restaurant. Same discounts as at the Copper Manor (owned and operated by the same people). **711 Silver Heights Blvd., 538-2916.**

Holiday Motor Hotel—$$
Has 80 rooms, pool and restaurant. On U.S. 180 going out of town to the east, **538-3711** or **1-800-828-8291.**

CAMPGROUNDS

COMMERCIAL

KOA-Silver City

On U.S. 180 east, right in town. Offers 75 sites with all KOA amenities. Priced at $15.95 for two people with all hookups. Rest room and hot showers. Television reception is excellent without cable. Run by some of the friendliest people I've met in all my statewide travels. **388-3351.**

Logans RV Park

On U.S. 180, west of Silver City. Has 20 sites. **538-3331.**

PUBLIC

Don't forget the nearby **Gila National Forest** for camping sites.

———— WHERE TO EAT ————

The Red Barn—$$

708 Silver Heights Blvd., right close to the three motels I've recommended. Good for steaks. **538-5666.**

Holiday Motel Restaurant—$$$

On U.S. 180 going east. Offers a well-rounded menu with lots of choices. **538-3711.**

Even in the middle 1860s Piños Altos went in for culture, as witness the Opera House.

═══════ Piños Altos ═══════

Some half-dozen miles north of Silver City on N.M. 15, Piños Altos cannot be called a ghost town, for too many people still live there. Gold was discovered here in 1837, and the town sprung up. But Apache Indians stayed on the warpath, and many miners lost their lives. To solve the problem, the original settlers held a powwow with the Apaches. One legend has it that Mangas Colorado, a famed chieftain of the Apache, came to town to discuss some differences of opinion with the local gentry. Although he came under a flag truce, he was subjected to a rump kicking and a horsewhipping. This treatment undoubtedly prolonged the Apache wars by at least 20 years. But finally the Indians and the miners got together for another powwow. As a result of the conference, it was agreed that a big cross would be placed atop the high point of the mountains, and as long as the cross was there, no more killing would occur. From that day forth, the Apache no longer killed miners at Piños Altos.

Most famous of all the buildings in this semi–ghost town is the **Buckhorn Bar**. You can still buy a drink there, just as you could since the 1860s. Its heavy bar fixtures were brought from San Francisco by mule-drawn wagon, which must have been quite a feat in those days B.I. (Before the Interstate). Two mannequins grace the Buckhorn. One is Indian Joe, who sits dejectedly at the end of the bar, ostensibly waiting for service. The other is a delightfully clad Debbie De Camp. The story is that when Debbie died in a public brawl, her sisters of the night scrawled this memorial over her room: "Shed a tear for Debbie De Camp / Born a virgin and died a tramp. For 17 years she retained her virginity, / A real good record for this vicinity."

In truth, Debbie's last name was Moore, but there was no way to make that rhyme with "tramp."

Other famous buildings include the **Piños Altos Mercantile** building and the **Opera House**. It seems strange to me now, but those early miners found a lot of money and had very little use for it. They couldn't buy much more than drinks and a night at one of the brothels. So they invested their money in Culture with a capital C. In the last half of the 1860s the Opera House in Piños Altos opened for business. It was certainly one of the most elegant entertainment palaces in the area.

Piños Altos means "High Pines" in Spanish. N.M. 15 from Silver City is not so crooked until after it passes through Piños Altos.

══ Gila Cliff Dwellings ══

Reached by N.M. 15 out of Silver City, the Gila Cliff Dwellings are the homes of a people of nearly 2,000 years ago. The earliest dates confirmed by archaeologists are A.D. 100 to A.D. 400. It was about the year 1000 A.D. that the beautiful cliff homes were built.

First we have to get there. The National Park Service pamphlet says that the dwellings are 44 miles from Silver City, then adds, "Driving time two hours." History tells us that the streets of San Antonio, Texas, were laid out following the paths used by cattle going out from the Alamo to graze. Perhaps N.M. 15 follows the meanderings of that peculiar rattlesnake, the sidewinder. It has the most curves per mile of any road I have ever driven.

You can avoid some of the tortuous route by taking N.M. 35 north from San Lorenzo to its junction with N.M. 15. Although N.M. 35 is not exactly straight itself, it is far superior to N.M. 15 and takes you through some lovely mountain country and along the beautiful Mimbres Valley. On the way in, you might want to stop at Lake Roberts for a rest period. More about the lake later in the Lake Roberts section.

Once you've completed the drive, go first to the visitors center and examine the exhibits and borrow a pamphlet so that you will better understand the things you'll be seeing on the walk up to the dwellings. Then drive less than a mile to the parking lot at the cliff dwellings themselves. The trail up is fairly steep and it crisscrosses the tiny stream that flows down to the Gila River. The trail is about a mile long, and it rises 180 feet above the valley floor. The walk is fairly strenuous but there are many resting benches and level stretches where you can catch your breath. I'm an overweight 71-year-old, with both diabetes and hypertension to slow me, and I have no problem with the path to the Gila Cliff Dwellings.

Undoubtedly, the little stream that provided drinking water was one of the biggest reasons for the ancient ones to choose this hidden side canyon for their home. The fact that it would be fairly easy to defend against raiding parties might have figured in their decision also. The total population of this place probably never exceeded 25 families, but the site was occupied for more than a thousand years. The solid rock-walled buildings were constructed of a conglomerate that was present right at the building site, so building was easier than might have been expected.

We know little about the people who lived here. We named the earliest ones the Mogollon culture (pronounced "muggy-owen"), and the last occupants were called Pueblo Indians. For some reason that we do not understand, they abandoned this site about A.D. 1300 and perhaps joined other pueblos farther southeast. We do know that there was a great drought across the southwest from A.D. 1275 through A.D. 1300, and perhaps this had something to do with their departure.

There is no sign of hostile actions by these people, but then they were too few in numbers to wage war. Why did they hide away in this spot, one of the most inaccessible in all of North America? We probably will never know why they came, nor can we be sure why they left. They did leave us their hometown, now guarded by the National Park Service and the U.S. Forest Service, which administers all of the Gila National Forest surrounding the national monument.

A word of warning about the narrow, dangerous, snakelike road back to Silver City. Although it is possible to drive it with a big motor coach, as I have, it is a workout for the shoulders. The driver must be very careful going around curves, which is 99 percent of the time. If you're taking N.M. 15 all the way back, you'll get a chance to visit Piños Altos.

There is a good **campground** right at the Gila Cliff Dwellings, administered by the forest service. Just a few miles on the road back to Silver City, you can camp at the **Gila Hot Springs Vacation Center**, where all hookup sites go for $10 per night. **536-9551.** Calling the same number will get you information about light housekeeping units there, about guided hunting, fishing and backpacking trips, and about renting horses for your own trips into the Gila country.

A view of the Gila Cliff Dwellings, north of Silver City.

════ Lake Roberts ════

On the way into the Gila Cliff Dwellings National Monument, by either route, you will pass Lake Roberts, which is a beautiful mountain reservoir, formed by damming up a stream in the pine-clad mountains. This is a lovely spot, a good rest stop on the route to the monument and a good place to fish for rainbow trout and have a picnic. There's a launching ramp to accommodate small boats, but you must remember that only electric motors are allowed on the lake.

Lake Roberts has a surface area of 72 acres, two nice forest service campgrounds and numerous trails leading up into the forest from the lake. If you are continuing on up into the Gila Cliff Dwellings, you might want to leave long trailers here in the big parking lot. To really enjoy the trip to Lake Roberts you should be in possession of two publications. One is a forest service map to the Gila National Forest, sold for $2 at every ranger station and in Silver City. The second is a "Hi-way 61-35 Mimbres River" brochure, put out by the **Mimbres Business Association, Box 61, Faywood, NM 88034**. It is more readily available at the visitors information center in Silver City.

For more information on where to stay, contact **Lake Roberts Cabins and RV Park. 536-9929.**

A view of Lake Roberts, one of the best fishing lakes.

Glenwood

Ninety miles northwest of Silver City on U.S. 180, the pleasant little village of Glenwood lies at the foot of the high mountains, right where Whitewater Creek comes spurting out of the most beautiful canyon in New Mexico. Its deeply shaded streets and air of quiet peace makes it a welcome spot for a traveler arriving from the bone-dry, treeless plains to the north.

Definitely not tourism oriented, Glenwood doesn't trumpet its attractions, but they are there just the same. I recommend it as a good place to headquarter while you do a little exploring.

HISTORY

The first notice of this area came from Fort Bayard–based soldiers who fought the Apache. Some of them were smart enough to know gold when they saw it in the creek beds of this land of the Apache. One of them was named Cooney. Discharged from the army in 1875, he began to work his gold and silver claims. Five years later the Apache killed him. His neighbors must have thought a lot of Cooney, for they built him quite a tomb. You can see it today if you're driving a car or pickup. It's on the road leading into the mountains from Alma, just 4 miles north of Glenwood, on U.S. 180. Signs show the way east from the highway.

Alma itself is full of history, for this is where Butch Cassidy's wild bunch headquartered. And when the Apache rose up and killed poor old Cooney, the whites "forted up" in Alma and waited out the insurrection, but not without considerable loss of life.

SEEING AND DOING

Right in Glenwood, you'll see signs pointing the way to the **catwalk in Whitewater Canyon**, which is the area's number one attraction. The Helen Mining Company developed 13 mining claims up the incredibly rough canyon. To work the claims, it built a 4-inch metal pipe, 3 miles long, to bring water down to where it could run the generator that powered the mill. As the mill prospered and the town's population grew, the 4-inch pipe proved no longer adequate, and a new 18-inch line was built. Can you imagine loads of 18-inch pipe being hauled from the railhead by teams of sometimes as many as 40 horses?

To build and to service the pipeline, it was necessary to build a rough catwalk along the walls of the canyon. The mining was over just 10 short years after it started, and there were few people to drink the water coming out of the 18-inch pipe. The catwalk fell into disrepair until the Civilian Conservation Corps rebuilt it in the mid-thirties. Aided by the catwalk, tourism began as a trickle, but few people saw the beauties of the fantastic canyon. The present catwalk was built by the forest service in 1961.

Now it is relatively easy to walk up through Whitewater Canyon on the catwalk. It is a bit scary at times where the catwalk clings to the side of the sheer cliff by means of metal rods sunk into brace holes in the solid rock. Even in midsummer, very little sunlight reaches the floor of the canyon. Despite the lack of strong sunlight, the entire canyon is forested, forming a cool, shadowy place when the summer sun scorches southwestern New Mexico. There seems to be a slight cool breeze blowing down the canyon almost all year long. The songs of birds and the sounds of the creek below are the only things that break the peaceful silence.

Another canyon near Glenwood—**San Francisco Box Canyon**—exhibits petroglyphs of the ancient Indians who roamed this country before the Apache came. You cannot drive to it, and it is quite a long walk. If you are into petroglyphs, check at the forest service ranger station on the south edge of Glenwood. Get a map of the area and some local advice before starting out to hunt up the petroglyphs.

———— WHERE TO STAY ————

ACCOMMODATIONS

Whitewater Motel—$$
Has 14 rooms. On U.S. 180, **539-2581**.

Lariat Motel—$$
Offers nine rooms. On U.S. 180, **539-2361**.

Los Olmos Guest Ranch—$$$
Operates a large number of stone cottages, with a central dining room. But be sure to call ahead for information as to availability and for rates. On Main Street in Glenwood, **539-2311**.

CAMPGROUNDS

When I asked in Glenwood about camping, I was told that nothing was available. But the truth is far different. Campers have their choice of two fine campgrounds. I must have asked the wrong people.

The Catwalk Trailer Park

At the edge of Glenwood, on the road leading to the famous catwalk. Offers 20 sites with all hookups at $10 per site. The campground is operated by Mr. and Mrs. Ray Crum, a congenial and knowledgeable pair. **539-2329.**

Oaks RV and Trailer Park

Outside of the tiny village of Alma, just 4 miles north of Glenwood. At the south edge of Alma, you'll see signs pointing the way to Cooney's Tomb. If you look even closer, you'll see a sign pointing the same way, advertising the Oaks Park, which is operated on the honor system. You pick your site, slip your $10 into the envelope and drop it into the slot. All hookups are provided, good water pressure, excellent new conditions. There is no rest room with showers, but with your modern RV, who cares? The park is owned and operated by Mrs. Toni McKeen. **539-2513.**

A flimsy looking, but quite safe, catwalk carries the visitor back into scenic Whitewater Canyon, outside of Glenwood, New Mexico.

═ Hillsboro and Kingston ═

These two places, each interesting in its own right, are reached via N.M. 152, which runs from Silver City through a mountain paradise over Emory Pass, from whose eminence you can see Kingston at the foot of the Mimbres Mountains. You can see 9 miles farther to Hillsboro, sitting on more level country. On a clear day, you can lift your sights just a bit more and see the sparkle of Caballo Lake, on the Rio Grande.

N.M. 152 is much cussed by tourists who wind their way across its sinuous length. They admit that it is lovely country, but "why so damned many curves?" If you want to visit these two towns—quaint and historic Hillsboro and ghost town Kingston—you can do it the easy way, by driving west from Interstate 10 from Caballo. If you are in the Silver City area or heading that way, you should allow half a day for driving time, and go see them. After all, what's your hurry?

Kingston existed because the famed Solitaire Mine was discovered there, and silver started flowing out of the mountains in 1882. The usual mining boomtown mushroomed. Within months, Kingston had more than 1,800 people and 22 saloons to service their thirsts. There was something about mining that developed great thirsts.

When the cultured element decided that it should have a church, the people passed the hat in the 22 saloons and netted more than $1,500, which was real money in those days. Gunfights were frequent, despite the calming effect of the church. There was money to be made, so the town prospered with the opening of the Calamity Jane, Caledonia, Black Colt and Little Jimmie silver mines. Apache chief Vittorio raided it, as he raided almost everything in the Mimbres Mountains that he had first claim to. The exuberant town even named its new hotel "Victorio" in his honor. Lillian Russell played in the theater at Kingston, and that storied beauty did not work for free.

But the silver played out, and Kingston died. Today there are few people living in Kingston and many reminders of the glory that once was this mining town. The sign at the junction with N.M. 152 bears a sign announcing that the Spit and Whittle Club meets here. Don't let that block you. Go in anyway, and take a good look at Kingston.

If you are interested in taking an in-depth look at Kingston, you should stay at the **Black Range Lodge**, operated year-round. This histori-cal bed and breakfast has been opened—and closed—before, so please call ahead for information and rates. **895-5652.**

Hillsboro qualifies as both historical and quaint. But the description as "quaint" is negative in my book. Too many people move into quaint places and try so hard to preserve their quaint nature that the whole place begins to look like a carnival sideshow. Hillsboro isn't quite in that classification, yet. Highlight of the year now is the **Annual Apple Festival**, which takes place in the first week of Sept. But an apple festival is a letdown from the elevated status Hillsboro once had. Back in the 1870s this was the center of an incredibly rich mining district, producing more than $6 million worth of gold and silver. Settlers each nominated a name for the town. All names were placed in a hat, and one drawn was "Hillsborough," which was shortened to Hillsboro.

One of the mines in Hillsboro was the legendary **Bridal Chamber Mine**, some 16 miles south of Hillsboro on N.M. 27. Miner John Leavitt found the fabulously rich lode on a claim leased from the Sierra Grande Company. On the very day that Leavitt made his find, the manager of the Sierra Grande Company was killed by Apache. The great silver find lay only 30 feet below the surface, and the riches flowed until 1893, when the silver panic made mining uneconomical. Today only a few reminders of the once-flourishing town are left.

In the shady, quiet streets of Hillsboro, you will find much of the 1880s still on view. Be sure to stop in at the **Country Store** for a cup of coffee and a piece of pie. Most times, it is the only place to get anything to eat.

Javelinas are found in the extreme southwestern corner of the state, where a limited-permit hunting season is allowed. These are juveniles, of course.

Reserve

Reserve was so named because an early forest ranger made his headquarters there. The name signifies forest reserves. The town is 33 miles north of Glenwood. Take U.S. 180 to its junction with N.M. 32, then go another seven miles on that road. This is a quiet town, serving ranching and farming industries in the surrounding area. But it was not always quiet. This is where Deputy Sheriff Elfego Baca held off a mob of Texas gunfighters in a battle that lasted 33 hours. Although the Texans riddled the building from every angle, they somehow missed puncturing Baca's hide.

Baca was a remarkable character. He read law in the offices of Judge H.B. Hamilton in Socorro and was admitted to the bar in 1894 at the age of 29. In 1919 he became the sheriff of Socorro County. At that time Reserve was known as Frisco and was 137 miles away but still in the same county. When gunfights and other disorderly conduct became too violent in far-off Reserve, Elfego Baca went out to put a stop to it. During the course of the pacification of Reserve, Baca arrested one of the Texan cowboys who was shooting up the town. When the cowboys decided to free their buddy, Baca took his prisoner into the house owned by Geronimo Armijo. He ordered the family out and set in for the siege, during which more than 4,000 shots were fired into the house, according to court investigations of the incident.

According to Elfego Baca, the only things not struck by bullets in the Armijo house were himself and a statue of Neustra Señora Santa Ana (Our Lady, Saint Anne). Another deputy, named Ross, arrived on the scene, and Elfego Baca surrendered himself and his prisoner, with the provision that he be allowed to keep his shooting irons.

Today, the people of Socorro stage the **Elfego Baca Shoot**, which is fought with golf clubs. Contestants drive golf balls off the top of the mountain and continue to strike the same ball all the way down to Socorro. It's an exhausting competition, and it honors the Socorro resident who helped tame Reserve.

Outside of the Elfego Baca story, my only interest in Reserve is as a jumping-off spot for elk and deer hunters and for the restaurant known as **Grandma T's**, which serves excellent Mexican food and sandwiches.

═══ Datil and Datil Well ═══

Datil lies on U.S. 60, west of Magdalena by some 34 miles, at the junction N.M. 12. This was once a pivotal stopping place on the historic hoof way, where untold thousands of cattle and sheep were driven from ranches to the west (as far as Arizona), to the railhead at Magdalena.

To accommodate the livestock, wells were dug about every 10 miles along this route. The Bureau of Land Management has constructed interpretive signs along the way on U.S. 60. The bureau also built a lovely campground at **Datil Well**, 12 miles west of Datil. The camp sites are well designed and laid out around a circular path through the piñon trees. Drinking water is provided at a central position, and of course there are no hookups at the sites. My only complaint is that there doesn't seem to be a level campsite in the entire campground. Small detail, but irritating. If you have automatic leveling devices, you'll be okay. If not, bring along lots of leveling blocks to put under the wheels. I feel guilty about complaining, for the campground is free.

In Datil, you'll find an old-timey restaurant and motel named the **Eagle Guest Ranch**, which I want to recommend wholeheartedly to the hungry traveler. One of the finest steaks I ever enjoyed was right here. Portions are more than generous to satisfy ranch appetites.

There's a healthy elk herd in the Gila and Apache National Forests. Glenwood and Reserve are centers of hunting activity for these big deer.

Quemado Lake

The town of Quemado (Spanish for "burned"), on U.S. 60, can provide food and second-class accommodations for the weary traveler, but its real importance is its location, where you turn south on N.M. 32, headed for Quemado Lake.

The artificial reservoir is formed by a dam across Largo Creek. This tall-pine country is a lovely place for one of New Mexico's finest fishing lakes. Rainbow trout are the big attraction here. The last time I was at the lake, there were five senior citizens fishing from lawn chairs on the bank. They were using such plebeian baits as marshmallows and corn.

I asked, "Any luck?" and I got broad grins. Among them, they were just three trout short of having their five-person limit! I looked the fish over carefully: small heads and thick, fat bodies. These trout were in good condition.

There is no camping allowed on the land administered by the state game and fish department (with the forest service), but the game department does provide a campground on Forest Road 13D, 2 miles east of the dam. Quemado Lake is a long way from any population center, which probably accounts for the good fishing. Isolated? Yes. Lovely? Yes. And very good fishing for rainbow trout.

The famous Buckhorn Saloon in ghost town Piños Altos, north of Silver City.

═══ The Very Large Array ═══

Thirty-nine miles west of Socorro on U.S. 60, we come across the amazing spectacle of 27 huge satellite dishes, each mounted on its own railroad car, all pointing in one direction! This is the Very Large Array radio telescope, usually called the VLA. These huge satellite dishes measure 82 feet across and 94 feet tall. Each weighs 235 tons. By traveling the 13-mile legs of the Y-shaped railroad system, the dishes can take on many different formations. Concentrating the dishes close together, radio astronomers have the equivalent of the wide-angle lens. But stretching out the dishes into longer arrangements gives the equivalent of a telescope lens. There is something eerie about the scene from a distance, and I imagine the scientific world using them like a hand cupped behind the ear, listening intently. What are we listening for?

Radio waves are produced from the farthest stretches of the universe. By intercepting these tiny, weak signals and concentrating them with the big saucers, scientists are able to feed the signals into computers that draw a map of the part of the stellar universe that the VLA is pointed at. These radio maps are amazingly accurate. Not only can the computers draw a picture of relatively close things—like our planets and our sun— but they can also map regions of outer space so distant as to be invisible to our finest optical telescopes.

Why was the VLA placed out here in the desolate isolation of the Plains of San Agustin? Because the plains afford a chance to lay out a level field of this great size, because the air is dry and free of vapors that can distort the radio signals and because there is very little man-made static to interfere with the clarity of the signal.

Some of the radio signals being received by the VLA may come from the original Big Bang at the creation of our universe. They may have been 70 million light-years away. How far is a light-year? One light-year is equal to the distance traveled by light in one of our earth years. That figures out to 5.88 trillion miles. Now just multiply that figure by 70 million, and you'll know how far away 70 million light-years is. I cannot comprehend it; most people cannot.

Visiting the excellent displays at the visitors center will help you understand what the national astronomical radio telescope is doing. One side remark of a radio astronomer caught my attention. He said that all of the energy captured by the VLA since its inception did not equal the total energy expended by a mosquito in taking off!

Many people have the idea that the VLA is listening for intelligent communication from outer space. This is not the purpose nor is anything like that planned. But I like to speculate that one dark night on the Plains of San Agustin some operator of the VLA will hear a signal that says something like, "Hello, Earth! How are things down your way?"

In any event, please go to the visitors center first. Then take the walking tour for half an hour. Get up close to these behemoth satellite dishes. Think about the immensity of the universe. Excellent explanatory booklets are available for $3 in the visitors center. Admission is free. Open daily 8 A.M.–6 P.M. Don't miss it!

Ruins of mining at the ghost town Kelly, just 3.5 miles south of the town of Magdalena.

Magdalena

Twenty-seven miles west of Socorro on U.S. 60, Magdalena was named for Mary Magdalene of biblical renown, because an early Spanish priest thought that a rock formation near the town resembled her head. Although it got its start as a mining center, it boomed after 1885, when the Atchison, Topeka and Santa Fe built a spur line to Magdalena from Socorro. Now it was possible to get the ore to smelters; now it was possible to ship the livestock of western New Mexico. Cattle and sheep were trailed to Magdalena, then herded into railroad cars.

There was a U.S. Army post at Pueblo Springs, just north of the present town of Magdalena. Idle soldiers got to prospecting and found rich veins of silver. In 1886 Colonel J. S. Hutchason of the U.S. Army opened the first mines, and in the next 60 years more than $60 million of ore was mined near Magdalena. After gold and silver, the miners also found lead, zinc and copper. The town of Kelly came into being just south of Magdalena to better serve the mines.

Ores are finite and always play out in the end. But cattle and sheep are renewable resources, and they kept coming, some of them trailed as far as 120 miles to reach Magdalena. At one time, Magdalena was the biggest livestock shipping point west of Chicago.

Today Magdalena offers two motels. They are the **Western Motel** ($$), **854-2415**, and the **Woman on the Mountain** ($$), **854-2754**. Two fairly good eating places are **Evetts** ($), **854-2449** and the **Magdalena** ($) **854-2696**. Don't worry about finding them. Magdalena is not that big.

Author Cadieux's motor coach parked alongside park headquarters at Pancho Villa State Park, Columbus, New Mexico. The old railroad station across the street is now a museum of the days of 1916.

Kelly

Definitely an authentic ghost town, Kelly has no occupants, no ticket takers, no commercialism. It does offer a small Catholic church, the tipples and foundations of huge mining smelters and equipment, dangerous cave-ins and total silence, except for the wind whistling through old frame-house remnants and the song of the cactus wren.

Kelly is 3.5 miles south of Magdalena. Turn from U.S. 60 just to the west of the U.S. Forest Service ranger station. It's a good idea to stop in and talk about Kelly with the forest ranger. His name is Wasser. He's a good source of information about the old ghost town and its history, unless he gets transferred away before you get there. I hope not, for he is a valuable asset to anyone who wants to visit Kelly.

It seems that an old army colonel, J. S. Hutchason, discovered a rich vein of lead at the Kelly site. He began working it with profit. Then he found a second lead deposit, which he gave to his friend Andy Kelly. Kelly began working the claim, and it turned out to be worth more than the colonel's original find. So the colonel promptly jumped the claim, the one named the Graphic. Kelly lost his mine, but he gave his name to the town.

Life was often violent in Kelly. The Apache raided often, for they tried hard to keep *their* land. The cowboys who trailed livestock into Magdalena were bored, so they often shot up Kelly for recreation. The miners at Kelly got even by shooting up Magdalena in their turn.

An adobe smelter did the original refining of ores from Kelly, and oxen pulled the wagons down the rail at Magdalena. The town really grew—seven saloons and two churches. Over its long history, more than $29 million came out of the Kelly mines. After the precious and semiprecious metals were gone, miners found out that they could recover zinc carbonate—a mineral valued for manufacture of paints—and a lot of that went to market.

Drive as far as the Catholic church, the only structure still functioning in Kelly, and leave your vehicle in that parking lot. There's no one around 90 percent of the time. Then walk, carefully, up the rock-cluttered road to the remains of the Kelly mines and smelters. Take nothing but pictures, and leave nothing but footprints. It is even hard to leave footprints in this rocky soil. Take your time, and try to imagine what it was like in the 1870s and 1880s.

Ghost Towns

Ghost towns are places that once figured in the history of the Land of Enchantment but died. Most of them have been completely abandoned; a few still have one or two families lingering on in the solitude. To me, there is something fascinating about wandering through the streets where history was made. Sure, there's nothing there now, but I find it fascinating that $6 million worth of silver was taken out of this place before it was abandoned. I'm the kind that listens to the wind sighing through the branches of a pine tree that has grown up right through the floor of what was once a saloon. I wonder about the people who lived there, who loved there and fought there, and who all too often died there.

If you share my interest in ghost towns, here is a list of 19 of them, with instructions as to how to find them. What is there to see? Go take a look.

Cerillos is 27 miles south of Santa Fe on N.M. 14. Here the pre-Columbian Indians mined turquoise, which had religious significance. There was a big gold strike here in 1879, and mining boomed, with gold, silver, copper, turquoise, lead and coal. There was mining all through the region in those days. Lots of ruins and a few occupied homes. Several times used as a movie set.

Chloride. Take Interstate 25 to its junction with N.M. 52 north of Truth or Consequences. Go northwest on N.M. 52 about 27 miles to Winston, then drive 1mile west to Chloride. Harry Pye discovered silver ore here while freighting for the military. When his government contract was finished, he started working the claim. Apache killed him. Lots of strange things happened here, according to the legends. A man named Love was out working his claim when nature called. He was caught with his pants down and attacked by a grizzly bear. Despite his handicap, Love killed the bear. Badly mauled, he rested until the next day, then walked to town. Chloride was also the site of a tar-and-feather party. An elderly physician was caught writing shocking letters to other men and women of the town. Residents took him to the edge of town, applied the tar and feathers, and sent him packing.

Colfax, 15 miles northeast of Cimarron on U.S. 64, was a coal-mining town. The ruins of a big hotel and a couple of other buildings can still be found.

Elizabethtown is about 6 miles north of Eagle Nest on N.M. 38. Once a booming mining town. The miners thought they had a good copper mine, but when they started working it, they found gold. Elizabeth-town boomed and boasted of seven saloons. Lots of gunfights and vigilante hangings. The gold played out, and a 1903 fire removed most of the town. You can still see the stone remnants of the Mutz Hotel.

Golden, halfway between Albuquerque and Santa Fe on N.M. 14. Gold was discovered in 1839, and the boom started in 1879. Was the center of mining activity for a big area. Miners found so much gold that they had their own stock exchange! Lots of tourists these days.

Kelly, just 3.5 miles south of Magdalena, which is on U.S. 60 west of Socorro. Kelly started out with copper, silver and gold and ended up mining zinc carbonate. Rough-and-ready mining town. Nobody lives there now, but a Catholic church is still used for worship and there are the remains of a big mining industry. See Kelly section.

Kingston, just off of N.M. 152, between Caballo on Interstate 10 and Silver City. A few people still live here, where 1,800 miners once patronized 21 saloons.

La Bajada. Go 20 miles south of Santa Fe on Interstate 25, then turn on the Cochiti Lake road. Drive 3 miles, then look for a sign on a right turn. La Bajada is Spanish for "the descent." This tiny village grew up there, where the road coiled around as it crept down the treacherous descent. The modernization of the highway moved the road to the other side of the hill, where it came almost straight down the slant. La Bajada never did amount to much; now it is almost gone. A few residents still operate a gallery, and there's an adobe church in this lovely spot.

Lake Valley is 17 miles south of Hillsboro on N.M. 27. More than 2 million ounces of silver came out of the Bridal Chamber mine here. Mines prospered from 1878 until 1893, then started to fade away. A few buildings still remain.

La Liendre is at the end of N.M. 67, which doesn't show on most state maps. But if you leave Las Vegas on N.M. 104 and start looking for it about 23 miles southeast of Las Vegas, you'll probably find N.M. 67. This is a very old Spanish community, dedicated to raising sheep. Today a few buildings still remain. Be sure to close any gates you open on the way in and out.

Loma Parda, a few miles out of Watrous (on Interstate 25) on N.M. 161, has a strange history. Lieutenant Colonel E.V. Suimner was horrified to find his soldiers, stationed in Santa Fe, were patronizing the red-light district. To remove temptation, he had Fort Union built on the bare plain east of the mountains, near a tiny hamlet of Loma Parda, and moved his men over there. But the red-light district simply moved from Santa Fe to Loma Parda. When Fort Union was abandoned in 1891, the customers were missing, and Loma Parda declined. A few buildings still stand. The saloons are gone, but there is still a church, which might prove that good triumphs over evil—but I doubt it.

Mogollon is about 9 miles east of Alma on N.M. 78. Alma is on U.S. 180, just north of Glenwood. Once a booming, roisterous town that produced $20 million worth of gold, silver and copper. Butch Cassidy and the Sundance Kid worked out of here. James Cooney, who was first to find the gold, sold his claim during an attack by Apache. Cooney wanted to go east and marry his sweetheart. But the Apache killed him before he could get away. A few families still live here in this lovely spot on the banks of Silver Creek.

Piños Altos is just north of Silver City on N.M. 15. Lots of people live there but the remains of its lawless past qualify it as a ghost town. Visit the **Buckhorn Saloon** and the **Opera House.**

Shakespeare is on the south edges of Lordsburg in the southwest corner of the state. See Lordsburg, and be sure to check in advance if you want to go in to see what is left.

Steins is 300 yards off Interstate 10, just 3 miles from the border of Arizona. Now commercialized but worth the small tour fee, and you can see much of it for free.

Trementina is an authentic ghost town, for no one lives here anymore. Not easy to find, it is about 46 miles east of Las Vegas on N.M. 104. Turn to the right just before the bridge. If you get lost, ask local residents. A woman named Alice Blake decided to do good for some Spanish Catholics who lived here. She arrived in 1900 and promptly began building a Protestant hospital and mission church. By sheer strength of will and hard work, she became the ruler of the tiny community, the principal of the school and the postmistress. Trementina means "turpentine," which was one of the things sold by the residents. Alice Blake died, and by 1950 Trementina was deserted. Lots of ruined homes still standing, but no one there.

Watrous, just off Interstate 25 north of Las Vegas, can hardly be called a ghost town, because it is still occupied by a few families. A mighty interesting pioneer town. During the heyday of the Santa Fe Trail, before the establishment of Fort Union, Watrous was the western terminus of the trail, the place where wagons waited for numbers. In numbers there was safety, so wagons waited until there were enough wagons to travel without fear. Then they set out on the most dangerous part—the run into Santa Fe. Lots of pioneer buildings still exist, including what is probably the oldest Protestant church in New Mexico.

White Oaks is 11 miles northeast of Carrizozo on N.M. 349. George Wilson discovered the North Homestake lode here in 1879 and promptly sold it to his friend, Jack Winters, for $40, a pony and a bottle of whiskey. Three years later, the mine had yielded more than $3 million (1880 dollars, remember!) in gold and silver. Boomtown White Oaks had an opera house, and the stately **Hoyle's Castle** still stands in faded grandeur. The town staked its fortune on the arrival of the El Paso and White Oaks Railroad, which never came. When the rails went to Capitan instead, White Oaks just up and died. Easy to visit.

Winston is right alongside of Chloride, and we already told you how to find Chloride. Originally called Fairview, it was founded in 1881. Leading citizen Frank Winston helped out financially when the silver boom died. In return, the residents named the town after him. Still are a few people here, but Winston is definitely a ghost town.

Index

The Fulcrum Travel Series
— 6x9, paperback —

*Written by locals, loaded with insider tips for
natives, newcomers and visitors*

THE COLORADO GUIDE *REVISED EDITION*
Bruce Caughey & Dean Winstanley

The definitive travel and outdoor guide to Colorado
written by two third-generation Coloradans is the most
reliable single resource with over 1,400 entries for
discovering this spectacular Rocky Mountain State.
Over 45,000 copies sold.

ISBN 1-55591-089-0, $16.95
656 pages, b/w photographs, maps

THE ALASKA HIGHWAY
AN INSIDER'S GUIDE
Ron Dalby

The most easy-to-use, fun-to-read guide to the entire
Alaska road system. It offers everything the traveler needs
including mileages, distances to campgrounds and
services, highway hazards to beware of and key points of
interest along the way.

ISBN 1-55591-067-X, $15.95
220 pages, b/w photographs, maps

Also of Interest

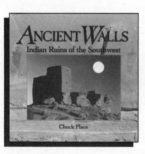

ANCIENT WALLS
INDIAN RUINS OF THE SOUTHWEST
Chuck Place

Photographer Chuck Place opens a window into the
mysterious world of the ancient peoples of the
Southwest. *Ancient Walls* vividly illustrates the lifeways
of the native civilizations before the coming of the
Europeans. This stunning volume features twenty-seven
archaeological sites in Arizona, Colorado, New Mexico
and Utah under National Park Service management.

ISBN 1-55591-126-9, $19.95
112 pages, 100 full-color photographs

Fulcrum titles are available at your favorite bookstore or call us
directly at **800/992-2908**

 Fulcrum Publishing

350 Indiana Street, Suite 350 • Golden, Colorado 80401-5093